The Borders of Nightmare
The Fiction of John Richardson

John Richardson was Canada's first native-born poet-novelist and 'The Father of Canadian Literature.' Michael Hurley offers the first detailed account of Richardson's fiction rather than of his life or sociological importance.

Hurley makes a convincing case for Richardson as an important early cartographer of the Canadian imagination and the originator of 'Southern Ontario Gothic.' He explores Richardson's influence on James Reaney, Alice Munro, Robertson Davies, Christopher Dewdney, Frank Davey, and Marian Engel.

Arguing that *Wacousta* and *The Canadian Brothers* hold central places in our literature, Hurley shows how these two works established a set of boundaries that our national literary discourse has largely kept hidden. Focusing on the protean concept of the border in the fiction of this man from the periphery, *The Borders of Nightmare* underlines the importance of boundaries, margins, shifting edges, and the coincidence of equally matched opposites in necessary balance to both Richardson and subsequent writers.

In an age of postmodernism these novels – riddled as they are with discontinuities, paradoxes, ambiguity, and unresolved dualities that problematize the whole notion of a stable, coherent national or personal identity – anticipate and define a number of concerns that preoccupy us today.

MICHAEL HURLEY is a member of the Department of English, Royal Military College of Canada.

MICHAEL HURLEY

The Borders of Nightmare
The Fiction
of John Richardson

UNIVERSITY OF TORONTO PRESS
Toronto Buffalo London

© University of Toronto Press 1992
Toronto Buffalo London
Printed in Canada

ISBN 0-8020-5009-3 (cloth)
ISBN 0-8020-6940-1 (paper)

Printed on acid-free paper

Canadian Cataloguing in Publication Data
Hurley, Michael
    The borders of nightmare: the fiction of
    John Richardson
    Includes index.
    ISBN 0-8020-5009-3 (bound) ISBN 0-8020-6940-1 (pbk.)
    1. Richardson, John, 1796-1852 – Criticism and
    interpretation. I. Title.
    PS8435.I33Z68 1992   C813'.3   C91-095730-4
    PR9199.R52Z68 1992

The lines from 'Progressive Insanities of a Pioneer' and *The Journals of Susannah Moodie*, from Margaret Atwood's *Selected Poems 1966–1984*, copyright © Margaret Atwood 1990, are reprinted by permission of Oxford University Press Canada. The lines from 'A Place: Fragments,' from Margaret Atwood's *The Circle Game*, are reprinted by permission of Stoddart Publishing Company Ltd., 34 Lesmill Road, Don Mills, Ontario, Canada. The lines from 'The Runners,' from *Selected Poems* by Al Purdy, are used by permission of the Canadian Publishers, McClelland & Stewart, Toronto. An earlier version of the material in chapter 5 has appeared as 'Wacousta as Trickster' in the *Journal of Canadian Studies* 26:3 (Fall 1991) 68–79.

This book has been published with the help of a grant from the Canadian Federation for the Humanities, using funds provided by the Social Sciences and Humanities Research Council of Canada.

For Kay Hurley (née MacDonald) and Will Hurley,
and for Nancy MacMillan

Contents

ACKNOWLEDGMENTS

1 **Introduction: The Borderline Case of Major John Richardson, Ex-centric** 3

2 *Wacousta*: **'Break Boundaries'** 27
Circles and Squares 34
Border Blur 43
An Ear for an Eye 54
'Break Boundaries': Exchanging Identity 58

3 **Border Doubles: Twin Poles of the Canadian Psyche** 69
Spiralling Repetition and Replay 78
The Struggle-of-Brothers Theme 83
Wacousta: Poseidon and The Wild Man 91
Governor de Haldimar: 'Moral Monster' and Establishment
  Manticore 95
Addiction to Perfection 98
Of Shadow Kings, Dark Fathers, and Father-Hungry Sons: Zeus
  and the Patriarchy 105

4 *The Canadian Brothers*: **Narcissus and Circe on the Border River** 110
Gorgons and Vampires 117

Through the Looking-Glass 123
Narcissus 126
Polyphemus 133
The Temple of Doom: Circles and Squares Revisited 137
  Ascent 144
Constructing and Deconstructing National Epics: Scott, Cooper,
  and Richardson 152

5 **The Shadow Cast by Southern Ontario Gothic** 156
The Ungrateful Dead: Southwestern Ontario *Senex* and *Mort-Vivants* Figures 166
Native Canadian Gothic: Wacousta as Trickster, 'The Enemy of
  Boundaries' 183
More Gothic Outlaws and Border Wolves 195

6 **No End in Sight: Seeing Double Hooks, Haunted by No Lack
of Ghosts ... and Making Richardson Safe** 202

NOTES 209

INDEX 225

Acknowledgments

I have been blessed with the friendship of several wonderful teachers and colleagues over the years, two of whom it gives me great pleasure to acknowledge here: James Reaney and Les Monkman. I am grateful to be among a growing community of people inspired and sustained by the imaginativeness, passionate insight, and generosity of spirit of these two gifted individuals. Without Les Monkman's support and expert assistance throughout every stage of this project, this book would not have been published. I also owe a debt of gratitude to Dianna Symonds who long ago – with characteristic patience and insight – encouraged a very apprehensive MA student to risk enrolling in Dr Reaney's much celebrated 'Ontario Literature and Culture' course at the University of Western Ontario.

I continue to be challenged by and to take delight in the illuminating work of American poet and dynamic explorer of the male psyche Robert Bly. Bly's workshops with Canadian author and Jungian analyst Marion Woodman have nourished both my teaching and the present study, and their influence will be readily apparent. Their lucid and moving books and presentations as well as the contributions of feminist scholars such as Jean Shinoda Bolen and Riane Eisler have helped render visible patterns in Richardson and our literature (and in myself) that had remained elusive or inchoate. In addition to Bly, I would like to honour here other figures associated with the men's movement in North America whose endeavours have directly or indirectly affected mine, among them Robert Moore, Michael Meade, James Hillman, John Lee, Tim Wilson, Ray Jones, Michael Kaufman, Harvey Schachter, Mac Freeman, Mac Gervan, Bob Kneebone, Chris McDonell, Steve Rush, Greg Forbes, Eric Andel, Brian Howell, and others from the Kingston/Thousand Islands region too numerous to acknowledge here.

Some of the material in this book, no less than its author, has undergone numerous incarnations, beginning in 1976 with lengthy published articles and conference papers and, in 1984, a PH D thesis. The latter was conducted under the able supervision of Dr Douglas Spettigue at Queen's University; William F.E. Morley, Richardson's bibliographer, and Donna Dumbleton at Queen's Special Collections, provided invaluable assistance, as did the Canada Council and Ontario Government Scholarships. The hospitality of David Beasley, Richardson's biographer, ensured a pleasant and productive weekend in New York City. Throughout these years and continuing into the present, I have enjoyed the wit and wisdom of Mary McGillivray, surely one of our most perceptive commentators on Bliss Carman. In bringing me together with such colleagues and friends, the spirits of place of Southeastern and Southwestern Ontario have proved adepts at the delightful dance of synchronicity.

My thanks for learning – and unlearning – experiences generated by my students as well as colleagues during three and one-half years of teaching at Queen's, several years at Kingston's 'twin' university, The Royal Military College of Canada, where the carnivalization of the garrison proceeds apace, and at various destinations along the modern-day circuit-rider's route from Belleville's Loyalist College to Collins Bay Penitentiary, and at Later Life Learning classes throughout Kingston. The encouragement, humour, camaraderie, and easy-going casualness of RMC's Department of English and Philosophy have created a congenial atmosphere in which to share ideas and perspectives; thank you Stephen Bonnycastle, Donna Campbell, Michael Mason, George Parker, Eleanor Rogers, Anne Skabarnicki, Tom Vincent, Don Binnie, and their families.

The true story of how this ever-changing manuscript found its way onto a word processor is known only to Addie Searle whose skilfulness, kindness, and laughter will always be treasured by myself and the entire English department and to Vivien Stanfield whose dexterity at the key-board, resourcefulness, and unfailing common sense are also much appreciated. I wish, too, to thank my publisher, editor Gerald Hallowell, manuscript editor James Polk, and editorial assistant Laura Macleod.

My limitations as a reader and a critic are many and will be readily apparent. Although my fascination with Canadian post-modernism is obvious, my growing interest in other aspects of contemporary literary theory probably will not be. I can only hope that theorists may find in this study more than just an unfortunate recrudescence of outmoded criticism. Taking delight in a plurality of critical approaches, I am grateful for the endeavours of literary critics of all stripes and feel neither qualified nor inclined to judge or police the work of others, especially those of a different critical orientation or persuasion. This is my reading of Richardson and other writers; I do not pretend to Olympian clarity or scholarly 'objectivity' or to a unitary view of the Canadian nation or to speak authoritatively for any collectivity, even when I use 'we' and other problematic or contentious terms.

Finally, a word about the people to whom this book is dedicated. My parents who read and told me stories and encouraged me to do the same have been truly remarkable in their generosity and understanding over the years. The creativity and vision of my wife Nancy MacMillan, as well as her support and enthusiasm, have inspired and sustained me in this and other projects. I thank all of you with all my heart.

THE BORDERS OF NIGHTMARE

... John Richardson, the father of our literature and the creator of those endlessly absorbing romances – *Wacousta* and *The Canadian Brothers* ... Richardson's work is not just 'good in parts.' The problem is, as usual, that there are parts of us unable as yet to deal with this writer's complex vision ... in short, Richardson is always writing about that strange Border River which flows at the edges of our souls ...

JAMES REANEY

Major John Richardson's novel *Wacousta*, appearing in the middle of the nineteenth century, suggests the paradigm of contradiction that continues to shape English-Canadian fiction... Richardson, in his struggle to violate that material into a story, portends our later coming.

ROBERT KROETSCH

In the absence of reassuring conceptions of a national destiny governed by a benign providence, Richardson's historical fictions emerge with gaps, contradictions and discontinuities more amenable to the expectations of the post-modern reader than to the reader in search of a neatly coherent nationalist ideology.

LES MONKMAN

CHAPTER ONE

Introduction:
The Borderline Case
of Major John Richardson,
Ex-centric

Both his personality and his work are extremely valuable keys to getting our tradition firmly rooted. To begin with, he's part Ottawa, part Canadian, part Scots-Canadian – representing the sort of families the Border lands turned out at the end of the French regime and the beginning of the British. This means that he's able to see back into Indian culture, go to Paris and Montreal and survive, balance Jacobite Scots rebel blood against the English snobs and Tories who wanted to make Ontario into a land of forelock-tuggers.

JAMES REANEY[1]

John Richardson, regarded as 'The Father of Canadian Literature' by James Reaney and others, has also been dubbed 'our certified madman.'[2] If so, it is a madness that he seems to share with later Canadian writers, especially postmodern authors. My study situates Richardson within this wider context. In so doing, I want to suggest that in the novels of our first native-born poet-novelist are adumbrated imaginative patterns which illuminate the work of Richardson's successors in the canon of English-Canadian literature.

Just as interrelationship is the hallmark of Richardson's fictional universe, so it is of my allusive critical approach. This is, first and foremost, a study of an early cartographer of the Canadian imagination, one illuminated by references to English-Canadian literature in general, including both canonical and 'ex-centric' authors. (While occasionally indulging in such problematic phrases as 'the Canadian imagination' or 'the Canadian sensibility' or, indeed, in the idea of a literary canon itself, I am aware of these concepts as constructs – arbitrary, distorting, but not unuseful, as recent studies continue to demonstrate.) Although once marginalized, ignored, and even censured in his own country (while praised abroad), Richardson is an important writer whom critics are now placing at the centre of a Canadian tradition mapped out primarily by Northrop Frye, Margaret Atwood, D.G. Jones, John Moss, and Dennis Lee as well as one identified by Linda Hutcheon in *The Canadian Postmodern*. No thorough and comprehensive textual analysis of Richardson's work attending to questions of form, structure, and ways of telling, and directed toward establishing patterns of expression, imagery, and theme has been undertaken to this point. While I consider all of his novels, my focus is primarily on the five-volume, 1,430-page epic of the founding (and premature death?) of this country – our first national prose epic – composed of *Wacousta; or, The Prophecy: A Tale of the Canadas* (1832) and its sequel *The Canadian Brothers; or, The Prophecy Fulfilled: A Tale of the Late American War* (1840). It is these works which experiment with the romance form of the descent narrative, raise the question of feeling at home here, dramatize unresolved tensions, and indeed problematize the whole notion of a stable, coherent national or personal identity, which have made Richardson one of our most resonant ancestral voices.

More specifically, I am concerned here with the protean concept of the border in the fiction of this man from the periphery. His phantasmagorical borderland, a dual universe in which worlds collide as well as coincide, complementing and running into one another, provides the touchstone for his epic's thematic, imagistic, and structural patterns. The multiple borderlines (of which the border river abysses in *Wacousta* and the sequel are but two) represent mental as well as topographical dichotomies; the strange terrain Richardson explores, maps, and constructs, reveals what Robert Kroetsch in a 1987 essay celebrating Frye identifies as 'the basic fissure, the Lacanian gap perhaps, that so informs the Canadian psyche.'[3] Indeed, Richardson shares with Kroetsch what Hutcheon identifies in the latter as a 'delight in borders as places of interaction, places where things can happen: on the margin, off-centre, ex-centric.'[4]

Romance itself has been called a kind of 'border' fiction where the field of action is the borderline of the human mind where the actual and the imaginary intermingle. Borders are of enormous importance in the imaginative life of any Canadian; as the title of Marshall McLuhan's essay 'Canada: The Borderline Case' suggests, our perspectives have something to do with boundaries, margins, shifting edges, contrasting patterns, and opposites in tension. For Kroetsch, Robertson Davies and others, this pattern of equally matched opposites always lies behind the multiplying theories of Canadian literature. The tensions generated by borders, or by what I define in chapter 2 as 'border blur' (a term adapted from b.p. Nichol via Michael Ondaatje) and 'break boundaries' (adapted from McLuhan), are expressive of a fundamental dualism in our art and society and give rise to the familiar Canadian double vision and voice.

Richardson's predilection for doubles, split selves, and love triangles seems to issue from a psyche fascinated with balancing or undoing one element by another (for readers of Sheila Watson, a very double-hook sort of sensibility). This tendency plays havoc with conventional notions of identity and up-ends any notions of a separate, distinct, and isolate self in a manner forecasting the fiction of Watson, Ondaatje, Kroetsch, P.K. Page, and others. It creates a mosaic borderland world of implosion, interrelationship, and potential equilibrium. Such devices of character linkage give ample scope for displaying the border phenomenon of unstable, fleeting, or multiple identity, of a self divided or spilling into another self. Borders between characters are strangely abrogated. As in a dream – or nightmare – figures explode, implode, split up, coalesce, fragment, reassemble, and defy closure. In novels from *Wacousta* to *The Monk Knight of St. John*, the paradigmatic double and triangle are refigured again and again throughout the text in a dizzying concatenation of such 'character loops.' Each one is a sort of 'retelling' in which the core double and triangle are further displaced, 'disseminated,' or blurred. The original relationship is thus from the beginning both reflected and concealed in such shards and traces, which function much like the text's other embedded stories. Lives reduplicate one another, giving rise to that eerie sense of doubleness, of reflections within reflections, of mirrors mirroring mirrors also found in the fiction of writers as diverse as Atwood, Davies, Munro, and Ondaatje.

The twins, split selves, doubles, and doppelgänger figures so prominent in the descent imagery of romance mesh efficaciously with the border dialectic of Richardson's work. Similarly, in *Wacousta*, two cultures, one immigrant, the other indigenous, apparently without any relation to each other, progressively intertwine and fuse in a curiously complementary fashion. Here, too, there is opposition in which the opposing forces endlessly turn into one another. Mapping these 'break boundaries' or points of reversal, of paradoxical inversions of identity, is important, for such border crossings are of the essence of Richardson's art. Dualities are simultaneously underlined and undermined, paradoxically subverted even as they are inscribed. And while the characters themselves remain largely oblivious to this process, readers are obliged to be more attentive, though up to now many of the patterns I describe have gone critically unremarked.

Perhaps this is partly due to *Wacousta*'s tortured textual history. Since critics in the past up to Gaile McGregor in *The Wacousta Syndrome* (1985) have unknowingly relied on seriously flawed editions of *Wacousta* which distort Richardson's intentions – especially the New Canadian Library edition, the most corrupt and unreliable – many have produced faulty criticism from faulty texts. Douglas Cronk was the first to make this assertion and to direct readers to the only authorial edition, the original 1832 volume. My PHD thesis on Richardson (1984) and the present book are the first extended studies to avail themselves of the research in Cronk's indispensable contribution to Richardson studies, an MA thesis entitled 'The Editorial Destruction of Canadian Literature: A Textual Study of Major John Richardson's *Wacousta; Or, The Prophecy*.' I quote liberally from the 1832 text, especially passages deleted from subsequent editions. The first page reference in brackets after every quotation from *Wacousta* is to this original edition, the second to the scholarly and more accessible CEECT (Centre for Editing Early Canadian Texts) edition (1987) skilfully prepared by Cronk.

While this is a critical examination of Richardson's work marked by close textual analysis, I also try to situate it within historical, social, and cultural contexts. I have not felt it necessary (or spatially possible), however, to outline significant events in his life, contradictory views of his personality, or repeated clashes between this marginalized ex-centric artist and representatives of the garrison mentality of the age. David Beasley's biography, *The Canadian Don Quixote: The Life and Works of Major John Richardson, Canada's First Novelist* (1977), supplies interesting factual information in this regard. Writing as a biographer rather than a literary critic, Beasley does not, of course, undertake such critical explorations as I embark on here; his pioneering work, the result of a great deal of enterprising research, offers new information on Richardson's life and times, but not on his fiction per se. References to the latter usually stress the extent to which his novels are autobiographical.

Likewise, Gaile McGregor writes as a cultural analyst rather than as a literary critic, one intent on the documentation and interpretation of social and cultural history and trends. While perceiving Richardson as a seminal figure in both Canadian literature and culture, one whose perspective is far from idiosyncratic, *The Wacousta Syndrome*, despite its title, is by no means focused on Richardson. Only seven pages at the outset are allotted to Richardson; these form a very generalized comparison of *Wacousta* to Cooper's *The Last of the Mohicans* based on a single theme, the differences in their handling of the landscape. This, in turn, serves primarily to introduce a longer discussion of how nature has been depicted in Canadian painting and to open up on the larger sociological issues relating to both art and literature which concern the analyst in her engaging cultural study. As a result of relying on the faulty 1923 edition of the novel, her brief comments on Richardson and Cooper are unfortunately often inaccurate or misleading.

This current study, then, is the first detailed examination of Richardson's work, rather than of his life or his sociological importance. It is my intention to read him primarily in terms of our received notions of Canadian literature, making frequent references to canonized texts and critics, both to assess his status as 'The Father of Canadian Literature' and to explore how texts and national literatures are constructed. Nevertheless, my focus reflects an awareness of the extent to which Richardson's writing is related to his experiences, of how literary texts and autobiography overlap and blur. Anyone familiar with his autobiographical outpourings knows that this writer wears as many hats and flows in and out of as many amorphous, everchanging, and often contradictory selves as his metamorphic fictional characters.

The personae assumed by Richardson in the course of his life include the following: intimate of London and Parisian literary circles; would-be recluse from white society welcomed by native peoples of Walpole Island in the St Clair River between Canada and the United States; 'a product of the mingling of the two races (native peoples and whites) which could not have failed to interest Tecumseh,'[5] obviously a spiritual ancestor for Richardson, one to whom he sought in vain to have a monument erected; impassioned advocate of the rights of native peoples, women, French Canadians, and black slaves in the Barbados; songwriter – his 'All Hail to the Land' opens a new music hall in New York City in 1850 with a two-hundred voice choir and the largest orchestra ever heard there; by turns a contentious and conciliating individual very sensitive to slights – fancied and otherwise; amateur naturalist and acquaintance of Audubon's; gambler; duellist; founder and feisty editor of a series of newspapers which bedevil garrison, government, and middle class with disclosures of fraud, bureaucratic mismanagement, and corruption; devoted husband; historian obsessed with the Border War of 1812 as our War of Independence against the United States which should have generated a myth of national character allowing Canadians to find genuine community with one another, their past, and the land; world traveller; typhoid survivor; POW at age sixteen; favourite of General Brock; defender of Lord Durham;

desperate office-seeker; petitioner of various governors-general for pension funds for needy artists; student of genealogy fascinated by synchronicity, a phenomenon which also intrigued his somewhat psychic wife; a proud and often irritating defender of his honour as a gentleman; an impetuous flouter of respectability, proprieties, and conventional boundaries; lampooner of petty officialdom, praised by George Woodcock for 'a laudable tendency to be politically independent in an age of patronage';[6] gardener; major; poet-novelist; trouble-maker; delighted reader of Cervantes, Sterne, and Radcliffe; special correspondent to the London *Times* on Canadian affairs, especially the 1837 Rebellion; son of an army surgeon who treats both whites and native peoples and later becomes a stern judge; grandson of a famous fur-trader; student of chivalry; ill-mannered, temperamental complainer on occasion; celebrator of the erotic energy of sexual desire in *The Monk Knight of St. John*; 'a very eccentric Christian' according to the obituary notice in *Pick's*;[7] spellbound listener to his French-speaking grandmother's tales about border warfare, Ponteac's capture of Fort Détroit, Jacobite outlaw ancestors, and voyageurs; the first Upper Canadian to have a volume of verse published in Great Britain; denouncer of American history books in Canadian schools; a Knight of St Ferdinand; and, depending on who you ask, 'Canada's First Novelist,' 'Canada's First Professional Native-Born Novelist,' 'Canada's First Poet-Novelist,' 'Canada's First Male Novelist' (with Julia Catherine Beckwith-Hart as 'Canada's First Novelist').

A designation such as 'The Father of Canadian Literature' lifts us out of the round of 'who's on first, who's on second' and roots us in an ongoing quest for genealogy, relationship, and influence in which the current study and Richardson's works themselves participate. Of course, finding or reclaiming one's father is not an easy, quick, or entirely painless process, but it is often a necessary and illuminating one. And surprising. What an ancestor to unearth, this Major John Richardson, what a strange, colourful, energetic, maddening, exotic, and downright familiar face he has! Surely in this progenitor it is possible to trace the lineaments of our oft-remarked dual, split, multiple, and contradictory selves.

Consider the following. Richardson, creator of the anarchic outcast Wacousta (whose American-born descendants are border outlaws) and the puritanical lawgiver Governor de Haldimar (whose descendants, 'the Canadian brothers,' belong to the garrison's ruling élite), is the product of a powerful border family consisting at once of fiery rebels and fur-traders as well as influential members of a mini family compact. Throughout his life, this inherited double vision and voice is strengthened as he remains connected both with members of the local power structure of the Old Northwest (as Southwestern Ontario – then Canada's western frontier – was once known) and of 'the first opposition in Upper Canada,' marginalized men like Joseph Brant, chief of the Six Nations Indians, and John Norton, an adopted Mohawk, writer, champion of native peoples' rights, and one possible historical model for Morton/Wacousta.[8] The same bête noire of the military establishment with whom the commander of British forces in Canada eventually orders no officer to associate proves, as superintendent of the Mounted Police along the troubled Welland Canal, a disciplinarian and vigilant enforcer of the law. The same man who wittily protests that 'Canada is too red-coat ridden,' too restricted by the garrison's herd mentality dictating that 'every duck waddles at the same gait,'[9] is also a proud major who seeks employment as a civil servant. Richardson, the borderline case, lives *between*, both inside the dominant culture and outside it, both reinforcing and interrogating the ideologies of his society.

Richardson's multinational ancestry likewise allows a shifting dual, even multiple perspective, one tolerant of diversity and difference and suspicious of cultural 'universals.' Despite some unconvinced critics, Beasley, Reaney, Woodcock, Desmond Pacey, and others assert that Richardson's grandmother was an Indian woman of the Ottawa tribe. Woodcock describes the dark-skinned Richardson as 'an early native Upper Canadian and, being a quarter Indian, somewhat more a Métis than Louis Riel.'[10] Sensitivity to racial prejudice – always downplayed in Canada – may lie behind some of the many scrapes he got in, and sheer contrariness others. His lifelong quest to assimilate and balance European culture and the wilderness seems to be cued by a number of things: French, Scottish, and half-Indian relatives and ancestors; an intimate familiarity with various dialects and bands of the borderlands; revulsion at a militant white society savagely wielding 'Christian bayonets'[11] as expressed in his narrative poem *Tecumseh* (1823) and twenty-six years later, in *A Trip to Walpole Island and Port Sarnia*, in the admonition that 'what the good Missionary, Mr. Jamieson, terms Pagans' might better be approached as teachers who could 'give a useful lesson to the whites';[12] unheeded attempts to make Tecumseh – as Riel and Big Bear have become – the stuff of our imaginative life, an important ancestor whom a white society that persists in seeing itself as a country without a mythology might consider adopting; a keen interest in those white men who had undergone the 'metamorphosis' into an Indian, as he terms it in 'A Canadian Campaign';[13] the strong pull to return to the bush and live among the native peoples as recorded in an intriguing article published in *The Literary Garland* (1849).

Richardson's life and fiction curiously foreshadow the attempt to close the gulf between an immigrant and an indigenous mentality that Frye sees animating recent Canadian writing. In *Fear and Temptation: The Image of the Indigene in Canadian, Australian, and New Zealand Literatures*, Terry Goldie calls this 'indigenization,' 'the impossible necessity of becoming indigenous.'[14] Interestingly enough, contemporary novelists have attempted on occasion to create characters who embody just that blend of races and perspectives found in Richardson. (And am I, too, trying to construct a Richardson congruent with this time and place, a double of my community's and my own needs and desires?) Born on 4 October 1796 on the Canadian side of the Niagara River border (which the narrator of Tom Marshall's 1989 novel *Voices on the Brink: A Border Tale* describes as one of the insane places on the earth), Richardson – 'our certified madman' – seems to have grown up learning how to juggle alternate realities, bridge or accept gaps, compare mythologies, and to maintain a tightrope balance between equally matched opposites wedded in mutual dependency. And seeing double still remains a peculiarly Canadian tendency.

Or so I shall suggest throughout this work. Chapter 2 is an in-depth study of the concept and the image of the border and its various ramifications in Richardson's work, especially *Wacousta*. Implicit in this concept is the complex balancing and mingling of apparent opposites which define the Canadian border, in contrast to the American frontier à la Cooper with its lone, independent individualists, as a world of simultaneity, interrelationship, and total interdependence. As in subsequent chapters, there are several sections: the presentation of 'the borderline case'; the contrasting yet complementary shapes of the dual worlds of fort and forest as they proclaim themselves through the border iconography of straight line and curve, as well as of eye and ear; and an inquiry into 'break boundaries.'

Chapter 3 pursues and complements this analysis. It explores how these same dualities work themselves out in the intricate fusings and permutations of identity in doubles (doppelgängers) and love triangles, and in the elaborate orchestration of parallels, multiple perspectives, and exact symmetrical correspondences between characters, settings, and situations. Allusions are made to similar character configurations elsewhere in our literature. Besides constituting the twin poles of the Canadian psyche as I read its presence in our literature, the De Haldimar-Wacousta relationship (like that of Linton and Heathcliff) conforms to a recurrent romantic convention which Richardson tailors to reflect the border dichotomy between civilization and wilderness. The third section of this chapter discusses this double in terms of the struggle-of-brothers motif which Frye sees as central to Romantic fiction and drama. This motif finds its archetype in Cain and Abel and expresses itself in the paradoxical relation – partly antithetical, partly complementary – of civilized and rude nature.

The emphasis here and in section four is on Wacousta as romantic lover, idealist, artist, story-teller, voice, a multifaceted identity obscured in most editions. Richardson's articulate, titanic quester after ideal beauty revels in Eve and untamed nature and clashes with a taciturn, repressed authority figure who tries to silence him; he is the anticipator of a whole band of outcasts from the established culture ranging from Douglas Le Pan's Rusty and

Leonard Cohen's F., through Aritha Van Herk's Arachne and James Reaney's Will Donnelly, to Rudy Wiebe's Riel, MacLennan's Jerome Martell, Chris Scott's Giordano Bruno, Mitchell's Bens, Callaghan's Peggy Sanderson, and O'Hagan's Tay John. Such figures show us what happens when the borders are abolished, when the dark or mad shadows blot out the genteel surfaces. Where the emphasis is on the twin configurations of group or cultural identity in chapter 2, chapter 3 presents this intense overlapping and merging of identity which the compressional, implosive borderland engenders from the standpoint of the major characters themselves.

The last three sections of chapter 3 concern themselves with the figure of Governor de Haldimar as 'moral monster' and manticore. As 'the monster of the status quo' (Joseph Campbell's term), De Haldimar is firmly in control of what Michel Foucault terms the 'systems of power' which control the 'Truth' of a culture.[15] This puritanical misogynist with his (male?) rage for order and, to a lesser extent, stern Magistrate Grantham in *The Canadian Brothers* stand squarely at the beginning of a long line of repressive or austere establishment representatives in our literature. In a later chapter, their symbolic descendants are traced in analogous characters in Davies, Wiebe, Reaney, Atwood, Kroetsch, Sinclair Ross, Scott Symons, F.P. Grove, Marian Engel, George Bowering, and Mordecai Richler. In this context, it becomes clear that Richardson's epic plumbs deep-seated cultural fears and prolonged national anxieties. Our interest in this seminal writer belongs in this larger context. While reflective of my own peculiar habit of mind, this approach may also recall Frye's thoughts on the interconnections weaving together all works in the literary universe and Atwood's comments on the Canadian love for synthesis; it also honours contemporary notions of intertextuality and parallel script and Foucault's interestingly worded claims that 'the frontiers of a book are never clear-cut,' that 'it is caught up in a system of references to other books, other texts, other sentences: it is a node within a network.'[16]

In the final four sections of chapter 3 and throughout chapter 5, I discuss the works of Richardson and others within the context of insights into the male psyche provided by both recent feminist scholarship and the growing literature of the men's movement in North America, especially its 'mythopoetic' wing identified with American poet Robert Bly, Jungian analyst and theologian Robert Moore, and mythologist and story-teller Michael Meade. Their combined mapping of this inner geography, marking the territory and its boundaries with mythological and archetypal signposts, proves particularly congenial to my approach to Canadian literature. Analyst Jean Bolen's lucid commentary in *Gods in Everyman* on the figures of Zeus, Poseidon, and Hermes as aspects of the masculine psyche and cultural historian and futurist Riane Eisler's thoughts on the motif of interconnectedness and her distinction between dominator and partnership societies in *The Chalice and the Blade* (1987) and *The Partnership Way* (1990) offer new perspectives for literary critics; here, they help me clarify important patterns in *Wacousta*, *The Canadian Brothers*, and *The Monk Knight* which extend throughout our literature. I am especially indebted to two key works of the men's movement: Bly's *Iron John: A Book about Men* (1990) and Moore's *King, Warrior, Magician, Lover: Rediscovering the Archetypes of the Mature Masculine* (1990). References in Richardson's autobiographical writings suggest he was familiar with some variant of the ancient story of Iron John/The Wild Man that inspires Bly's fascinating revaluing of masculine experience. Bly's commentary on this powerful archetype who takes his place in the community of beings inside the male psyche along with those listed in the title of Moore's study, proves invaluable to my discussion.

De Haldimar and Wacousta are two archetypal forces battling over the possession of the New World. Richardson is unable to see these figures except as equally matched opposites in mutual dependency, even as Michael Ondaatje cannot envision his Bolden and Bellocq as other than two equal and opposite forces balancing at a common point: 'Drawn to opposites, even in music we play. In terror we lean in the direction that is most unlike us.'[17] This is, I suggest, a tension within Richardson himself: he is on both sides at once. Like Kroetsch, Reaney, and other artists who work on the periphery, he is fascinated by problems of identity which seem to be problems of equilibrium. In any case, a principle of balance is maintained throughout his major works. In the original edition, Richardson is intent on balancing the attractiveness and repulsiveness of his authority figure and his disorder figure; each is an ambiguous mixture of positive and negative traits, and the balanced appeal to our romantic sympathies and to our sober judgment is such that we are often pulled both ways simultaneously. The novels seem both to seek and to resist a point of balance between all sorts of opposites which the border river generates and defines: order and anarchy, fixity and flux, sobriety and romance, enclosure and open space, fragment and totality, margin and centre, the fantastic and the realistic, civilization and the wilderness, the day world and the night world, fact and fiction. That these become curiously intermingled in what we may come to recognize as 'border blur' suggests that the myth of the border is the coincidence of opposites.

The special features of Richardson's sensibility – an ironic double vision and voice, ambiguity, a strong tragic sense, and an intuitive feeling for the spirit of place – are again apparent in *The Canadian Brothers*, the focus of chapter 4. In this sequel, the author deftly interweaves the working out of Ellen Halloway's curse of 1763, prophesying the extinction of the race of De Haldimar, with the military incidents of the Border War of 1812. The collision between the antagonistic families of the Mortons and the De Haldimars is paralleled by that between the warring nations of the United States and Canada. This section canvasses the ways in which the sequel inherits the border dualism of *Wacousta*, as well as its effectiveness as a descent narrative, a form which critics from Frye to Bowering regard as a persistent Canadian narrative strategy. With the aid of Frye's *The Secular Scripture*, a work as exciting and helpful to me as to writers like Kroetsch and Reaney, I trace the descent of Gerald Grantham (De Haldimar's descendant) from his little town in the sunshine across the border into the night world of romance. Readers familiar with this text or works by mythologists Joseph Campbell, Jean Bolen, and Michael Meade will recognize the descent narrative's familiar emphasis on growing confusion of identity, labyrinths or prisons, cruelty and love, metamorphosis, mirrors, doubles, and twins. Like *Wacousta* which bespeaks the author's strong archaeological pull, this is also a 'descent' narrative in the genealogical sense; it, too, features memory-laden characters obsessed with recovering traces of ancestors and unearthing a past which keeps flowing into the present. As in *Wacousta*, Richardson uses a mirror-like border river as a metaphor for a double focus; here, too, almost every action and character is reflected over and over again as if caught in two facing mirrors. The resultant cases of duplication involve balanced symmetry and the active equipoise of opposite forces. The sequel is also structured via 'break boundaries,' that intermingling of contrarieties which shapes Richardson's haunted, blurred borderland.

Again, the Jungian emphasis on the tendency for things to run into one another, on opposites overlapping and coinciding, distinguishes this work as it does those by Kroetsch and Davies – indeed, the Canadian sensibility itself as these two authors conceive of it. The motif of the struggle of brothers and the demon-lover are once more interwoven with the doppelgänger theme, the latter given one of its familiar variants as the narcissistic mirror-reflection. What results is an imaginative retelling of the myths of Narcissus and Circe in North American terms; this blending of documentary realism and mythic patterning prefigures Southern Ontario writing from Munro to Ondaatje, much of which situates itself on what is called in *Fifth Business* 'the borderland between history and myth.'[18] As in *Wacousta*, the Narcissus archetype lies behind the myriad permutations of identity. The border conflict is developed in terms of the struggle-of-brothers motif: Richardson presents a classic confrontation between those doubles, the disciplined, law-abiding Canadian garrison officer and the half-civilized backwoodsman and outlaw from the United States.

That Governor de Haldimar's descendants are Canadians and Wacousta's Americans is of considerable importance. Richardson plants the two interwoven family trees in his borderland to reflect the differences between two nations and two sensibilities which are described as diametrically opposed in their principles. Although – or perhaps because – the opposites begin to blur into one another, at least in the psyche of the tragic protagonist, the story crystallizes differences between the romantic and the ironic sensibility. The Canadian brother emerges from his descent with an ironic awareness of the self and others that contrasts with the romantic and solipsistic sense of being belonging to the American outlaw he has almost turned into. Rather than light out for the territory, he now decides to return home, to social order and community. At the end of chapter 4, the complementary and interlocking nature of *Wacousta* and *The Canadian Brothers* is discussed. Among other things, the former addresses itself to an exposé of the garrison mentality, while the latter exposes the dangers inherent in the seductive but profoundly dangerous American credo of individualism. Through linking the two historical crises of 1763 and 1812, the struggles of an emergent nation to contend with the exigencies of the environment and to assert itself against the pressures of a mother country and a neighbouring giant to the south are dramatized.

The assumptions that underlie the gothic and its sister genres, the mystery and the horror story, are the sources of Richardson's conceptual framework no less than of Atwood's. Indeed, he anticipates her notion that important images and archetypes in Canadian literature are tied to concepts of monsters, doubles, ghosts, and the gothic. Their writing reveals that certain preoccupations of Canadian experience awaited projection in the gothic form. Moveover, as the opening section of chapter 5 maintains, this mode is uncannily appropriate for articulating the spirit of place of Southwestern Ontario, a 'haunted' region which Munro, Davies, Reaney, Atwood, Timothy Findley, and Graeme Gibson have called absolutely gothic. Richardson uses features commonly associated with the gothic novel, Jacobean revenge tragedy, romantic tragedy, and Romantic poetry. That he is painstakingly selective in his sources soon becomes evident as we note what things in the tradition he chooses to develop, play down, alter, or omit. A cursory review of various types of ambiguously split gothic hero-villains is undertaken in order to help us appreciate the adaptation of this figure to a Canadian locale. Such writers as Walpole, Young, Radcliffe, Lewis, Maturin, Godwin, Hogg, and the Shelleys, I suspect, sustain Richardson in his attempts to shock a garrison culture into an awareness of what a chamber of horrors its own smugly regarded world really is. Richardson's nightmarish borderland features twin tyrants because both garrison and wilderness are menacing, as Margot Northey, John Moss, and Dennis Duffy have observed.

Richardson's border doubles take on an iconic character which permits a grand staging of our collective Canadian neurosis, our notorious fractured psyche. In its characters and structure, the epic gives expression to that contradictory wish for both freedom and stability, so frequently identified as characteristic of the Canadian personality. As the second section of chapter 5 shows, Governor de Haldimar, who embodies the flaws of the British imperial system, is an extreme gothic manifestation of a decaying, antiquated social order and its obsession with stability, restraint, and limitation. A severe and inflexible empire-builder, his character conforms to the *senex* archetype, the lineaments of which I attempt to trace with the help of Stephen Larsen's *The Shaman's Doorway*. In exiling feeling, joy, and sexuality, in walling out artists (Sir Reginald Morton/Wacousta is an accomplished painter), women, native peoples, and the natural world, the celibate founder of British North America incorporates the deficiencies of the *senex* and the patriarchy into the social order over which he presides. Richardson's imaginative diagnosis of the type of man who shaped this country in his own attenuated image is confirmed by later Canadian writers as well as by Bly, Moore, and Bolen.

While similar incarnations of prudence and propriety are discussed in other Canadian novelists, the emphasis is on the reappearance of the *senex* and related *mort-vivants* figures in works by authors from 'Souwesto' (artist Greg Curnoe's name for Southwestern Ontario), in particular, Reaney, Munro, Davies, Gibson, Raymond Knister, and Christopher Dewdney. If, as has been said, the (official) voice of Ontario reflects the victory of deadening form over feeling, in Richardson's canon readers overhear the first heated exchange in that tempestuous debate. The possibility that eerie, gothic Souwesto might become – or indeed has already become – a kind of mythical country, like the American South, is canvassed here. I also assess Richardson's role as the first mythologist of this fascinating region of haunted garrisons, farms, and small towns – all of them 'deep caves paved with kitchen lineoleum,'[19] often so thick and dulled by the yellow waxy buildup of a puritanical ethos as to obscure the world of wonders within from the unsuspecting or the inattentive. Born in the 1950s in Southwestern Ontario myself, to a white, English-speaking, working-class couple of Canadian, Irish, Scottish, and English ancestry, with American relatives over the border in Buffalo, with a sensibility responsive to, and galvanized in the mid–70s by, the local – the particular – the different – perspectives of James Reaney, I approach Richardson first as a regional writer. For me, he is a novelist very rooted in a distinct geographical, historical, and cultural world. I have tried not to confuse Ontario with the rest of this multicultural mosaic when I blithely generalize/totalize about things 'Canadian.'

Wacousta's character is an amalgam of border-legend, tall-tale, and historical figures as well as gothic and Romantic hero-villains. Focusing on Native Canadian gothic, the third section of chapter 5 investigates Wacousta's resemblance to the ambiguous figure of Trickster in North American Indian mythology. Typical trickster motifs are found throughout the story; given Richardson's lifelong interest in Indian cultures, these may signal his awareness of such tales. Reference is made to writings by native peoples as well as Bly, Bolen, and especially Paul Radin's *The Trickster* with its commentaries by Karl Kerényi and C.G. Jung. As the enemy of boundaries, the trickster is the perfect foil for the European garrison with its compulsion for fixed borders and rigid demarcations. Jung associates the trickster with the doppelgänger, the shadow, the unconscious, and Hermes; Richardson's wolf-double anticipates similar outcasts haunting more respectable social representatives in Ross, Mitchell, O'Hagan, Atwood, and Davies.

In the chapter's last section, I examine how the gothic spirit of

Souwesto erupts again in the gruesome story of *Westbrook, the Outlaw; or, The Avenging Wolf: An American Border Tale* (1851). This narrative of another border monster prowling the untamed wilderness is contrasted with two works featuring an American forest setting which, significantly, lack a gothic atmosphere and demonstrate Richardson's understanding of American mythology, especially that crystallizing around outlaw figures: *Hardscrabble; or, The Fall of Chicago* (1850) and *Wau-Nan-Gee; or, The Massacre at Chicago* (1851). Like so many of Richardson's novels, these three emerge out of – and conflate – local legend and historical material. With its echoes of the Richardson brothers' experiences as adolescents during the War of 1812, *The Canadian Brothers*, for instance, blurs the borders between the autobiographical and the fictive; in its use of what historians refer to as Kentucky's 'Beauchamp Tragedy' (which also fascinated Poe), the novel initiates that linkage between the American South and Southern Ontario oft remarked on by Munro, Findley, and Reaney. Intertexts of this generational tale are also present in the first volume of the epic. *Wacousta* incorporates stories told by Richardson's parents and grandparents, portraits of relatives, and aspects of the journal of fur-trader and friend of the family Alexander Henry. The latter chronicle also attracted Thoreau who declared it capable of sustaining a great national epic; Leslie Fiedler, in turn, contends that the Canadian fur trader is the inventor of the Western myth, thereby linking American and Canadian writing.[20]

The documentary impulse is strong in Richardson the historian/journalist/memoirist/novelist. He delights in blurring the borders between document and myth, the historical and the fictive, the factual and the legendary. His imagination, no less than Bowering's, Wiebe's, or Findley's, feeds on facts. As Richardson comments in *Eight Years in Canada* (1846), he writes 'with a view to show how truly it has been remarked that the romance of real life is often more stirring than that of fiction.'[21] 'Fiction can't compete with real people or events; that's why I'm drawn to historical subjects,' says Ondaatje.[22] Similar observations on 'the romance of real life' from Munro, Reaney, and others might be cited. It may be this double awareness in Richardson which allows him to be, in Woodcock's words, the artist 'who – in *Wacousta* and *The Canadian Brothers* – first showed that Canadian history was interesting enough to be matter for literature.'[23]

Conversely, literary technique becomes 'matter' for history as this double awareness finds expression in playing with the boundaries between history-writing and fiction-writing. The fictionalizing impulses at work in the non-fictional *War of 1812* (1842) with its pronounced oral tone and texture recall its fictional counterpart published two years previously, *The Canadian Brothers*; in the latter, the past is often reconstructed via a historian's discourse and a participant's memories. In each work, the author is also actively engaged in rewriting received, official, 'objective' (i.e. American) versions of historical characters (Tecumseh, Brock) and events (the Border War, its causes and who 'won' it); he does so in ways not unrelated to subsequent strategies and sub-versions adopted by Wiebe, Findley, and Reaney. Such transgressions of generic boundaries, I need hardly add, anticipate postmodern obsessions and much more sophisticated, self-conscious experimentation.

Throughout my study, it becomes apparent that the dual nature of the morally ambiguous Byronic hero, as well as of other archetypal figures of enormous appeal to the Romantic mind which surfaced in Mary Shelley and Emily Brontë, is more alluring and useful to Richardson than characters in Scott and Cooper. Richardson proposes certain ideological and aesthetic ways of understanding and representing Canadian life that are different not only in degree but also in kind from those pursued by Scott and Cooper in articulating their own cultures. In both Richardson and Cooper, there is a debt to, and a movement away from, Scott, both an inscribing and a subverting. Both New World writers are highly selective, rejecting outright certain motifs, even modes, while adapting, reshaping, and dismantling others. Out of such building blocks, the two create radically different fictions answerable to the imaginative needs of their own communities. The manner in which the Waverley Novels, the Leatherstocking Tales, and *Wacousta* and *The Canadian Brothers* play – or parody – the role of national epics is instructive (as I emphasize at the end of chapter 4). Much can be learned from how we choose to tell – and retell – our stories, and what Richardson, obsessed with locating the metanarrative of an emergent nation, finds over and over is a disturbing set of contradictions, paradoxes, fragments, double-hooks, and discontinuities. The quotation from Leslie Monkman which helps initiate this study emphasizes this point; it continues by suggesting that 'the discontinuous narratives of Bowering and Findley emerge as Canadian rather than simply post-modern through their links to a tradition extending backwards to Richardson in which the difficulties in constructing authoritative versions of the past in the realms of either fact or fiction are explicit; in Kroetsch's terms, "disunity is our unity."'[24]

Unlike Cooper, Richardson is fascinated not by a marriage of males but by a struggle of brothers over a woman. Not an American Adam but a Canadian Cain haunts his imagination. And so does Eve. Not a lone white man bereft of ancestry and in flight from history but doubled figures enmeshed in generations-spanning interrelationships obsess him. Richardson's struggle with the concept of the hero/a hero betrays an uncertainty and confusion undetectable in Cooper or Scott. Nor is the idyllic American Dream frontier experience anything like that of the nightmarish Canadian borderland. In general, quests for genealogy, split and shared selves, and the darker aspects of existence registered by Richardson in his gothic portrayal of a heart of darkness are glossed over or denied in the optimistic, unified world-view of both Scott and Cooper. While they refuse to grapple with forces of disorder and irrationality or to sound the abyss, the gaps, absences, and fissures which riddle Richardson's universe, these early Canadian descent narratives plunge into the underside of consciousness or 'The Belly of the Whale,' as Joseph Campbell calls it. Authority figures and romantic outcasts, both with their visions of glory, hook twice the darkness in an exploration of nihilism, violence, madness, and fragmentation of identity that is still being carried on in the work of Ondaatje, Reaney, Davies, Kroetsch, and Atwood.

Unlike Scott and Cooper, in Richardson instead of answers we have questions. Instead of resolution, we have doubt. Blur smudges clarity, disunity and multiplicity 'threaten' unity, and a double or multiple voice – hesitant and ambivalent – drowns out any single authoritative one. Faced with the possibility of being inscribed and defined by two of the master narratives of the time, Richardson opts to 'uninvent' the worlds constructed by the British and the American novelists, worlds of sharp boundaries, sharp (national and personal) definition, sharp focus. Hawk-eye. Ivanhoe. Such easily recognizable heroes and opposing villains as well as confident, neat, and coherent national trajectories are, in my reading, invoked and parodied (another form of doubling) in Richardson's blurred, broken, incomplete, unwieldy, ragged, and contradictory borderland.

Scott's passionless protagonists eventually embrace a middle-class, materialistic society which swallows up a 'primitive' one. This is anathema to Richardson who throughout his life condemns what he satirizes as 'this age of improvement,' 'of utilitarianism and of progress,' 'that "go-ahead" system which lays so emphatic a value upon time' and breeds a 'matter-of-fact people' 'absorbed in the pursuit of pounds, shillings, and pence.'[25] Inimical to the arts, the spirit of Eros, and native peoples, this same patriarchal system, which grows 'arrogant by the humiliating sale of the most petty articles necessary to human existence,' declares war on woman: 'As it is, what are women? Slaves, literally the slaves of men, and regarded principally because they are necessary to their own selfish ends,' we read in *The Monk Knight*. The double standard of a materialistic sexist culture is satirized, and the narrator recommends 'more liberality on the part of him who arrogantly, but falsely, deems himself the first of creation.'[26] This culture also declares war against the land; protesting the destruction of ancient stands of forest near his hometown, Richardson laments that 'these solitudes ... should have been thus invaded and destroyed ... now everything was so altered, so *civilized*, that I regarded whatever met my eye with a feeling of bitter disappointment ... I loved the ground, not for what it was, but what it had been.'[27] Perhaps only the remarkable 'mystic' David Willson and his Children of Peace at the beautiful Sharon

Temple in Sharon, Ontario, are among those Anglo-Saxon Canadians in the first half of the nineteenth century who shared and could as passionately articulate a similarly unconventional outlook. No wonder Richardson appeared at times to a somewhat axe-happy, smug, dour, and overly pragmatic pioneering society a perverse, mad heretic living on its fringes. And – to compound his sins – writing.

What Scott's and Cooper's societies (and often his own) call universal truth or natural or unchangeable, Richardson frequently contests and parodies. *Wacousta* challenges and demystifies the British imperial and military system, with General Brock in the sequel excusing Ponteac's 'uprising' and castigating the British commanders who brought these disasters upon themselves. *The Canadian Brothers* asks what it is to be a Canadian, an American, a native person, and a European. In it, the American myth of the noble outlaw and the sacred temple of the forest is exploded in the graphic portrayal of the loathsome, cannibalistic Desboroughs which tellingly inverts Cooper's models of the good and true American. It would be hard to imagine a figure more unlike Cooper's celibate, woman-fearing frontier Christian, the uncouth Natty Bumppo, than the passionate romantic Sir Reginald Morton or the ribald Wacousta. And just as Richardson's major characters are not granted immunity from violence and death, his fledgling colonies and emergent nations do not bloom into immortality under a benign providence but remain communities under threat, ones which border on dissolution, teeter over an abyss, and collapse.

Unlike Scott's and Cooper's novels, Richardson's offer no easy or unproblematic versions of national identity, no satisfying endings, but instead ironically refuse the resolution of contraries. Both a national epic and a parody of one, the story commenced in *Wacousta* begins eerily one midnight in 1763 and ends several generations later with the warring descendants of both 'founding' families perishing together in the hellish border river abyss separating Canada and the United States; the armies of both countries are likewise swallowed up by this dark chasm/graveyard, with the suggestion that history, no less than the ancient curse on the families, moves in endlessly recurring cycles within an indifferent and perhaps malevolent universe. Fourteen hundred and thirty pages later, is this 'national epic' telling us there is no nation and no story to tell? And is that it – our story? Somehow or other, Richardson manages both to authenticate our experience and to interrogate or question it. A writer capable of such magic acts I find worth paying some attention to. And if he is the first to do so, he is certainly not the last. Approaching Canadian literature through the fiction of John Richardson proves an intimidating initiation, one which combats any notion that ours is or can be seen as a literature of certainty, easy comfort, stability, or security.

The 'border blur' dimension to Richardson's best work has its closest analogue not in romances by Scott or Cooper but in that gothic masterpiece outside 'the Great Tradition,' *Wuthering Heights*, published over fifteen years after *Wacousta*. Allusions to Brontë recur throughout my analysis; her book – like Mary Shelley's – reveals a similar preoccupation with intertwining families, transformations, revenge, the fusion of opposites, violent exchange of identity, and a struggle of brothers. Such novels offer us a glimpse of what Audrey Thomas, describing her own writing, calls 'the sense of the other, the dark side of ourselves, the nightmare side.'[28] In Richardson, this glimpse is granted through an *enantiodromia*, the process in which things turn into their opposites, a phenomenon dramatized by subsequent authors and explored by the Canadian Jungian analyst Marion Woodman in works with break-boundary titles like *The Pregnant Virgin* and *Addiction to Perfection*.

My last chapter seeks to avoid any 'final words' on the ongoing border-blur and break-boundary process, choosing to encapsulate rather than enclose this study with a perspective on Richardson offered by the late Souwesto writer Marian Engel. It is difficult, besides, to resist ending a discussion of Richardson with a reference to an author who found herself on occasion as controversial a figure as Richardson; she, too, shares a similar concern with nature and sexuality, ancestry and the presence of the past, paradox and mystery, not to mention gothic experiences on the margins and peripheries, as well as more genteel, puritanical ones within conventional bounds. Engel's observations and ones by Hutcheon, Kroetsch, and Reaney help us assess the continuity of concern between Richardson and other Canadian writers among whom he assumes his position as 'The Father of Canadian Literature.'

CHAPTER TWO

Wacousta: 'Break Boundaries'

The theatrical experience in front of you is designed to give you that mosaic-all-things-happening-at-the-same-time-galaxy-higgledy-piggledy feeling that rummaging through a playbox can give you.

JAMES REANEY, *Colours in the Dark*

The square mind sees everything in simple, detached, objective, three-dimensional terms. But the new mind sees things in multiple terms – it sees many things at once, all intersecting, conjugating, interrelating.

SCOTT SYMONS, Interview, *Eleven Canadian Novelists*

... Billy needs to believe in a dichotomized universe, in which the domain of consciousness is wholly separate from the domain of instinctual energy. But while *Billy the Kid* accepts the primacy of those two domains, it then shows them as overlapping, coinciding at every point ... The dualism of savage fields ... is a dualism of simultaneity.

DENNIS LEE, *Savage Fields*

'A roaring of tense colours and interlacing of opposites and of all contradictories, grotesques, inconsistencies: LIFE.'

AUDREY THOMAS, *Blown Figures*[1]

A line from Marshall McLuhan's essay 'Canada: The Borderline Case' encapsulates the theme of my study, and also intersects with the preceding quotations: 'The borderline is an area of spiralling repetition and replay, of both inputs and feedback, of both interlace and interface, an area of 'double ends joined,' of rebirth and metamorphosis.' Richardson's Canada is a land of multiple borderlines, psychic, social, and geographic in McLuhan's sense. Both *Wacousta* and its sequel, *The Canadian Brothers*, constitute just such an imaginative 'world of the interval, the borderline, the interface between worlds and situations'; they dramatize 'areas of maximal interplay and subtle interpenetration' in ways not unrelated to contemporary Canadian novelists whom Linda Hutcheon argues are McLuhan's true spiritual heirs.[2] Richardson's phantasmagorical border region – a paradoxical universe in which dual worlds simultaneously collide as well as coincide, in which opposites run into one another, becoming inextricably intertwined – provides the touchstone for his epic's thematic, imagistic, and structural patterns.

The following two chapters are devoted to a study of *Wacousta; or, The Prophecy: A Tale of the Canadas* (London: T. Cadell 1832).[3] The chapters on this work form a unit, focusing on the image and on the concept of the border as one possible way into the labyrinthine world of *Wacousta*. The complex balancing and mingling of opposites in Richardson's border world are apparent in the unexpectedly complementary alignment of the differing cultures of European and native peoples and in the uncanny conflations of temporal and spatial boundaries. This chapter has several sections: the presentation of 'the borderline case'; the contrasting shapes of the dual worlds of fort and forest as they proclaim themselves through the related motifs of straight line and curve and of eye and ear; and 'break boundaries,' points of reversal, of paradoxical inversions of identity.

Form and content are nowhere so happily wedded in Richardson's canon as in *Wacousta*. In his analysis of Hawthorne's romances with their gothic overtones and revenge-obsessed doppelgängers, Richard Chase emphasizes the American author's desire to find in romance 'a neutral territory, somewhere between the real world and fairy-land, where the Actual and Imaginary may meet, and each imbue itself with the nature of the other.' This mingling, crossing, and interplay occur in the neutral region of '"betweenness," the world of the interval, the borderline' McLuhan investigates. For Chase, this simultaneous overlapping and interpenetration is a structural feature of the romance genre itself: 'romance is ... a kind of "border" fiction, whether the field of action is in the neutral territory between civilization and the wilderness ... or whether ... the field of action is conceived not so much as a place as a state of mind – the borderland of the human mind where the actual and the imaginary intermingle.'[4] Carl Klinck opines that *Wacousta* 'may appeal to the poetically-minded as a gigantic symbol for something in the frontier places of every mind.'[5] Naming *Wacousta* as 'the prototype' of 'frontier exile' in Canadian literature, John Moss similarly asserts that 'exile, in this novel, is a state of mind; the frontier, a state of consciousness.'[6]

Historian W.L. Morton's observations on the role of the northern frontier in the Canadian imagination are apposite here: 'The line which marks off the frontier from the farmstead, the wilderness from the baseland, the hinterland from the metropolis, runs through every Canadian psyche.' Commenting specifically on this statement in *Divisions on a Ground*, Northrop Frye remarks that 'This last line might be equally true of the psyches in Colorado or Arkansas or Oregon: what is different is that in the United States wilderness and baseland can be assimilated by a uniting consciousness. In Canada, the wilderness, symbolized by the North, creates a kind of *doppelgänger* figure who is oneself and yet the opposite of oneself.' Relating this 'split within the psyche that Morton mentions' to themes of metamorphosis and 'descent to the darker levels of one's consciousness,' Frye finds that the writer 'becomes both a daylight consciousness and a dark shadow of that consciousness which identifies, very often, with a continuously martyred nature.'[7] Such is obviously the case with Richardson. He early learned to see with a double vision and speak with a divided voice.

Richardson's fictional mapping of the border surfaces the hidden contours of our society and of our psyches. The multiple borderlines in his major works represent mental as well as topographical dichotomies. Such a strategy of cultural dialectic is central to our fictional and national heritage. In *Another Time*, Eli

Mandel avers that 'Our perspectives ... have something to do with boundaries and contrasting patterns.'[8] This observation receives fuller statement in Mandel's essay 'The Border League: American "West" and Canadian "Region"': 'Obviously, the metaphor of the frontier and the actuality of the border still exercise a profound hold on the imagination of writers in this country. It's difficult to see how it could be otherwise.'[9]

Wacousta and its sequel tacitly enact a sort of cosmology of the borderline and their contrasting yet complementary cultural and character configurations are expressions of the dual worlds they delineate. Richardson's epic explicates a world of alien experience; it focuses on the explosive (and implosive) collision between Europe and North America in the former work, and between Canada and the United States in the latter. He picks up our story from the beginning: the Conquest, the Treaty of Paris in 1763, Ponteac's Rebellion, and the War of 1812. Fascinated by the way these events cast their shadow in his own backyard, he begins 'seeking ancestral roots within a bordered region,' to borrow a phrase Dick Harrison uses to describe 'the developing Canadian western mythology.'[10]

Mandel notes that Kroetsch is right to locate the central concern of Canadians as the regional myth of origins.[11] As Richardson's entire canon, from *Tecumseh* and the 1812 flashback in *Écarté* through the border war tales culminating in the grotesque story of *Westbrook*, attests, this is one of Richardson's central concerns as well. It no doubt accounts for the fascination of James Reaney, another mapper of the Southwestern Ontario region ('Souwesto'), with these works and his play *Wacousta!* (1979). As Carl Ballstadt has observed, even though historical documents are basic to Richardson's fiction, they are shaped to reveal a myth of European adjustment to the New World.[12] As in Rudy Wiebe, Matt Cohen, Robert Kroetsch, Timothy Findley, George Bowering, James Reaney, and other contemporary Canadian authors, there is a strong 'sense of history merging into myth, of theme coming out of a perception of the land, of geography as a source of art.'[13] In Richardson, this is both a tendency of the genre he works within and the result of a conscious desire to create the first

Canadian novel, to tell the story of a nation 'hitherto untouched by the wand of the modern novelist.'[14] In its emphasis on the balancing and intermingling of opposites and the ambiguity, contradictions, discontinuities, and dark confusion this often generates, this cosmology is profoundly different from that of Scott's Waverley Novels or Cooper's Leatherstocking Tales. It is answerable to the Canadian locale and psyche.

Scott roots his historical romances in times of national crisis which contrast civilization and lawlessness, usually represented by England and Scotland, as in the rebellions of 1715 and 1745 which also figure in the Scottish 'Eden' episode in *Wacousta*. As critics have noted, prudence, common sense, restraint, bourgeois respectability, and order invariably win out over the lure – finally adjudged irresponsible and juvenile – of romantic impulses and the imagination. The battle lines are clearly drawn; there is no confusion between virtue and vice, no moral ambiguity, and terror, and all eruptions of the irrational are rationally contained. In his 1829 'Introduction' to *Rob Roy*, Scott refers to a 'strong contrast betwixt the civilized and cultivated mode of life on the one side of the Highland Line, and the wild and lawless adventures which were habitually undertaken and achieved by one who dwelt on the opposite side of that ideal boundary.'[15] For Scott and his legion of readers, this proved a highly reassuring, adaptable – and entertaining – *modus operandi*, one perfectly suited to his vision of the geographical and historical situation.

In Richardson, such a contrast is more apparent than real. Far from being an absolute division (as it often is in Cooper's black-and- white world of Manichean opposites), this either/or mentality is dramatized as an unfortunate component of the European or garrison world-view, not as a determinant of his own. Through a vast web of interlocking parallels, correspondences and echoes, and doubled plots and characters, Richardson is at pains to undermine, subvert, or reject such tidy dualisms; indeed, they prove difficult to maintain in the enigmatic Canadian borderland in which the two domains repeatedly overlap and coincide. Where the scale falls to the side of lawful society in Scott and to wild frontier in Cooper, in Richardson there is a balanced pull, a tension between opposites, if only because either alternative, garrison or wilderness, civilized 'rationality' or primitive wilderness, seems inadequate and confining at best, menacing and death-dealing at worst.

A rigidly dichotomized universe is a product and a reflection of the garrison mentality. It is valid only from the limited point of view of the combatants themselves. That mentality has been described as 'a tendency to polarize everything into the for and the against.'[16] Richardson invites the attentive reader to make the connections between the worlds his individual characters fail to see. As distinctions between the two domains blur and opposites mingle, a great deal of irony is sustained, and a lurid gothic light is generated that is not found in the literature of Scott and Cooper, with whom Richardson is sometimes associated. Such is the ambiguity and ambivalence infusing what Robert Lecker calls Richardson's 'intermingled vision'[17] that it is hard to tell which is the 'civilized' and which the 'savage,' which the order and which the opposing chaos.

In Richardson's epic, historical incident and our own homegrown legends, journals, tall tales, Indian mythology, and regional and family history are memorialized and romantically shaped to exploit – and subvert – the contrast between these two realms underlined in Scott's novels. As in Shakespeare's plays juxtaposing the realms of the court and of the 'green world,' in the Waverley Novels, or in the polarized cosmos of calm, ordered Thrushcross Grange and the tumultuous, elemental Wuthering Heights, topography complements the contrasting character types. Richardson adapts and stylizes the physiography of Southern Ontario and the Detroit border region, at the time a part of British North America. The landscape is a character in its own right, a powerful presence shaping the psychological dramas being unfolded.

Moreover, topographical contrasts reinforce historical and cultural ones. The dual worlds of civilization and nature, garrison and wilderness, alien British soldier and native Indian, intellect and impulse, reason and passion, order and disorder, stasis and mobility, the familiar and the unexplored, consciousness and unconsciousness, the prosaic and the magical, reality and dream are focused and brought into convergence along an 'ideal boundary' or border: a haunted ravine, an 'abyss, the depth of which was lost in the profound obscurity' (II, 148; 239). Or, at least, this is the dialectic which first seems to suggest itself.

This crack between worlds is a threshold symbol of the night-world of romance (which for Frye and Campbell involves descent narratives, growing confusion of identity, labyrinths or prisons, cruelty and horror and death, metamorphosis, mirrors, Narcissus, twins or doppelgänger figures). An ominous, mirror-like river, 'imperceptible to the eye in the "living darkness"' (II, 148; 239), deriving 'its source far within the forest,' flows out of this heart of darkness through a wild, dark, and thickly wooded ravine. A fragile bridge spans it. The exact centre of the 'Bloody Bridge' (also its historical name) is repeatedly emphasized. Here civilization and its structures intersect with nature and its forms. The spot images the violent point of intersection between the rigid military-social order of the English garrison and the spontaneous, seemingly irrational life of the North American Indian. (Richardson specifies the various tribes, the Ottawas foremost among them.) Such a fundamental cleavage reflects 'the incongruity between a highly sophisticated imported culture and a bleakly primitive physical environment' which for Frye underlies the curious affinity between the spirit of Canadian literature and that of Anglo-Saxon culture.[18] Garrison and wilderness constitute two solitudes, like the two men who preside over them, Colonel de Haldimar and Wacousta. Tragically, neither one is able to connect or bridge the double realms, to attain wholeness or at least some measure of harmony; each twin or twinned group remains unbalanced, one-sided, excessive, extreme.

Fate being an ironical but precise choreographer, the exact centre of the bridge over the abyss is the site of the violent deaths of both intertwined families, De Haldimars and Mortons, law-and-order representatives and outcast criminals. The historical failure to close what Frye terms the 'vast gulf between an indigenous and an immigrant mentality' is horrifically symbolized by a bloody tomahawk in the head of an executed British soldier who is slumped over a coffin on the border bridge midway between fort and forest. 'The possibility of eventually closing this gulf,'[19] which Frye sees as the quest of contemporary Canadian authors, is one that haunts Richardson, increasingly preoccupying him and underlying his art; it is also the most conspicuous theme of Reaney's *Wacousta!*.

The Canadian Brothers likewise ends in a ravine-abyss with the Niagara border river running through it, 'a chasm into which the sunbeam had never yet penetrated.' Fulfilling Ellen's prophecy, it becomes the graveyard of those classic doubles, Canadian garrison officer and American outlaw-frontiersman, Grantham and Desborough, the descendants, respectively, of the European garrison patriarch and the half-white, half-Indian wilderness criminal. The vast gulf between Canadian and American is represented by another casket and another Morton: the femme fatale Matilda, Wacousta's American descendant, who entrances Gerald Grantham, De Haldimar's Canadian descendant, is 'a beautiful casket which, on opening, is found not to contain a gem of price but a subtle poison, contact with which is fatal.'[20]

Circles and Squares

The tension between these two kinds of reality, their inveterate opposition, and, at the same time, their continuity and even their contiguity provides the form and content of *Wacousta*. Richardson is the first Canadian novelist to explore and map what Atwood calls our 'inescapable doubleness' and to suggest something which transcends this 'violent duality.'[21] Within *Wacousta's* dual universe, each world is defined by its own peculiar shape. Civilization's constructs are predominantly square, nature's forms circular. Everything on the European side of the border river is a right-angled monument to the intellect, to 'rationality' or what Margaret Avison refers to as 'straight thinking.'[22] Fort Détroit presents the four equal sides of a square. (Richardson retains the French spelling to suggest the layered nature of colonialism and further to underscore the British Empire builders' alien status at the time of 'the Conquest.')

In the following passage, one of many missing from most editions, thereby upsetting the delicate balance of opposites, we see the garrison's arrogant imposition of its own imported, abstract grid on a curving landscape. It is an attempt to enclose, conquer, and control the realm of nature by translating any kind of 'tricky' space into the straight, the flat, the uniform, and the rational. 'The direct military road runs in a straight line from the fort to the banks of the Détroit, and the eastern extremity of the town. Here it is intersected by the highway running parallel with the river, and branching off at right angles on either hand; the right, leading in the direction of the more populous States; the left, through the town, and thence towards the more remote and western parts, where European influence has yet been but partially extended' (I, 231; 128). 'The appearance of geometrical patterns in the human environment,' notes Frye, is 'a symbol of aggressiveness, of imperialistic domination.'[23]

Such is the order of Western European man, caught at the precise moment it is struggling for a foothold in the New World. Informing the Conquest as much as the conquest of the land and the Indian, it is an arrogant and militant vision of order; as *The Canadian Brothers* attests, it will shape and determine the perceptions and assumptions of the culture that will emerge out of this symbolic fort, the only one of nine along the border the Indians could not suppress. And it is to the exposure of its inadequacies and the alienation which it fosters that Richardson addresses himself here and elsewhere. That he should be roused at the same time to celebrate the group heroism occasioned by the struggle to survive and endure is part of the ambiguous double vision he has bequeathed to us.

Inside the walls of the fortress, this cultural ideal of order and rationality rigorously expresses itself in an obsession with geometrical and mechanical exactitude. A brief reminder of the story may help to clarify this compulsion. It begins at midnight in September, 1763 with the violent ringing of an alarm bell echoing in the 'death-like silence' (I, 49; 29). 'The English garrison of Détroit,' besieged from without by a federation of various Indian tribes, is 'thrown into the utmost consternation by the sudden and mysterious introduction of a stranger within its walls' (I, 25; 16). It is the first of a bewildering array of enigmas thrown out by the fast-paced narrative. The 'unseen visitant' (II, 39; 179) is the shadowy Wacousta who disturbs the slumber of Colonel de Haldimar. As we learn later, he torments him with threats of revenge for the Colonel's betrayal of friendship, for the treacherous seduction of the anima-like Clara Beverley (thus robbing Wacousta of the ideal his passionate, romantic sensibility has enshrined), and for the loss of honour – and identity – through a court martial on false charges engineered by De Haldimar. Branded a traitor and an outlaw, Wacousta drifts to the margins of society as his double, the ambitious De Haldimar, climbs the ladder of promotion.

Although all this happened twenty-four years before in the Old World, Wacousta finds Canada a perfect climate for preserving the past; he swears that in no other country in the world could his dark revenge wreak such havoc. Once a handsome British gentleman and artist, the baronet Sir Reginald Morton, he has grown hideous and grotesquely taller, a 'gigantic' (III, 221; 461) embodiment of the Canadian landscape itself which is called Nature's 'gigantic offspring' (I, 33; 20). Now second-in-command to Ponteac, he furthers his plans to exterminate the De Haldimar family by urging the Indian chief to check the spread of the white race before they become a conquered people like the French.

Alarmed by the inexplicable and irrational appearance of this unknown intruder inside the 'hermetically closed' (I, 28; 18) fort, to restore order the garrison is filled with 'armed men, distributed into three divisions, and forming, with their respective ranks facing outwards, as many sides of a hollow square, the mode of defense invariably adopted by the Governor in all cases of sudden alarm' (I, 56; 32). Thus, they form a square within the larger square of the fort. And exactly in 'the centre of that centre' (I, 58; 34) not the escaped Wacousta but his (unknown) nephew Frank Halloway confronts the military machine.

He is another round peg in a square hole: Wacousta's double-by-duplication, he is likewise an impulsive, passionate individual whose real name is also Reginald Morton. And he, too, is arraigned and falsely accused of being a traitor by Colonel de Haldimar in an eerie, torch lit court martial. On the following morning, Halloway is again 'reconducted into the square ... in the immediate centre' (I, 199; 111). At the end of Volume 3, Wacousta's second trial mirrors that of Halloway: 'the prisoner stood nearly in the same spot where his unfortunate nephew had lingered on a former occasion' (III, 328; 519). The laws of geometry govern life – and death – in *Wacousta* as much as those recognized in its voluminous legal codes. Throughout the work, such symmetry reflects the need to control, wilfully to check and dominate the impulsive, the spontaneous, or the irrational. It is a direct manifestation of the excessive 'caution and vigilance of no common kind [which] were increasingly exercised by the prudent governor' (I, 25; 16). Dennis Lee's insights into similar designs in Michael Ondaatje's superb *Billy the Kid* help illuminate *Wacousta*. In both works, we find men mechanizing themselves, 'taking an airless delight in the precision of diagram or machine.' Such 'mechanical icons seemed to promise power over the organic domain without, and the separation of the ego from the organic domain within.'[24]

The steps taken to preserve life end up sacrificing it. Such ironic reversals alert us to the fact that a garrison culture, by its very nature, perpetually hooks twice the darkness in its self-righteous attempt to hook twice the glory; what is gained in security and stability is lost in the sacrifice of spontaneity and vital energy. To quote from *Divisions on a Ground*, 'What we are now beginning to see is that an original belief in the rightness of destroying or ignoring a so-called "savage" culture develops toward a contempt for our own.'[25] In that case, it again becomes hard to distinguish between the 'primitive' and the 'sophisticated.' In Richardson, as in E.J. Pratt, precise military detail is a manifestation of highly disciplined, group-oriented movements. But although he, too, celebrates perilous enterprises and the heroic struggle to survive against all odds, unlike Pratt he fiercely questions the 'unquestionable' values and assumptions of garrison society. As De Haldimar's fate makes apparent, wilfully to dominate the realm of nature and the Indian is also to declare war on one's own instinctual nature, to mechanize oneself.

The realm of nature and the Indian on the other side of the

border ravine is just as consistently one of circles and curves. Indian tepees, arranged in concentric circles in the very heart of the dark bush, are sheltered within a series of 'undulating hills' 'crowned with thick and overhanging forest'; this mass of trees extends in a 'circular sweep ... around the fort' (I, 264–5; 146). The tiny square of the fort is at the centre of a vast circle, everywhere surrounded by the frontier. In Richardson's introduction, also omitted from the NCL edition, we are told that it 'stands in the middle of a common ... bounded by woods ... untouched by the hand of civilization' (I, 19; 12).

A similar arrangement is echoed in the position of the schooner carrying Madeline away from the burning ruins of Fort Michillimackinac across Lake Huron: 'To all appearance they were yet in the middle of the lake for around them lay the belting sweep of forest that bounded the perspective of the equidistant circle, of which their boat was the focus or immediate centre' (III, 16–7; 349). 'In Canada, wherever one is, the frontier is a circumference,' writes Frye.[26] Although from the perspective of the claustrophobic, terror-stricken garrison the New World environment manifests the lineaments of hell or a vast labyrinth concealing demonic monsters, Richardson suggests that another perspective is possible. Locale and native peoples belong to one another. At the same time that it appears nightmarish to the European, it is also described as a bush garden, a New World Eden closed off to the closed minds of the immigrants. 'A sort of oasis of the forest' (II, 155; 243), the Ottawas' encampment where Wacousta lives is the counterpart of the Old World mountain-top 'oasis of the rocks' (III, 209; 455) where Sir Reginald Morton woos his beloved 'child of nature' (III, 220; 461). Unlike the Europeans, the Indians accommodate themselves to the flowing contours of the land. Their oasis presents 'the appearance of a mound, constructed on the first principles of art.' The 'conical shape' (II, 155; 243) of the irregularly spaced teepees harmonizes with the curving landscape.

Unlike the strictly regulated and segregated grouping of officers, artillerymen, common soldiers, and women in the garrison, a haphazard mass of Indian men, women, and children relax idly on the ground, in physical contact with one another, undismayed by the lack of privacy, of 'private space.' There is a shaggy, tactual, almost sculptural dimension to the descriptions of their bodies and clothes; this is particularly true in Wacousta's case. The circle motif is present in the seemingly incidental detail of some Ottawas lying with their feet close to the camp fire, so that they 'diverged like so many radii from their centre' (II, 155; 243).

Richardson appears to be the first Canadian writer to articulate the grammar of strife between straight line and curve so ubiquitous in our literature. Atwood, for instance, notes in *Survival* that throughout Canadian writing 'The order of Nature is labyrinthine, complex, curved; the order of Western European Man tends to squares, straight lines, oblongs and similar shapes.'[27] *Wacousta*'s shaping imagery of circles and squares reinforces the thematic polarization of the New World into two antagonistic yet complementary forces. Richardson's inauguration of this way of symbolically mapping the conflict between civilization and nature, European and Amerindian, may stem from his intimate knowledge of garrison life in North America, Europe, and the West Indies; so, too, his (alleged) Indian ancestry and lifelong familiarity with the Indian tribes of the border region may have sensitized him to these configurations.

Certainly, both his fiction and non-fiction disclose an acquaintance with native Indian customs, legends, and symbol systems, particularly with those creation myths dealing with twins and trickster figures. Richardson's imaginative deployment of straight line and curve marks the absorption of the North American Indian sensibility into our literature from its beginnings. Such an incorporation is one that contemporary poets and novelists are striving to effect; Reaney's *Wacousta!* and Don Gutteridge's *Tecumseh* (with the inclusion of long quotations from Richardson's *War of 1812* and his *Tecumseh*) suggest recognition of a writer responding to and utilizing his immediate environment.

The faithfulness of this translation of the everyday details of border life receives corroboration in the poignant reminiscences of medicine-man Hehaka Sapa or 'Black Elk':

It is a bad way to live, for there can be no power in a square. You have noticed that everything an Indian does is in a circle, and that is because the Power of the World always works in circles, and everything tries to be round ... The sky is round, I have heard the earth is round like a ball ... The wind, in its greatest power, whirls. Birds make their nests in circles, for theirs is the same religion as ours ... Our teepees were round like the nests of birds, and these were always set in a circle, the nation's hoop, a nest of many nests ... But the Wasichus have put us in these square boxes. Our power is gone and we are dying ... [28]

'The Circle and The Square,' a chapter in the autobiography of story-teller and medicine-man 'Lame Deer,' is relevant to our appreciation of what Richardson is doing in *Wacousta*. He speaks of 'wavy lines,' 'whorls, spirals and zigzaggy lines,' 'circles within circles,' and squares: 'The white man's symbol is the square. Square is his house, his office buildings with walls that separate people from one another. Square is the door which keeps strangers out, the dollar bill, the jail. Square are the white man's gadgets – boxes, boxes, boxes and more boxes ... corners and sharp edges ... You become a prisoner inside all these boxes.'[29] No better gloss on these motifs in Richardson can be found than these two complementary reflections.

Fraught with multiple ambiguities which undercut the simple polarity which the book may seem at first to suggest, the line between the two worlds wavers and fades, even as the doubles blur into one another. Initially, the circle-square motif might indicate that we are dealing with two cultures so entirely different that they exist separately without any apparent relationship with one another whatsoever. Yet gradually the reader sees that even on the basis of conflict alone, Indians and Europeans are alternately trying to attack and escape from one another, reversing identities as pursuer and pursued. They progressively become intertwined, until at certain moments both groups are confused and confounded. At the end, there is a conjugation of the two cultures which were so violently opposed at the beginning: both De Haldimar and his double Wacousta are dead; peace is declared, the doors of the fort open and Europeans and Indians intermingle; the new chief teaches games to the sons of the new colonel.

This is a conjugation of extremes which has been prepared for throughout by the structural fabric of interwoven correspondences between the cultures, between individual characters (usually doubles or those involved in love triangles), and between settings. Seemingly disparate episodes within the work parallel and echo one another. At the same time that Halloway is brought into the centre of the garrison square as a traitor and spy, his best friend who is at one point referred to as like a brother, Frederick de Haldimar, is in the forest at the exact centre of a circle of Ottawas presided over by Wacousta, who calls him a spy. The fate of each man and the dehumanizing way in which each is treated suggest that the gap between civilized and savage behaviour is not great, as Northey, Moss, and Duffy have also observed. The garrison can be a spiritual and moral wilderness, its savagery hidden beneath the mask of law and order; Halloway's trial is one in a proliferating series of scenes detailing what has been termed 'a herd mentality,' the group persecuting a scapegoat.[30] This sense of a radically contracted, compressional borderland where all things happen at once is intensified by three lengthy flashbacks. These create a multiple perspective; the same event is presented in differing contexts, heightening the web of interconnections between people and places. The fast-paced narrative sequence is initially disrupted at the point where Colonel de Haldimar and his soldiers defeat Ponteac's plans to take over the fort through the ruse of a peaceful council allowing the Indians full entry into the fort. The reader is returned to the opening incidents of the story, and more pieces of the puzzle are displayed in the narrative of Frederick's night-journey into the Indian encampment.

These same events are now seen from the point of view of those on the other side of the border ravine; it is as if two slightly out of focus pictures are being superimposed on one another, giving rise to a world of endless reduplication, of halls and mirrors. The flashback ends with a description of Frank Halloway's execution as it appears to the Indians and to Frederick; the latter, disguised as an Indian, escapes his captors and runs madly to the bridge at the same time that Ellen eludes the group of those restraining her, doffs her disguise of a soldier's outfit, and glides like a phantom towards the bridge. She crosses the bridge into the Indian world, abducted by Wacousta; Frederick crosses back into the garrison domain, rescued by his friends.

The breakdown in distinction between the two domains is also apparent in the way fort and Indian encampment mirror or duplicate one another. The view from the ramparts to the bridge is complemented by that from the elevated tent site. Wacousta's tent opens towards the fort; he watches them as they watch him, and both watch each other watching the border bridge in utter fascination and revulsion. Like the fort, the Indian encampment is protected by a defensive barrier and sports a flag. Corresponding to the fort's flagstaff, which is of tapering pine, the camp has one solitary pine, standing out as a landmark on a ridge. Wacousta is to be hanged from the former, but he escapes; Everard is tied to the latter, awaiting torture and death, but he, too, escapes. Such affinities between the two suggest a strange sort of interplay, of interpenetration.

This is further heightened by a variety of interwoven events creating a sense of a world of instant all-at-oneness and interdependence. Wacousta enters the fort at the same time and by the same means as its favourite son, Frederick de Haldimar, exits from it. Everard shoots from the ramparts at the shadowy Wacousta on the ground outside who almost instantly fires back. Wacousta throws his tomahawk at Colonel de Haldimar at the same time as someone fires at him, knocking off his white turban. Both groups subsist together and act and react upon one another at the same time in synchronized concert, as if on some gigantic feedback loop. These suggest the movements of a single, huge entity whose right hand does not know what its left hand is doing. Could this strange entity be a 'Border Double,' its two halves, here in conflict, 'sophisticated' European immigrant and 'primitive' North American Indian culture? As Wacousta remarks, people and events seem to be interconnected 'by some fatality of coincidence' (III, 276; 491).

Dennis Lee, describing the 'interplay' characterizing similar conflicts in *Billy the Kid* and *Beautiful Losers*, employs terms which are helpful in interpreting *Wacousta*: 'the coincidence of opposites' and 'the dualism of simultaneity.' He presents these within the context of 'the dualism of savage fields,' the strife of 'world' and 'earth' or, very roughly, civilization and nature. Earth assaults world and world assaults earth, notes Lee, as if they had nothing in common. But the books' own vision of the two domains is very different: 'it shows them coinciding completely, each person and thing a member of both domains at once.' They overlap and intermingle 'like two fields of force in a single space, rather than standing over against each other like two armies on a battle-field.'[31] This recalls Hawthorne's 'neutral territory ... where the Actual and the Imaginary may meet, and each imbue itself with the nature of the other'; Chase's 'borderland of the human mind where the actual and the imaginary intermingle'; Frye's wilder-ness 'doppelganger figure who is oneself and yet the opposite of oneself'; and McLuhan's borderline 'area of maximal interplay and subtle interpenetration,' 'the space between two worlds, constituting a kind of double plot or action.'[32]

Border Blur

For a long time, the EYES did not have it.

ROBERT KROETSCH [33]

Besides the straight line/curve motif, 'eye versus ear' imagery constitutes another of the complementary pairs of opposites structuring Richardson's *Wacousta*. Both motifs are inseparable; together they advance the configuring of garrison and tribal worlds. The 'bias' of the garrison culture is reflected in sharp, visual detail emphasized in the description of the fortress; in the ever present telescope which defines the garrison dweller as the watch does Gulliver; and in the repeated references to characters fixing their eyes in the distance, especially on the fatal bridge which exercises an almost hypnotic influence. Whenever the narrator describes the fort layout or military procedure, he does so in a realistic, almost documentary style. Minute, concrete particulars of everyday, domestic life are inventoried with a strongly pictorial emphasis forecasting that of other writers from this region such as Munro, Findley, Davies, Dewdney, and Reaney. Yet that very clarity, so reassuring to the British garrison with its precarious foothold in this strange border world, repeatedly begins to blur.

In the following passage, one of many not included in the NCL edition, Richardson is concerned to provide the reader with a firm impression of massiveness and solidity. He also conveys the British obsession with enclosing space within an abstract grid, hacking the universe up into discrete, visual segments. Since this effect is created through a cumulative piling up of detail, it is necessary to quote at length.

> The barracks of the officers, consisting of a range of low buildings, occupied the two contiguous sides of a square, and in the front of these ran a narrow and covered piazza, somewhat similar to those attached to the guardhouses in England ... On the other two faces of the square stood several block-houses, a style of structure which, from their adaptation to purposes of defence as well as of accommodation, were everywhere at that period in use in America, and are even now continued along the more exposed parts of the frontier. These, capable of containing each a company of men, were, as their name implies, formed of huge masses of roughly shapen timber, fitted into each other at the extremities by rude incisions from the axe, and filled in with smaller wedges of wood. The upper part of these block-houses projected on every side several feet beyond the ground floor, and over the whole was a sheathing of planks, which, as well as those covering the barracks of the officers, were painted of a brick-red colour. (I, 200–1; 119)

Such documentary realism with a specificity Munro or Ondaatje might appreciate yields a clear blueprint from which we could reconstruct the entire fort block by block. It is a factuality noticeably absent from Cooper's Leatherstocking Tales, which eschew realism. The stress here is on visual order, precise demarcation, uniform and continuous shapes and sizes, efficient and practical management of space. This tendency to split, divide, and compartmentalize as a means of control and domination extends beyond architecture itself to embrace every aspect of garrison life; on a psychological level, it is exemplified in Colonel de Haldimar himself, a very split man indeed. Richardson coaxes metaphors out of blockhouses the way Melville is said to squeeze poetry out of blubber.

To the dismay of the visually oriented garrison, everything outside the solid square structure of the fortress is an insubstantial blur. The eye proves an unreliable guide to the New World environment, for the wilderness is a world of flux, of constantly moving shapes, shadows, blurred boundaries, and outlines. The forest blurs, dissolves, and merges separate things as well as people. The daylight world of facts and figures, so realistically evoked, is invaded and permeated by the fantastic, bizarre, and unreal atmosphere of the nightworld of romance. As the solid becomes insubstantial, the line dividing the ordinary and the unearthly begins to waver, blur, and fade.

Throughout *Wacousta*, eyes and ears are strained to the uttermost. Telescopes compulsively scan – almost frisk – the landscape for clues to the mysterious nature of their new surroundings. Charles de Haldimar's exclamation at the outset of the work as he stares into the 'impenetrable obscurity' enveloping the garrison, trying to spot the mysterious midnight intruder, is representative of dozens of such utterances: 'I do begin to fancy I see something ... but so confusedly and indistinctly, that I know not whether it be not merely an illusion of my imagination' (I, 49; 29). A recurrent moment in this work and in the sequel occurs when the flux gradually, suspensefully, resolves itself into more distinct, 'intelligible' shapes – at least temporarily.

In the opening chapters, the garrison is embedded in an eerie darkness which recedes at dawn only to be replaced by an enshrouding mist, 'a rolling sheet of vapour retiring back upon itself, and disclosing objects in succession, until the eye could embrace all that came within its extent of vision.' Eventually, 'a dark speck upon the common' is perceived, yet 'so indistinctly, they could scarcely distinguish it with the naked eye.' The speck metamorphoses into 'the dark shadow of a human form' (I, 89–90; 50–1). Typically, this engenders endless speculation arguing the ambivalence of perceptible reality: it is successively held to be the carcass of a wolf, the corpse of an Indian, the body of the midnight intruder, the missing Frederick de Haldimar, 'the devil himself' (I, 119; 67). Yet to name is only to misname.

Finally, it is discovered to be the hideously disfigured corpse of Donellan, Frederick's servant, a man 'remarkable for the resemblance he bore, in figure, to Captain de Haldimar' (II, 141; 236), one of many doubles in the text. Inexplicably clothed in Frederick's uniform, the body is covered in a 'disguise ... of blood and brains' (I, 126–7; 71). The incident typifies subsequent encounters with the unexplained and unknown outside and inside the fortress walls. A mystery which no one can unravel, it gives rise to unlimited 'conjecture' (I, 82; 47), one of the most frequently used words in the story. And as one puzzle is solved, two more sprout up to baffle the sorely tried reasoning powers and strained eyes of the anxious Europeans. 'The Canadian sphinx,' as Frye puts it, has 'brought her riddle of unvisualized land' to a people terrified and haunted 'by a sense of the unreality of the unseen.'[34] And the eyes did not (do not?) have it.

The border river and the surrounding wilderness, declaring themselves a realm of the unexplored, the unconscious, and the magical, seem a particularly congenial abode for this horrific 'sphinx.' The eye fails completely at the borderline, the gap, the juncture of the two domains: the ravine is literally a realm of the unseen, 'an abyss, the depth of which was lost in the profound obscurity that pervaded the scene.' It is the bed of 'a narrow stream, so imperceptible in the 'living darkness,' and so noiseless in its course' (II, 148; 239). It is certainly not the only river-ravine symbolizing divided landscapes and psyches in Canadian literature.[35] Wacousta, the shadowy, gigantic creature who alone appears undaunted by the perils of this abyss he so easily navigates, is as unvisualizable as the landscape he haunts; he is the 'unseen visitant' (II, 39; 179), suddenly appearing beside those who fear him most. Those De Haldimars who cross the borderline become similarly invisible ghostlike figures. At the bridge, riddles of identity and genealogy become more grisly, evoking a characteristically gothic *frisson*.

During his second frenetic midnight journey into the wilderness, Frederick de Haldimar, barely able to see, is surprised by the apparition of the 'threshold guardian' (Campbell): the lycanthropic Wacousta guarding the entrance into this other world. But first he encounters his 'familiar,' the wolf-dog Onondato 'whose eyes glared like two burning coals through the surrounding gloom' (II, 41; 180). Initially, it, too, is a formless blur in the exact centre of the bridge: 'The dark shadow of something upon its centre caught his eye, and a low sound like that of a dog lapping met his ear. While his gaze yet lingered on the shapeless object, endeavouring to give it a character, the clouds which had so long obscured it passed momentarily from before the moon, and disclosed the appalling truth. It was a wolf-dog lapping up from the earth, in which they were encrusted, the blood and brains of the unfortunate Frank Halloway' (II, 39; 179).

People and landscapes continually go in and out of focus. We may provisionally call this phenomenon in *Wacousta* and *The Canadian Brothers* 'border blur,' adapting that term from Michael Ondaatje who, in turn, has taken it from b.p. Nichol; in Ondaatje, as Eli Mandel observes, it is associated with the 'possibilities of the Western as a means of exploring perceptual reality.'[36] In Richardson, the border blur motif, like the play of circles and squares, serves the larger myth of European adjustment to the New World environment; it suggests the perceptual and psychological disorientation arising both 'in the primitive world' where, Carl Jung notes, 'things do not have the same sharp boundaries they do in our "rational" societies,' and in that unknown realm which Campbell describes as 'always a place of strangely fluid and polymorphous beings, unimaginable torments, superhuman deeds.'[37]

An 'obstructive blur' may attend all border crossings. Addressing himself to 'the riddle of unvisualized land' in Tom Thomson's painting, Northrop Frye states that 'focusing on the farthest distance makes the foreground, of course, a shadowy blur'; in these incubus-haunted landscapes, 'one has the feeling of something not quite emerging which is all the more sinister for its concealment.'[38] Such is also the case in *Wacousta*. As a bewitched detachment of soldiers cautiously approaches the fatal bridge, they 'fancied they beheld the dark and flitting forms of men gliding from tree to tree along the skirt of the wood; but when they gazed again, nothing of the kind was to be seen, and the illusion was at once ascribed to the heavy state of the atmosphere and the action of their own precautionary instincts' (I, 267; 148).

Border blur, as it appears in Richardson, seems to be an integral aspect of our own tradition of North American gothic. Like the haunted explorers of the New World who 'investigate the nature of the country' in Al Purdy's *The Runners*, Richardson's European immigrants suspect that

the forests are making magic against us –
I think the land knows we are here,
I think the land knows we are strangers.
Let us stay close to our friend the sea,
or cunning dwarves at the roots of darkness
shall seize and drag us down –

'Afraid of this dark land, / ground mist that makes us half ghosts, / and another silence inside silence,' the scouts for Eric the Red, like the alien British, are 'hungry for the home islands.'[39] Spooked by the 'violent blur' of the atmosphere, Atwood's Mrs Moodie is also caught up in illusions,

watching the bear I didn't see condense itself among
the trees, an outline tenuous as an echo

...
It absorbs all terror[40]

Likewise confronted with the unknown and the unlived in, Richardson's garrison inhabitants fill in the visual blur with the monstrous apparitions of hallucination. The gigantic, spectral Wacousta and his wolf-dog Onondato preside over a land of the dead populated by the shades of Hades; the Indians are perceived by the British as shadows, ghosts, monsters, spectres, mad animals, giants, and demons eerily gliding through a hellish wilderness, not unlike the way the Congolese natives strike the intruding Europeans in Conrad's *Heart of Darkness*. 'Examining the edge of the forest above and below, I was almost certain I could see movements – human forms gliding here and there,' 'flitting indistinctly against the gloomy border of the forest,' says Marlow on board a steamer whose 'outlines blurred as though she had been on the point of dissolving.'[41] In *Wacousta*, 'the schooner glided with a silence that might have called up the idea of a Stygian freight,' firing at howling spectres flitting through the darkness; the captain vows that 'This is sailing through the heart of the American forest with a vengeance' (III, 52; 368), well aware that Canada – Southern Ontario certainly – is one of the dark places of the earth.

Richardson's borderland is a gothically flavoured realm of 'incubus and *cauchemar*.' *Wacousta* emerges out of an unexplored country where – as the subtitle *The Prophecy* suggests – nature speaks in riddles and oracles and vast empty silences. As the wide assortment of spectres and monsters attest, the land has not been imaginatively digested. 'A large tract of land,' observes Frye,

> may well affect the people living near it as too much cake does a small boy: an unknown but quite possibly horrible Something stares at them in the dark; hide under the bedclothes as long as they will, sooner or later they must stare back. Explorers, tormented by a sense of the unreality of the unseen, are first: pioneers and traders follow. But the land is still not imaginatively absorbed, and the incubus moves on to haunt the artists. It is a very real incubus. It glares through the sirens, gorgons, and centaurs, griffins, cyclops, pygmies and chimeras of the poems which followed the Greek colonies.[42]

What is essential in Richardson's portrait of the borderland is akin to what Frye detects in painters like Tom Thomson: 'the imaginative instability, the emotional unrest and dissatisfaction one feels about a country which has not been lived in: the tension between the mind and a surrounding not integrated with it.'[43] The garrison responds to the world outside its palisades as to a mysterious enemy code, one that demands deciphering yet resists all efforts to crack it. Despite feverish speculation about the enigmas of nature and Indian, most conjecture proves partial or misleading or completely erroneous. Perception becomes problematical. Closure at the rational level is continually subverted. In various ways, the British have encountered their blind spot.

The act of judgment itself is called into question. Reason cannot be trusted. What the garrison fails to understand is that its blurred vision is largely the result of being filtered through their own cherished illusions, cultural blinkers, and imported inadequacies. Such distortion not even a thousand telescopes can clarify. What needs refocusing, Richardson submits, is not the telescope but a lopsided, unbalanced psychological outlook. As Atwood's Moodie realizes, 'Whether the wilderness is / real or not / depends on who lives there.'[44]

For the Indians and the 'Canadians' who live in harmony with each other on the borderland, nature is not a monster and North America is not an endless nightmare. Wacousta, referred to throughout as 'The Warrior of the Fleur de Lis,' is accepted by both the native people and the French Canadians; their anguish and their anger at being conquered by the British are expressed in Wacousta's revenge on De Haldimar and the garrison. Although forced into guiding the terrified Frederick and Everard through the bush, François alone remains relaxed, at ease, and good-humoured; on board the schooner as it sails through what for the British is a heart of darkness, he gorges himself on provisions and falls pleasantly to sleep. The Indians are at home in their 'unvisualized' land. For the British, they partake of its insubstantiality. Shadows and spectres, they float silently and effortlessly through the densest undergrowth; leaping and bounding, 'their dark and pliant forms' speed 'with almost incredible rapidity over the dilapidated walls, and fly into the very heart of the forest' (I, 113; 64).

In direct contrast to the silent, gliding forms of the Indians 'flying in air like so many Will-o'-the-wisps' (I, 123; 69), the soldiers plod heavily and wearily along their straight road to the bridge loaded down with rattling artillery and cumbersome uniforms. Long 'cooped up' (I, 230; 127) in the fort which announces their rare departure with a 'heavy clanking,' a 'dull creaking sound of the rusty bolts and locks that secured the ponderous gate' (I, 121; 68), their movements are stiff, mechanical, robotic. Frederick de Haldimar's first night-journey into the wilderness guided by the passionate, heroic Indian woman Oucanasta points up this difference. Orienting himself by eye in 'the mazes of the forest,' he trips awkwardly over roots and dodges branches. She moves noiselessly along 'a narrow winding path, less seen than felt in the deep gloom pervading the wood, and with light steps bounded over obstacles' (II, 146; 238).

To facilitate his movements and to escape detection, Oucanasta offers Frederick her moccasins. 'The civilized man' refuses, and suffers the narrator's irony. 'This was too un-European, – too much reversing the established order of things' (II, 149–50; 240). At her insistence, the established order is reversed, Frederick escapes immediate detection, and learns of the stratagem to seize the fort. Without the love and devotedness of this 'guardian angel,' even the excessive prudence and caution of Colonel de Haldimar, it is emphasized, would be of no avail against 'Indian ingenuity' (III, 336; 523). Even in such a 'trivial' detail as differences in footwear, Richardson is able to convey two kinds of sensibility: 'Had he retained his unbending boot, it must have crushed whatever it pressed; whereas, the pliant moccasin, yielding to the obstacles it encountered, enabled him to pass noiselessly over them' (II, 153; 242).

Intimidated by the vast open space celebrated by Cooper's frontiersmen, the garrison soldiers are constantly shown trying desperately to enclose themselves within or under various structures. Outside the fortress walls, they compulsively conceal themselves within the bomb-shelter, under the ends of the bridge, or, like Frederick, within the hollow trunk of a beech tree. Charles Olson's *Call Me Ishmael* offers one gloss on such obsessive behaviour: 'I take SPACE to be the central fact to man born in

America ... Some men ride on such space, others have to fasten themselves like a tent stake to survive.[45] Survival, rather than easy-riding, preoccupies Richardson's protagonists. The horror of feeling exposed and vulnerable in this immensity is rooted in the same fear that 'unstructured / space is a deluge' which fuels the progressive insanities of Atwood's pioneers. Armed with a mind partitioned by walls and fences and straight rows, a cultural ideal of geometrical order and the bias of 'eyes / made ragged by his effort / the tension / between subject and object,' this figure is a direct descendent of the type so deftly portrayed by Richardson in 1832.

> He stood, a point
> on a sheet of green paper
> proclaiming himself the centre,
>
> with no walls, no borders
> anywhere; the sky no height
> above him, totally un-
> enclosed
> and shouted:
>
> Let me out![46]

This is the shout of Governor de Haldimar, the builder of walls, the static 'tent stake.' Wacousta is the roving dream figure, energetically riding on space in the Scottish Highlands as in the borderland's undulating hills. Like the Indians, he is a shadowy spectre with no fixed form or shape, a trickster. This is how he appears throughout the first volume; he only begins to take on flesh and blood in the last volume. Like the ghost who appears as the clock strikes twelve in *Hamlet*, spurring conjecture as to its reality among the anxious guards of the beleaguered castle of Elsinore, the 'unseen visitant' at Fort Détroit impresses the sentinels as 'not a living soul' (I, 33; 20); 'it appeared impossible any thing wearing the human form could pass them unperceived, even in the obscurity that reigned around' (I, 39; 23).

Like energy without form, the fiery Wacousta is perpetually in motion, leaping, gliding, bounding. Hurtling through all barriers and crossing all boundaries, this trickster escapes from the fort three times and is the only one able to leap the border ravine between fort and forest. He runs with a speed deemed supernatural. He paddles a canoe with 'a quickness that rendered it almost invisible to the eye' until 'like some wild animal, instinct with life, it lashed the foaming waters from its bows' (III, 133; 412). Colonel de Haldimar, on the other hand, rigid, unbending, walks with a 'haughty and measured step' (I, 77; 44). Weighed down by worries and thoughts about the survival of the garrison and his own obsession with propriety and proper appearances, the movements of this emotional cripple become more strained and heavier as the revenge progresses. Such contrasting yet complementary traits reflect the intricate interrelations of a doppelgänger pairing described concisely by Wacousta: 'He, all coldness, prudence, obsequiousness, and forethought. I, all enthusiasm, carelessness, impetuosity, and independence' (III, 194; 447). Head, heart. Intellect, feelings. Reason, instinct. Mind, body. Garrison mentality, Indian or romantic sensibility.

Wholeness, psychological and cultural, requires a harmonious tension between these opposites; without these contraries is no progression, no growth, and, as Frye says, 'something anti-cultural comes into Canadian life, a dominating herd-mind in which nothing original can grow.'[47] To deny, repress, or to attempt to eradicate one half of this configuration, as a garrison culture so attempts, is to drive away the vital energy without which such a culture remains stunted; a gigantic, seemingly demonic Wacousta figure prophesying a dire revenge – what Frye calls 'dark, repressed oracular doubles concealed within each of us' – is both a product and a casualty of this scheme of things.[48] Richardson's garrison, excessively prudent and 'rational,' attracts what it fears and walls out because 'it' is its other half, distorted because driven underground, monstrous because unnaturally suppressed or cut off.

This ironic reversal reveals a culture sorely unable 'to connect' yet also bespeaks the need for an approach to wholeness through a reconciliation with, and an assimilation of what is sentenced to exile outside its heavily defended borders. As Robertson Davies advises,

> We must be aware of the darker side of our natures. We must know what lurks in the shadows ... What is demonstrated is simply the principle of *enantiodromia*, which is the tendency of things to run into their opposites if they are exaggerated. Excessive self-love becomes no love at all; extreme prudence ends up by spoiling the ship for a ha'p'orth of tar; a rejection of all that is coarsely vital in life brings a shrivelling of sensibility. As a very eminent psychiatrist once said to me: 'We attract what we fear.' What we fear is the portion of life that remains unlived. Our task, if we seek spiritual wholeness, is to be sure that what has been rejected is not, therefore, forgotten, and its possibility wiped out.[49]

An Ear for an Eye[50]

The eye proves an unreliable guide in Richardson's wilderness because this is primarily a world of sound. The forest is an auditory space. A swirling, undulating, pulsing blur echoing with a cacophony of piercing shrieks, yells, groans, and curses. It is evoked through imagery of hallucination, disorientation, and irrationality. The Indians are presented as beings of sound, disembodied voices speaking in the accents of the violated and forbidding landscape itself: 'A hundred tongues like the baying of many bloodhounds, again rent the air with their wild cries, which seemed to rise up from the very bowels of the earth, and close to the appalled ear of the young officer' (II, 192; 262–3). 'The ear of the red skins is quicker than the lightning' (II, 149; 240), states Oucanasta. In the forest, the Ottawas orient themselves through a wide variety of cries with specific intonation and meaning. To Frederick and a few others conversant in the customs and language of the tribe, these speak volumes; to most, however, it is the howling of demons.

The wolf-like Wacousta exults in sound, howling, screaming, bellowing. He soars on it as he rides on space. In this, he is not unlike Sinclair Ross's strange Judith West, an outcast from the false-fronted Horizon Main Street; she is associated with the vitality of the open prairie, with the wind in her hair as it is in that of W.O. Mitchell's Bens. It is a howling wind which she scales when she sings alone, 'something feral in her voice' able to 'ride up with it.'[51] Standing in the centre of the bridge after having killed Charles de Haldimar, Wacousta shakes both realms with his roaring: 'A yell, so terrific as to be distinctly heard in the fort itself, burst from his vast chest, and rolled in prolonged echoes through the forest' (III, 302; 505). The 'invisible' (II, 193; 263) Wacousta is initially presented not to our eye – even to the keen-sighted Everard he is little more than 'something dark, and slightly moving' which may be a wolf – but to our ear as a voice: 'a fierce, wild, and prolonged cry, expressive at once of triumph and revenge' (I, 51; 30). It is the voice of the outcast culture, here literally a voice crying in the wilderness. In the years following 1832, Wacousta will assume a prominent position in a chorus whose sound will be amplified by the powerful voices of Matilda Montgomery, Desborough, the Monk Knight, Westbrook, the Bens, the Donnellys, F., Eisengrim, Tay John, Judith West, Jerome Martell, Michael Hornyak, Coyote ...

Wacousta's cry echoes throughout the romance and is heard again at the end of volume 3. It is one of a series of things 'framing' the work and suggesting, in their reduplication, a cycle again about to repeat itself; a 'loud yell, but of disappointment and anger' (III, 357; 535), is uttered as the gigantic shadow, seen through a telescope from the safety of the ramparts, falls from the bridge into the mirror-like river in the bottom of the abyss. It is the last in a number of scenes of characters falling into reflections of themselves. Like 'that Shadow' Kurtz, a seven-foot-plus 'indistinct' 'wraith' who 'presented himself as a voice,' Sir Reginald Morton / Wacousta is both the eloquent, idealistic orator and artist whispering of love and the fiery, screaming 'animated image of death' presiding over a tribe of howling spectres that elevates him to 'a high seat among the devils of the land.'[52] Colonel de Haldimar, on the other hand, speaks in short, clipped sentences delivered in the kind of monotone Scott Symons characterizes variously as 'the voice of the Canadian Civil Servant,' of 'God's frozen people ... the WASP English Canadian,' of 'The

Blandman,' and of 'English-Canadian Cube Culture.' Significantly, not De Haldimar's voice but his penetrating eye is his most emphasized feature. He is constantly scrutinizing and staring at people, usually in an accusing, inquisitorial manner. To appeal to Symons again for illumination, this is the eye that prefers people and things 'detached in three dimensions at the end of a vanishing point – like looking down life at the wrong end of the telescope, which is what the Blandmind does. His is the civil servant's eye, the eye which labels everything. But in the cathedral everything – subject and object – are harmoniously linked. Everything is one, and many. You can't simply "square" the Gothic medieval cathedral.'[53]

Everything is one, and many, in the borderland, and everything happens all at once, 'suddenly' being perhaps Richardson's favourite adverb. In the context of border blur, this may be because 'To the blind all things are sudden.' Especially unnerving is the sudden alternation of sound and silence which defines Richardson's border world as it does the jungle in *Heart of Darkness*. 'While the adjutant was yet reading, in a low and solemn voice, the service for the dead, a fierce and distant yell, as if from a legion of devils, burst suddenly from the forest ... After the second yell, however, the woods in the heart of which it appeared to have been uttered, were buried in as profound a silence as if they had never yet echoed back the voice of man' (I, 85–6; 49).

This is an insistent and perhaps ineluctable silence in our literature. Discovering it in Pratt's poetry, Frye is moved to identify it as 'the symbolic silence of a moral chaos in which the creative word has not yet been spoken'; it is the silence accompanying the riddle of 'the vast unconsciousness of nature' which seems 'an unanswerable denial' of human and moral values.[54] The garrison walls provide no defence against sound. Ironically, such massive walls only help turn the entire borderland into a vast echo-chamber; as a consequence, both realms are fused in a tempestuous sea of sound which drowns out sight and shakes buildings and fractured psyches alike to their foundations. Visually oriented, extensions of their omnipresent telescopes in their fixed point of view, their desire to keep people and things at a safe distance, and their restricted, separative outlook, the Europeans are disoriented by the sudden loss of perspective: things are 'detached in three dimensions at the end of a vanishing point' in a magically discontinuous domain vibrating with yells coming from all directions at once.

Instructive here is a passage from Edmund Carpenter's 'The Eskimo and his Art,' an essay both Eli Mandel and Marshall McLuhan have found to be of interest. It condenses those concerns which have preoccupied us in this chapter. 'Auditory space has no favoured focus. It's a sphere without fixed boundaries, space made by the thing itself, not space containing the thing. It's not pictorial space, boxed-in, but dynamic, always in flux, creating its own dimensions, moment by moment. It has no fixed boundaries; it's indifferent to background. The eye focuses, pinpoints, abstracts, locating each object in physical space, against a background; the ear, however, favours sound from any direction.'[55]

The narrative of the fall of Fort Michillimackinac, its reabsorption by the land, and the narrow escape by schooner into an even more horrific heart of darkness is a superb passage that is illuminated by Carpenter's comments. In the first part of the chapter, the scene is 'shot' through the 'telescope, which had formed one of the principal resources of the cousins' (II, 266; 302), Clara and Madeline de Haldimar. They are standing at a window separating them from the 'savage scenes and unexplored countries' without, an archetypal Canadian pose. 'The forest ... formed ... the gloomy and impenetrable walls of the prison-house, and the bright lake that lay before it the only portal through which happiness and liberty could be again secured' (II, 237; 286-7).[56]

After the Indian attack, occurring simultaneously at Fort Détroit as well, the visual emphasis suddenly gives way. Perspective snaps in and out as the characters lose and regain consciousness. A sense of primeval chaos and disorder is powerfully conveyed through engulfing sound, as Clara de Haldimar faces her moment at the auditory whirlpool: 'The confusion of the garrison had now reached its acme of horror. The shrieks of women and the shrill cries of children, as they severally and fruitlessly fled from the death certain to overtake them in the end, – the cursings of the soldiers, the yellings of the Indians, the reports of rifles and the crashings of tomahawks; – these, with the stamping of human feet in the death struggle maintained in the council-room below between the chiefs and the officers, and which shook the block-house to its very foundation, all mixed up in terrible chorus together, might have called up a not inapt image of hell to the bewildered and confounding brain' (II, 280–1; 310).

Everything happens at once, everything and everyone 'mixed up in terrible chorus together.' It is a whirlpool of sound. The neatly compartmentalized garrison world is completely swallowed up, the sharply–defined distinctions, fixed points of view, and method-ical one-thing-at-a-time procedures fused with and obliterated by their opposites. McLuhan's understanding of the border clash between visual cultures and audile-oral-tactile ones is invoked here: 'The world of the ear is more embracing and inclusive than that of the eye can ever be. The ear is hypersensitive. The eye is cool and detached. The ear turns man over to universal panic while the eye ... leaves some gaps and some islands free from the unre-mitting acoustic pressure and reverberation.'[57] Quoting McLu-han's observation that 'Terror is the normal state of any oral soci-ety, for in it everything affects everything all the time,' Frye ends his 'Conclusion to a *Literary History of Canada*' by speculating that 'The Canadian spirit, to personify it as a single being dwelling in the country from the early voyages to the present, might well, reading this sentence, feel that this was where he came in.'[58]

'Break Boundaries': Exchanging Identity

While *Wacousta* dramatizes a dichotomized universe in which the domain of consciousness seems wholly separate from the domain of instinctual energy, it also shows them as overlapping. Under the intense compressional force of the borderland, the dual worlds intermingle or interpenetrate; there is a strange rediffusion or exchange of identity. The opposites begin to merge or coalesce, the borders and boundaries to blur. Inside the enclosed alien space of the garrison, the Indians metamorphose into their opposite. In the chapters portraying the artifice of Ponteac to possess himself of these two last British forts, the borderland intermingling of 'the Actual and the Imaginary' is vividly apparent. The lacrosse game is the Ottawas' 'Trojan Horse,' an example of 'Indian ingenuity.' It is designed to lull the anxieties of the enemy and deceive him into allowing them free entry into an unguarded fort.

Significantly, this is carried out under 'the guise of friendship,' the same phrase by which Richardson underlines Ensign de Haldimar's treacherous deception of his 'friend' Sir Reginald Morton. Forewarned of the trick through the combined efforts of Frederick and Oucanasta, the British match plot with counterplot, deception with counterdeception, secret with countersecret, disguise with counterdisguise until there ensues, as Robert Lecker perceptively points out, a 'breakdown in distinction between soldier and savage': 'both soldiers and savages become one in a single put-on.'[59]

In this hall of mirrors, the wily Ponteac meets his match; Colonel de Haldimar, nothing if not duplicitous, is no stranger to the arts of deceit and cunning and, as the opening scenes of the romance which he has 'conjured up' (I, 35; 21) attest, no mean manipulator of appearances. It is all a vast illusion. A game. And it is a game, strangely enough, in which either both sides win or they both lose, depending upon one's position on Atwood's victim scale, itself very much a game-theory creation.

This commingling of identity involves a medley of themes I have already engaged. Taken by surprise, as are the British when they are 'out of place,' out of their element, the Indians are overcome by 'stupefaction,' a term usually reserved for the soldiers, and dumbfounded by the 'almost magic' (II, 123; 225–6) change in appearance of a fort that at first glance seemed ineffectually guarded. Boxed in by innumerable claustrophobic blockhouses, the Indians confront rifles pointing from every angle of the square. Unlike the 'successful' massacre at Fort Michillimackinac, here there are no hellish sounds or furious, chaotic movements. The cries die in their throats, their limbs frozen in unnatural positions. They are rendered immobile and mute, the condition of frontier trauma the soldiers usually display.

Their sensitive ears prove as useless in the hermetically closed and congested visual world of the fortress as do the straining eyes of the Europeans in the echo-chamber of the forest wilderness. 'Choking up the gateway, in which they were completely wedged ... a dense mass of dusky Indians were to be seen casting their fierce glances around; yet paralysed in their movements ... After the first general yelling heard in the council-room, not a sound was uttered ... they now stood on the spot on which the further advance of each had been arrested, so silent and motionless, that, but for the rolling of their dark eyes, as they keenly measured the insurmountable barriers that were opposed to their progress, they might almost have been taken for a wild group of statuary' (II, 123–5; 226–7).

Spectral forms condense and solidify. An ever-changing, kinetic world suddenly comes to a standstill. The surprised Indians come under the 'spell' of the rational world and are cast into a new mould, to emerge a bizarre mirror-image of the stiff, heavy, mechanical soldiers. In the border crucible of implosion and compression, lines between twinned groups undulate and disintegrate, until both turn inside out. These simultaneous scenes at Forts Michillimackinac and Détroit are paradigmatic moments in *Wacousta*. They complement themselves in ways which invite us to bring the critical terminology of Atwood and Lee to our reading of them. The fate of the two forts illustrates the settler theme in Canadian literature which, Atwood speculates, breaks down into two aspects: 'straight line battles curve and wins, but destroys human life-force in the process' (Fort Détroit); 'straight line deteriorates and curve takes over again; that is, settlement fails' (Fort Michillimackinac).[60]

The corresponding episodes in Lee are the moment of 'world assault, in which men torment and slaughter the creatures of instinct;' and the complementary 'moment of earth assault, [in which] a human consciousness is pummelled and nearly demolished by instinctual energy.' Interestingly, Lee's study of *Billy the Kid* and *Beautiful Losers* leads him to posit a third paradigmatic moment: Earth-in-World. 'World needs to believe it has nothing in common with earth. And *Billy the Kid* shows world hypnotizing itself with that belief. But the book's own vision of the two domains is very different; it shows them coinciding completely, each person and thing a member of both domains at once.'[61]

Although Lee is delighted at finding this third 'moment' in these texts, he believes this is a recent phenomenon in our literature. However, Richardson, our first professional novelist with an international reputation, is, I suggest, the first to delineate such a moment. The patterns Richardson traces have their nearest analogues in the works of contemporary authors. The appearance of these patterns makes him an ancestral voice in our culture and suggests the continuity of the ways in which the Canadian imagination has developed in its fiction.

We may catch a fuller glimpse of the manner in which these two domains overlap in the exchange of identity overtaking those Europeans who wander too far from the shelter of the garrison walls and who cross over the border bridge. In a complementary reversal to that of the Indians inside Fort Détroit, the bewitched soldiers undergo a metamorphosis into screaming spectres; sometimes they are even hideously apparelled in Indian dress. This exchange or reversal is particularly true of major characters, especially Ellen Halloway (married to both Reginald Mortons) and the De Haldimars: Clara, Charles, Frederick and their cousin Madeline de Haldimar. Invaded by the wilderness, their bodies and their minds begin to blur, fragment, dissolve, and fade away. In the process, the forest rolls up the 'real' world of the garrison on its quickly spinning spool in order to unroll it as a haunted, phantasmagorical realm.

Ellen's transformation is the most dramatic, her identity the most fractured. Disguised as a drummerboy to escape detection by Colonel de Haldimar, she slowly accompanies the execution squad to the fatal bridge where her husband Frank Halloway (Reginald Morton) will be shot. Positioned midway between fort and forest, Halloway is first shot by the soldiers then immediately struck by Wacousta's (Reginald Morton's) tomahawk. At this moment, Ellen's shriek 'divided the air.' 'So wild, so piercing and so unearthly' is it that even the voluble Wacousta is humbled. Significantly, she now discards the soldier disguise, her last link to a garrison in which she and her husband were never fully integrated nor their true identities known, and runs toward the centre of the bridge. 'Flying with the rapidity of thought,' no longer stumbling, she 'resembled rather a spectre than a being of earth.' Ellen now presents 'the image of one whose reason has fled forever' (I, 276–7; 153). 'Turning with animal instinct on the hand that has inflicted its death-blow' (II, 102; 215), the border oracle, standing on Halloway's coffin, is precariously poised between the two worlds which grind away at her identity – a stance not unfamiliar in Commonwealth literature. From her double perspective, both tribe and regiment are equally threatening, equally 'inhuman' and 'devilish.' Yet her curse is on the man who has turned a blind eye on her sufferings, the 'inhuman murderer' (I, 278; 87) Colonel de Haldimar and all his children. Like Wacousta, like Sheila Watson's Coyote, she represents fate, retribution, and death.

Like Wacousta, she also becomes part Indian. Her spectral appearance, frantic energy, instantaneous movements, wild screaming and leaping, her bloody, half-naked appearance – all suggest that the border balance has come down on the side of nature and the Indian. The cultured European woman married to a fine gentleman is now the ghost. Coming upon her later in the bush, Clara is startled: '"Speak; who are you? Surely I should know that voice for that of Ellen, the wife of Frank Halloway!" A maniac laugh was uttered by the wretched woman. This continued offensively for a moment; and she observed, in an infuriated tone and with a searching eye, – "No, I am not the wife of Halloway. It is false. I am the wife of Wacousta."' (III, 171; 434). Once again, the exact centre of the bridge is a place of death and transformation.

This reversal or exchange of identity occurs at a ravine through which flows a mirror-like river. It is a very schizophrenic process: from British lady to immigrant commoner to drummerboy to spectral Indian to madwoman, wife of two Reginald Mortons. In her as in Wacousta, the infinitely complex and mind-boggling intermingling of contrarieties – the hallmark of Richardson's magical borderland – takes its fierce toll. Throughout volumes 2 and 3, we catch glimpses of a slovenly, begrimed, animal-like 'maniac' (III, 293; 500); she is like the narrator's prophetic drawing in Atwood's *Surfacing* of a European princess who grows fangs and is accompanied by a snarling wolf.[62] The lycanthropic Wacousta and his wolf-dog – the one discovered feeding on her husband's remains – keep Ellen company. Now entirely in Indian dress, totally unrecognizable, she takes on a grotesque New World identity, as Macpherson, Moss, and Northey note. Like the immigrants in Atwood's *Further Arrivals*, Ellen (as the De Haldimars)

> ... left behind ...
> one by one our civilized
> distinctions
>
> and entered a large darkness.
>
> It was our own
> ignorance we entered.[63]

Like Wacousta, Ellen begins to embody the crude violence of place. And it is her eyes that most mark the change: they are now 'wild and unmeaning,' giving her a vacant look betraying 'the almost utter unconsciousness' (III, 169; 433) which descends upon those who cross over into the boundless wilderness. At the end of the story, this mad wraith has come to haunt the garrison; as the last line informs us, search had been made for her, but she never was heard of again. Like Wacousta, Desborough, Tay John, Kristin, the Donnellys, and others, she has completely disappeared, absorbed back into the land again.

The De Haldimars fare no better. Soon after Wacousta abducts and takes to wife Ellen, his nephew's spouse, he takes Clara de Haldimar hostage. Distinctions between the two women blur. Both are frail and delicate beings who share similar physical characteristics and succumb to madness, Clara's being more Ophelia-like as befits a 'light herione.' Unlike Cooper's perfectly coiffed damsels in distress, Ellen's hair is totally dishevelled and matted and Clara's 'long hair hung negligently over her shoulders.' Matching her situation, she is clothed in both an Indian blanket and apparel 'strictly European' (III, 169–70; 433). Both are stained in blood. Her wilderness journey from burning Michillimackinac has left her, says Richardson, with every fibre of her brain racked almost to bursting, and filled only with ghostly flitting visions of the dreadful horrors she had seen. In her, too, civilizations's imprint is being bleached out.

Clara's cousin Madeline also becomes a nightmarish death-in-life figure. Glowingly described as a voluptuous 'Medicean Venus' (II, 253; 295) – a rare apparition in Canadian literature – all that seems left of her after the Michillimackinac massacre is a disembodied spirit with 'pale and spectral face ... dull eyes bent fixedly and mechanically' and 'a row of white and apparently lipless teeth' (III, 10; 345). She impresses the sailors as 'an immaterial being, sent from the world of spirits to warn them of some impending evil' (III, 1; 341). Floating like ghosts through an undulating, blurred landscape, enclosed in a bubble of semi-consciousness, the De Haldimars are fitting companions for the bubble-enclosed figures of Atwood's Moodies. Both De Haldimars and Moodies are culture-bubble spectres, out of touch with 'reality,' the land, each other, and their own unexplored instinctual natures.

Mrs Moodie, 'grown intangible,' speaks of 'the land I floated on / but could not touch to claim;' she is sorely unable, like Richardson's characters, to get a foothold, literal or psychological, in this immensity. Yet the land claims Mrs Moodie and her 'shadowy husband': 'he swerves, enters the forest / and is blotted out.' Again, the eye is the organ of control, of sanity itself:

> Unheld by my sight
> what does he change into
> what other shape
> blends with the under-
> growth, wavers ...
> ...

He may change me also
with the fox eye, the owl
eye, the eightfold
eye of the spider

Caught in the web of nature, unable to see her way out, her own identity evaporates, even her non-stop mind is stunned: 'I can't think / what he will see / when he opens the door.' These reflections emerge under the spell of 'the grey wolf under snow' in the poem *The Wereman*.[64] Mrs Moodie fears her husband may metamorphose into a wolf, her fears coming true in *Surfacing*. She, herself, returns to haunt the concrete wilderness of Toronto, a stubborn ghost hovering over Southern Ontario, a fitting companion for the spectral Ellen Halloway. Perhaps these lines from *The Circle Game*'s *A Place: Fragments* best catch Richardson's feel for border blur:

The people who come here also
flow: their bodies becoming
nebulous, diffused, quietly
spreading out into the air ... [65]

The De Haldimar brothers, like their descendants, 'The Canadian Brothers,' are also strangely 'altered' (III, 160; 428) by the North American borderland. Bearers of the torch of reason, their sanity is threatened – as it is in all of Richardson's characters – by sudden irruptions of the unconscious, of dark instinctual energy, and of the disturbingly irrational. They live under the volcano, on the very edge of complete breakdown and disintegration of identity. Despite heroic endurance and an ability to cope not patterned on his father's aggressively masculine and rational wilfulness, Frederick does not always succeed in keeping the wilderness at bay. Inside the circles of the Indian encampment at midnight, 'confused and distracting images ... crowded on his brain' (II, 179; 256). Trapped as in the ravine, his hallucinatory encounter with Wacousta belongs to the nightmares of the 'bushed.'

Taken prisoner, he is dressed as an Indian. Escaping Wacousta, he is seen flying across the ground with extraordinary speed, his whole attitude expressing despair and horror. Like others, he becomes so intermixed with the Ottawas it is difficult to distinguish him. On board the ghost-ridden schooner, not knowing whether he is awake or dreaming, he totters like a somnambulist. Finally, he, like all the others adrift in the bush, succumbs to vertigo. 'Like one bereft of all sense and consciousness of surrounding objects' (II, 332; 337), he leaves the empire of consciousness and passes into an impenetrable heart of darkness. The exultation of the intellect and of consciousness is abased. The solid, substantial world of the garrison dissolves into a blur large enough to absorb the universe.

The invasion of the wilderness is most poignant and complete in the figure of Charles de Haldimar. From the outset, possessed, like Ellen, of some of the 'mediumistic' qualities distinguishing Sir Walter Scott's mad characters, Charles has registered the full impact of Ellen's curse: 'it haunts me in my thoughts by day, and in my dreams by night' (II, 97; 212). He, too, becomes like those he fears, as if Wacousta, wendigo-like, has infected the accursed De Haldimars he abominates with the disease of death, despair, and self-destruction. Just as the garrison sets out to conquer and remould nature, the wilderness refashions the alien Europeans who resist it.

Torn by paroxysms of grief, prey to illusions and vague apprehensions, fearful for his sanity, Charles is soon reduced to a spectral 'deathlike image,' an increasingly morbid creature with 'lips bloodless and parted' (III, 125–6; 408–9). As in the case of Frederick, Clara, Ellen, and Wacousta, the law of the borderland seems to be that he can only enter the other world as an Indian: disguised as an Ottawa warrior, he attempts the rescue of Clara and his 'twin brother' (III, 312) Everard at the bridge. Again, the two groups coalesce. Paralysed by the dark shadow of the gigantic Wacousta looming above him in the moonlight, he is killed by the minotaur who has plagued his dreams in the exact centre of the labyrinth. It is the same spot where Frederick, also disguised as an Indian, had fallen before, apparently dead; here, too, his twin sister Clara is soon to perish.

Such bizarre metamorphoses are the concomitant manifestation of all border crossings in Richardson's writings. These reversals or paradoxical inversions of identity may be approached through the term 'break boundary.' In *Understanding Media*, McLuhan takes delight in 'showing that in any medium or structure there is what Kenneth Boulding calls a 'break boundary' at which the system suddenly changes into another or passes some point of no return in its dynamic processes.' Paradoxes are typical of the reversals that occur at break boundaries: from mechanical to organic, stasis to motion, etc. In McLuhan's investigation of the break boundary between tribal and literate men, he finds that 'One of the most common causes of breaks in any system is the cross fertilization with another system.'[66] In *Wacousta*, the border river-ravine and the bridge which spans it mark the symbolic interface between two disparate cultures. And it is here that we see most vividly the process by which one form alters another. Richardson's deft handling of this hydra-headed motif bespeaks his instinct for what is imaginatively central in the Canadian sensibility.

Break boundaries or points of reversal where opposites merge have exercised a potent and enduring fascination for Canadian poets, novelists, and critics. In *Divisions on a Ground*, Frye notes that 'there sometimes comes a curious Hegelian fatality into human life of eventually producing the opposite of what was originally aimed at.' 'This phenomenon of things reversing themselves is particularly noticeable when society fixes onto something as a symbol for its anxiety and tries to maintain it without change.'[67] This theme seems related to others discussed in his book, descent, doppelgängers and the frontier being the most relevant here. Romance, as *The Secular Scripture* conveys it, contains 'breaks in consciousness' occasioned by descents into demonic nightworlds, which involve 'a change so drastic as to give the sense of becoming someone else altogether.'[68] In his discussion of gothic literature, nightworld descents, and dualism, Robertson Davies emphasizes 'the principle of *enantiodromia*, which is the tendency of things to run into their opposites if they are exaggerated.'[69] In Mackenzie King, a sort of De Haldimar-

Wacousta double, one can see 'the opposites running into one another, and this is very Canadian.'[70]

Robert Kroetsch concurs with Davies's sense of break boundaries in comparing Canadian and American sensibilities: 'We're more Jungian in some way. We see opposites in necessary balance all the time.' 'Caught in the balance,' Canadians 'become fascinated by problems of equilibrium.' One can see this par excellence in *But We Are Exiles*, which Moss compares to *Wacousta*.[71] It is as redolent of mirrors, water-reflections, doubles as any of Richardson's work or Atwood's. Here, too, in playing off the differences between two sensibilities, 'The whole business of the night world and the day world has become kind of intermingled.'[72] Rudy Wiebe suggests that his historical fiction is about the collision of world-views and that what holds interest for him is 'the conjunction of the two things together.'[73] For Lee, the informing principle of *Savage Fields* is 'the recurrent conjunction of world and earth' and how they overlap and commingle.[74] In Mordecai Richler's writing, Eli Mandel discovers a development akin to 'Sartre's whirligig: an opposition in which the opposing forces endlessly turn into one another ... Richler's whirligigs involve paradoxical inversions of identity ... barbarians who are civilized; cultivated barbarians, and so on.'[75]

Such diverse references suggest that Richardson has struck a deep vein in his imaginative mining of the borderland. Chase's definition of romance as 'the borderland of the human mind where the actual and the imaginary intermingle' and McLuhan's sense of 'an area of spiralling repetition and replay' will help define the context of my following chapter: a study of *Wacousta*'s plethora of doubles and love triangles.

CHAPTER THREE

Border Doubles:
Twin Poles of the Canadian Psyche

In Canada, the wilderness, symbolized by the north, creates a kind of doppelganger figure who is oneself and yet the opposite of oneself ... The Canadian recurring themes of self-conflict, of the violating of nature, of individuals uncertain of their social context, of dark, repressed oracular doubles concealed within each of us, are now more communicable outside Canada in the new mood of the world.

NORTHROP FRYE, *Divisions on a Ground*

His own life was no longer a single story but part of a mural, which was a falling together of accomplices.

MICHAEL ONDAATJE, *In the Skin of a Lion*[1]

'Break boundaries' – points of reversal generating a paradoxical blurring, merging, or exchanging of identity – occur between specific characters in *Wacousta* as well as between the larger cultural groupings of regiment and tribe. In the preceding chapter, I sought to show how two cultures, one indigenous, the other immigrant, apparently without any relationship to each other, progressively intertwine and fuse in a curiously complementary fashion. Similarly, the twins, doubles, or doppelgänger figures so prominent in descent imagery participate in the border dialectic of Richardson's works. Here, too, there is opposition in which the opposing forces endlessly turn into one another.

Such doubleness gains in depth and impact from being reflected in the setting and structure of the work and is integral to the exposition of the central themes. Richardson's predilection for doubles and love triangles seems to issue from a psyche fascinated with balancing or undoing one element by another. This tendency plays havoc with conventional notions of identity. Lives reduplicate one another, giving rise to an eerie sense of doubleness, of reflections within reflections. Like the double exposure in a photo, under the intense compressional force of the borderland, characters and situations are superimposed over one another until it becomes hard to distinguish where one leaves off and another begins. Indeed, it soon becomes futile – not to say exasperating – to define identity in terms of separate and neatly isolatable individuals. Identity is communal; the focus is on groups rather than single characters.

Unlike many American frontier romances featuring a lone protagonist devoid of ancestry, *Wacousta* and *The Canadian Brothers* describe a claustrophobic world of uncles, nephews, aunts, cousins, mothers, fathers, daughters, sons, sisters, and brothers. All are caught in a web of family relationships which is so densely interwoven as to be labyrinthine in complexity. Two family trees take root in Richardson's borderland of the Canadian psyche: that of the respectable De Haldimars and that of the outcast Mortons, the former, according to Wacousta, destined to be the bane of the latter. Their branches become inexplicably intertwined to the point where they are indistinguishable; when the Wacousta limb is chopped off, the De Haldimar branch withers and falls to the ground soon thereafter. Moreover, they are set within the tightly knit society of the garrison, itself comprising tense groups who are 'by a communionship of suffering, isolation, and peculiarity of duty, drawn towards each other with feelings of almost fraternal affection' (I, 26; 16).

The major double, of course, is constituted by the De Haldimar/Wacousta relationship, a relationship examined in depth in this chapter beginning with the section entitled 'The Struggle-of-Brothers Theme.' To borrow a term from separate studies of doppelgängers in literature by Miyoshi and Tymms, this is a 'double-by-division'; it features two characters of opposing yet complementary temperaments who are strangely bonded.[2] In addition, there are also 'doubles-by-duplication' in which one figure is multiplied or mirrored in almost identical form. Here we have two Reginald Mortons. Both adopt pseudonyms, names and naming – as well as 'unnaming' – being of great importance in Richardson's works. ('Wacousta' is the uncle of 'Frank Halloway,' this family connection discovered by the former late in the story.) Besides a common name and lineage, they share similar physical and personality traits and meet the same fate.

Passionate, impetuous, high-spirited, energetic, daring, proudly independent, and defiant, both Reginald Mortons are men of strong feeling unafraid of expressing emotion in a constricted culture which limits and frowns upon such open expression. Tender, generous-hearted, and frank, both are impassioned lovers who risk all for love. Halloway's family rejects him after he, like Wacousta, refuses a marriage of convenience for one of affection. Marrying the woman he loves, Halloway is forced by adverse circumstances to conceal his status as a gentleman by birth and assume a new name and a lower rank. By fateful coincidence, Ellen Halloway becomes the wife of both Mortons. In each case as well, Colonel de Haldimar separates them from the woman they cherish.

Both Mortons form brotherly attachments with De Haldimars. Echoing Sir Reginald Morton's friendship with Ensign de Haldimar, Frank Halloway's best friend is Frederick de Haldimar who closely resembles his father. Such is their affinity that Clara de Haldimar avers that 'Frank Halloway ... loved my brother as though he had been of the same blood!' (III, 286; 496–7). Like his uncle in his youth, Halloway is selfless and altruistic: on the Plains of Abraham, he shows himself willing to sacrifice his life to preserve that of his friend, throwing himself in front of Frederick as one of Montcalm's favourite officers discharges his pistol. Ironically, this 'French' officer turns out to be Wacousta who recognizes the son by his resemblance to the father. Wacousta nearly kills his nephew; Colonel de Haldimar will be the next one to have Halloway shot.

Both Mortons fall victim to De Haldimar. He blackens their

honour and their reputation, has them court-martialled on trumped-up charges as traitors, and ensures their exile or execution. What Ellen describes as 'the persecutions of the Morton family' (III, 180; 439) in the Old World continue in the New, prompting her prophetic curse on the race of De Haldimar. A bitter Wacousta laments that his nephew has been rewarded for saving Frederick's life by 'an ignominious death, inflicted, perhaps, for some offense not more dishonouring than those which have thrown me an outcast upon these wilds ... what but ingratitude of the grossest nature could a Morton expect at the hands of the false family of De Haldimar!' (III, 287; 497). In the sequel, the last of the Mortons, locked in a death embrace with the last of the De Haldimars, perishes in the Niagara border abyss between Canada and the United States during the Battle of Queenston Heights.

Like the defendants themselves, the work's three trials seem to condense into one. Overlapping and paralleling one another, they suggest the cyclic nature of the herd mentality's insatiable appetite for scapegoats. During his second court martial, Wacousta stands on the same spot previously occupied by his nephew. He, too, insists on his status as a gentleman. Both ask for a delay in the proceedings pending Frederick's return, a request initially denied then granted by Governor de Haldimar in each case. Both are accused of conspiring with Ponteac and with François, the Canadian innkeeper; as in modern treatments of Louis Riel, each Morton is branded an outlaw and traitor to be exhibited as an example to native peoples so that 'when they behold your fate, they will take warning from your example; and ... be more readily brought to obedience' (III, 331; 521). Both the Reginald Morton within the fort and the one without are killed at the exact centre of the 'Bloody Bridge.' Frank Halloway's declarations that 'Appearances ... are against me' (I, 63; 36) and 'I am not indeed what I seem to be' (I, 140; 78) echo earlier statements by his uncle and suggest that the work's controlling irony lies in the abyss between appearance and reality.

The merging of the two Mortons is, perhaps, the most obvious example of a pervasive blurring of boundaries between characters in this borderland where identity is never static but always changing and indeterminate. Like De Haldimar and Wacousta, Charles de Haldimar and Sir Everard Valletort are doubles-by-division. 'Nearly of the same age,' 'the one was all gentleness, the other all spirit and vivacity' (I, 169; 94). Again, a passive and an active figure are bonded in strong friendship. They balance one another even as Wacousta's 'wild spirit was soothed by the bland amenity of his [De Haldimar's] manners' (III, 195; 447). Unlike that later relationship, 'not a shade of disunion had at any period intervened to interrupt the almost brotherly attachment subsisting between them, and each felt the disposition of the other was the one most assimilated to his own' (I, 169; 94). Indeed, in yet another important passage from the original 1832 *Wacousta* edited out of subsequent editions, Everard speaks of Charles de Haldimar as one 'whom I loved as though he had been my twin brother' (III, 312; 511). As in the case with Wacousta and De Haldimar and most doubles, they die within a short time of each other.

Such friendships represent a spirit of selflessness, camaraderie, and community that balances the mean-spirited herd-mind that often dominates garrison life. Recalling Richardson's *Frascati's* and anticipating a similar motif in his *The Monk Knight of St. John*, the bond between the two is further strengthened by Charles's desire that his friend wed his identical sister, his 'counterpart' (I, 174; 97) Clara, 'that dearer half of myself' (I, 194; 108). (An analogous relationship obtains in Ernest Buckler's *The Mountain and the Valley*; identities merge as the aggressive, energetic Toby and the reflective David are balanced by their common inspiration, the latter's twin sister Anna.) Both brother and sister, in turn, bear an uncanny resemblance to their deceased mother, Clara Beverley, and both are killed by Wacousta at the fatal bridge.

By the end of the story, the identities of Clara, Charles, and Everard have coalesced in bizarre fashion; as Clara suddenly materializes at the opposite side of the bed upon which her dead brother lies in state, Everard is disoriented by the dizzying reflections from this human hall of mirrors: 'Her likeness to her brother, at that moment, was so striking, that, for a second or two, the irrepressible thought passed through the mind of the officer, it was not a living being he gazed upon, but the immaterial spirit of his friend. The whole attitude and appearance of the wretched girl, independently of the fact of her noiseless entrance, tended to favour the delusion. Her features, of an ashy paleness, seemed fixed, even as those of the corpse beneath him' (III, 319–20; 515). The permutations of identity are infused with an unsettling gothic light that becomes even more tenebrous during the ensuing vows of love. Declares Everard, 'In you will I love both my friend and the sister he has bequeathed to me.' For Clara, he will be 'both a brother and a husband' (III, 322; 516).

Like 'The Canadian Brothers,' the De Haldimar brothers also reveal Richardson's obsession with balanced pairs of characters, an obsession to which he, like Kroetsch, will remain faithful throughout his oeuvre. 'Captain de Haldimar had none of the natural weakness and timidity of character which belonged to the gentler and more sensitive Charles. Sanguine and full of enterprise' (II, 177; 254), he is the allegro figure contrasting with the penseroso type his brother represents. While the active Frederick undertakes two heroic quests across vast distances and through the wilderness, his passive brother remains inside the fortress walls. Frederick is Colonel de Haldimar's favourite son; Charles is neglected, even rejected by his father, also named Charles, whose austere and puritanical nature is the opposite of his warm and emotional son's. In an epic informed by the Cain and Abel story, these two brothers, oddly enough, do *not* struggle; in the sequel, however, a similar tension between opposites is more exacerbated in their descendants as they quarrel over a woman (Wacousta's descendant) and one brother – inadvertently – kills the other.

Just as there are two Charles de Haldimars and two Reginald Mortons, so there are two Claras, mother and daughter. Abducting Clara de Haldimar from her father as he had Clara Beverley from hers, Wacousta sometimes confuses the two. Ravishing the former in the Indian oasis which parallels the Highland Eden of the latter, Wacousta – who has just told his other 'bride' Ellen Halloway that she has been the wife of two Reginald Mortons – swears that 'the love I have so long borne the mother [will] be transferred to the child' (III, 181; 439).

There is a similar commingling of identity among the five major female figures: Oucanasta, Madeline, Ellen, and the two Claras. Clara Beverley's capacity for uninhibited outpouring of affection is shared by Oucanasta, Ellen, and Madeline. The latter, possessing the 'voluptuousness' of 'the Medicean Venus' (II, 253–4; 295–6), shares her aunt's fearless nature and her sexual attractiveness. The portrayal of her impassioned meetings with her fiancé Frederick appears to echo that of the meetings between Morton and Clara Beverley. Madeline de Haldimar and Clara de Haldimar, first cousins, strike admirers at Fort Michillimackinac as a study in contrast, 'Venus and Psyche in the land of the Pottowatomies' (II, 260; 299).

Passionate and earthy, Oucanasta, the Ottawa woman at home in her forest oasis, is the true New World counterpart of Clara Beverley in her Scottish garden and is, I suggest, the true heroine of the work. Her love for Frederick goes unrequited, however; she is forsaken by the 'civilized' white man much as Keejigo is abandoned by Nairne of the Orkneys in D.C. Scott's *At Gull Lake: August, 1810*. Though fascinated by such liaisons which recall Richardson's own family history, garrison propriety is less offended by Frederick's marriage to his first cousin than to one of another race. Other parallels knit these characters even closer together. Madeline, for instance, bravely throws herself between her doomed father and the attacking Indians at the besieged fort which he commands. Later, she interposes between Frederick and Wacousta aboard the captured schooner; falling at Wacousta's feet, begging for mercy, she is spurned by the warrior even as the supplicating Ellen at the beginning of the story was rebuffed by Colonel de Haldimar and as a wildly distraught Clara de Haldimar at the end pleads at the feet of Wacousta.

Further blurring distinctions between Ellen and Clara de Haldimar are similar physical characteristics: both are delicate, fair-skinned, blue-eyed. Charles remarks that Clara 'had ever treated Ellen Halloway rather as a sister' (II, 103; 215). Both women are abducted and taken to wife by Wacousta who keeps them in his tent. As Charles is remarkable for his feminine appearance, female characters are sometimes made to look like men, thus blurring sexual identity. Like Clara Beverley who is disguised as a man as she leaves her Eden to cross over the abyss separating it from the garrison world below, Ellen is disguised as a drummerboy as she approaches the bridge over the border abyss dividing European from Indian. So, too, Oucanasta appears in the guise of a male warrior as she leaves the forest to enter Fort Michillimackinac to rescue Madeline.

Not surprisingly, the paradigmatic love triangle constellated by Wacousta, Clara Beverley, and De Haldimar also undergoes eerie multiplication. Shattered in the Old World, we catch reflections from it off a myriad of splinters in the New. Disclosed only towards the end of volume 3 in Wacousta's flashback, like a magnet it draws all the doubles and triangles whose significance may have escaped the reader, or seemed gratuitous, into meaningful patterns. A list which does not pretend to be exhaustive would include the following triangles: Everard-Clara de Haldimar-Charles; Oucanasta-Frederick-Madeline; Frank Halloway-Ellen-Wacousta; Everard-Clara de Haldimar-Wacousta; Clara de Haldimar-Wacousta-Ellen. Wacousta's liaison with François's daughter, Babette, moves us into 'love rectangles,' to borrow a term from Atwood's article on Rider Haggard.[3] As with each double, each triangle is an analogue to, and comment on, the others, tending to suggest by parody, analogy, or correspondence characters and situations not immediately present.

In Richardson's fiction, the ideal triangle emerges out of the dialectic of opposites. An active and a passive male character revolve around an anima-like female who effects or mediates a larger reconciliation or equilibrium between conflicting forces. On a personal and psychological level, this represents a Jungian integration of the personality. On the cultural level, the Apollonian and Dionysian elements are harmonized in a new, dynamic synthesis. Although such themes of reintegration and communion are central to Richardson's art, this 'ideal' is only realized momentarily in *The Monk Knight of St. John*, perhaps because it is set outside the hopelessly schizophrenic nineteenth-century Canadian milieu. Most often, it is as though an original wholeness were split into antithetical fragments which war on each other.

The core triangle in *Wacousta* is homeomorphic to all others. It is traced and retraced with a redundancy characteristic of the borderline which, we recall, McLuhan describes as an area of spiralling repetition, replay, and metamorphosis. One example must suffice to illustrate how *Wacousta*'s proliferating doubles and triangles are deployed by Richardson to recapitulate in miniature the thematic implications of the main plot and to anticipate its further development. The triangle involving Middleton, the Indian 'Venus' (II, 263; 300), and Baynton portrayed in the chapters on Fort Michillimackinac in volume 2, has complete congruity with that of the Wacousta–Clara Beverley–De Haldimar triangle revealed in volume 3. A variation on this theme, it is set in a comic rather than a tragic key. Chatting idly to Madeline and Clara about his friend Middleton, Captain Baynton remarks that he 'stole cautiously behind him, and saw that he was sketching the head of a tall and rather handsome squaw ... a Venus, a Juno, a Minerva.' As Middleton goes on duty, Baynton playfully teases him: 'I think I shall go and carry on a flirtation with your Indian Minerva' (II, 261–3; 300).

This brief interchange does not draw attention to itself and, indeed, is quickly forgotten in the avalanche of details concerning the Indian attack. It is not until the embedded narrative of Wacousta's flashback many chapters later that the attentive reader begins to see double – or triple. Wacousta tells of being alone in his room sketching a picture of the Highland Clara; he suddenly realizes that De Haldimar has silently entered and is standing looking over his shoulder. Instinctively, 'I asked him, laughingly, what he thought of my Cornish cousin' (III, 239; 471). De Haldimar feigns indifference; yet, later, when Wacousta – or Morton – is called away on duty, De Haldimar quickly seizes the opportunity and marries the inexperienced Clara. The exactness of the mirror image is blunted by the omission in the edited versions of Charles's fleeting allusion to Baynton and Middleton whom Everard fears may be potential rivals for Clara: 'the musical and sonnetteering Middleton' (I, 196; 100) is an artistic individual like Morton. De Haldimar, who does not appreciate 'the talent of so perfect an artist' (III, 239; 471), is reflected in the practical, scoffing Baynton with his polished manner.

Spiralling Repetition and Replay

The feeling one has is of entering a haunted world of reflections within reflections, of story within story that is also experienced in the work of Davies, Reaney, Munro, Atwood, Kroetsch, and many Canadian postmodernists. The original situation happens again and again one way or another. One set of relationships is constantly viewed or inflected through another in a kind of infinite regress. I will provisionally call this technique 'amplification by analogy,' a term borrowed from Edward F. Edinger's Jungian inquiry, *Ego and Archetype*.[4] For the most part, the parallels, which tragically evade the awareness of the characters themselves, are casually introduced without any editorializing whatsoever. Richardson leaves it to the reader to make the connection, a considerable act of faith in an audience which has only recently come to appreciate the depth of his artistry.

Despite such a complex web of interrelationships uniting everyone and resonating with ambiguity, the garrison inhabitants themselves perceive things in terms of simplistic, either/or categories, seeing a world of sharp borders and unbridgeable gulfs. The tragic irony of such blinkered vision is nowhere more dramatically underscored than in the network of correspondences between the garrison's major characters – especially those rebuked by Colonel de Haldimar – and Wacousta. Just as the line between Indian and European blurs, so, too, a curious overlapping of identity occurs among the De Haldimar brothers, Everard, Johnstone, and the warrior who seeks to destroy them. As I shall soon suggest, Richardson attempts, not altogether successfully, to create in Frederick de Haldimar a character who balances the Colonel's arid intellectual nature with Wacousta's fiery passions. Tall, handsome, heroic, Frederick shares the latter's adventurousness, daring spirit, and athletic prowess. Ponteac proclaims him a faster runner than the Indians; on one occasion, he even outruns Wacousta.

Both men are passionate lovers. Recalling the language Morton uses to describe his 'cousin' Clara, Frederick's cousin is to him 'a divinity whom he worshipped in the innermost recesses of his being.' Her 'almost superhuman voice' enchants him as Clara's does Morton. 'His brain whirling with very intoxication,' the enraptured Frederick is likewise a lover who obeys 'wild impulse' (II, 255; 296). Like Wacousta, he also undergoes a series of metamorphoses, disguising himself as a common soldier and a Canadian duck hunter, and at one point he is dressed as an Indian. Like both Mortons, Frederick is ordered arrested by De Haldimar for defying the law. Both men are believed dead on several occasions, although each seems unable to wound or kill the other. Wacousta, however, does kill Donellan who 'was remarkable for the resemblance he bore, in figure, to Captain de Haldimar' (II, 141; 236). That the first victim of the gigantic Wacousta is Donellan, the tallest and largest grenadier who is also Frederick's mirror-image, suggests the uncanny interdependence of all characters in this radically contracted borderland, down to the least of them.

At first glance, Charles and Wacousta seem to possess little in common. Yet both are men of feeling and sensibility who suffer from broken hearts in a society dominated by those who place value only on the intellect. Each sheds copious tears. Constantly worrying for the safety of his closest friend and Clara, Charles has violent paroxysms of grief which threaten to dislodge his reason; they parallel the fever and madness that plague Wacousta after he loses both Clara and his best friend. Giving vent to his emotion, Charles, like the Mortons and Everard, fears his reputation for courage will be assailed. Like these figures and Ellen, he, too, is intuitive and given to presentiments, making statements which later prove prophetic. (In folklore, meeting one's double foreshadows death or the onset of prophetic power.) Charles is also insulted by De Haldimar and, like Wacousta, impulsively moves to draw his sword to defend his honour. Given such resemblances, it is ironic that he should be the first De Haldimar killed by the Warrior of the Fleur de Lis.

We find other reflections of Wacousta in Johnstone and Clara Beverley's misanthropic father. The latter, also a Jacobite rebel, is an eccentric gentleman heart-broken by the loss of a beloved wife and disgusted with English society. Lieutenant Johnstone is another distorted image of the young Lieutenant Morton. Johnstone is a brave, fiery, and reckless Scot, the motto of his Highland ancestors 'Nunquam non paratus.' (This is the inscription on Richardson's own ring and recalls his Jacobite ancestry.) The head of his family was also branded a traitor by the English. Like Everard and Charles, the impetuous Johnstone is repelled by the obsequious Ensign Delme, a yes-man who recalls Ensign de Haldimar and is, appropriately, the last European shot by Wacousta. Delme insults Johnstone and twists his words, threatening to denounce him as a traitor. Once again, an outspoken, marginalized individual, critical of garrison administration, is associated with treason, his honour challenged in a public manner by a hypocritical representative of law and order.

Sir Everard Valletort also mirrors Sir Reginald Morton in surprising ways. Both are lively and adventurous baronets, heirs to titles. Everard is also somewhat of a romantic idealist out of step with garrison society; the narrator associates him, too, with the power of the imagination and the heart and the quest for ideal beauty. Active and impulsive individuals, each is linked with a more passive and retiring double. Such friendships involve them in love triangles with either Clara or her daughter. Both claim the latter as their bride, and Wacousta sees his own situation reflected in the Everard-Clara relationship. A disoriented Clara confuses the two men herself, imagining that she is in Everard's arms while actually being ravished by Wacousta. Wacousta ties Everard to the Indian flag-pole, and later the former is bound to the garrison flag-pole; both captives escape carrying Clara, reversing roles of pursuer and pursued. Likewise gifted with a keen eye and ear, Everard, too, is an expert rifleman; his first shot at the beginning of the border romance and his last at the end wound Wacousta.

Like both Mortons, Charles, and Johnstone, Everard begins to manifest many of the outcast stigmata. He is also unjustly accused and publicly humiliated by Colonel de Haldimar. It is Everard's 'undisguised perception' (I, 82; 46) of the man behind the Governor's mask of impartiality that draws down this severity. Again, it is the most frank and astute individuals who are victimized, pushed out of the centre of the garrison world to its borders. It is appropriate that it is Everard, a man appreciative of paradoxes, who alone voices Wacousta's Conradian status as 'one of us': 'That man, savage and even fiendish as he now is, was once possessed of the noblest qualities. ... Colonel de Haldimar has brought this present affliction upon himself' (III, 317; 514). Wacousta the wild man is not as primitive as the soldiers imagine, but they haven't known that until this point.

Such is the delirium of doubles, complementary personalities, twins, and modulations of the twin theme characterizing Richardson's border milieu. A product of the author's fascination with dualities and the convergence of opposites, the resultant vertigo is an essential part of the romance's intent: unlike the American frontier of independent loners, the Canadian borderland is a world of uncanny interdependence, a mosaic mesh in which the most disparate and seemingly autonomous groups of people become entangled. Paradoxically, the text confirms both the continuity and discontinuity of this scattered world. Characters seem irresistibly drawn together even when they are bitterly antagonistic. This skillful marshalling of doubles and triangles sustains a great deal of resonant ambiguity; multiplicity, fragmentation, incompleteness, and discontinuity are posited even as their opposites are suggested: unity, completeness, and continuity. It also generates psychic conflict in which anxieties are sharpened to the point of madness. The details of such interpenetrating lives are intricately wrought and attest to a very careful use of echoes – of phrases and images – always setting up parallels and correspondences. Again, this pattern of recurrence, of an unabashed use of coincidence and analogy, emerges out of a very McLuhanesque sense of the borderline as an area 'of maximal interplay and subtle interpenetration.'[5]

Such repetition and duplication is found in a number of Canadian writers, especially in recent years, as our literature has moved in the direction of fantasy. Richardson's proliferating Claras and Reginalds take their place among the doubled Annas,

Demeters, and Billys in Robert Kroetsch's *Badlands, The Studhorse Man*, and *Alibi* respectively; the three Maud's in F.P. Grove's *The Master of the Mill*; the array of Georges in George Bowering's *Burning Water*; the nine sisters named Mary in Marian Engel's study of inbred Southwestern Ontario in *The Glassy Sea*; and the numerous Marys in Brian Moore's *I Am Mary Dunne* who have almost as many selves as the protagonist in Alden Nowlan's *Various Persons Named Kevin O'Brien*. As I emphasize throughout this study, a very Richardsonian concern with the overlapping and fusion – and confusion – of identity, with the very notion of self as isolate, distinct, definable, enclosed, autonomous, is prominent in the work of many modern Canadian authors, with their radical challenges to the humanist notion of the self as coherent, unified, and stable.[6] The twins and other characters who are described as 'Siamesed' in Matt Cohen's Salem novels, no less than the 'characters [who] split, double, multiply, evaporate, condense, disperse, assemble' in Tom Marshall's *Rosemary Goal*, also set in gothic Southern Ontario, suggest the efficacy of Richardson's border model of a radically contracted Canada; 'maybe,' muses the protagonist of the latter work, a novelist fond of stories within stories, 'that's what this town is anyhow. A daisy chain, a sexual commune ... connections between everyone, the endless interrelationships that make us one people ... A cast of characters whose lives are all interconnected.'[7]

In two other books structured round an exchange of identity, we discover similar avowals which help place Richardson's modus operandi in a larger context. In Hugh MacLennan's *The Watch That Ends the Night*, the solidly middle-class George Stewart, who finds his double, the dynamic, reckless Jerome Martell 'to be inside me, *to be me*,' declares 'Each one of us is everybody, really.'[8] (Similar realizations are also shared by the protagonist of Chris Scott's postmodernist *Antichthon* and Leonard Cohen's *Beautiful Losers*.) *The Studhorse Man* is one of many Kroetsch tales of a bizarre swapping of identities; it illustrates what this writer, in conversation with Margaret Laurence, asserts as a very Canadian concern: 'the *doppelgänger* thing.'[9] Perched in an insane asylum bathtub, Kroetsch's mirror-gazing narrator recounts the epic story of his roving uncle and adversary into whom he appears to metamorphose; reflecting on 'the act of naming,' the mad historian discourses on 'the fact that we are all, so to speak, one – that each of us is, possibly, everyone else.'[10] Such observations by both madmen and conservative middle-class citizens may help to orient us when confronted by the dizzying prospect of Richardson's fictional world.

The Struggle-of-Brothers Theme

Colonel de Haldimar and Wacousta, like Gerald Grantham and Matilda Montgomery in the sequel, or Abdallah and the Baron in *The Monk Knight of St. John*, are doubles-by-division or by opposition. They are set within the dual cosmology they express – the border world of garrison and wilderness. Here the forces of restraint, repression, and reason present in the imported European culture presided over by Governor de Haldimar are at war with those of spontaneity, passion, and irrationality as expressed in the criminal outcast Wacousta and the North American Indian. In nineteenth-century Canada, the tragedy, as Richardson envisions it, is that no one bridges the psychological and cultural gulf between the two domains.

The De Haldimar-Wacousta relationship, like that of Linton and Heathcliff in Emily Brontë's *Wuthering Heights* (1847), conforms to a recurrent romantic convention which Richardson tailors to reflect the New World border dichotomy of civilization and wilderness. Frye's comments on the struggle-of-brothers motif in *A Study of English Romanticism* illumine all of Richardson's works and echo statements by Chase, Davies, Lee, and McLuhan cited in my earlier discussion of the 'intermingled vision':

The paradoxical relation of civilized and rude nature, a relation partly antithetical and partly complementary, is often expressed in Romantic fiction and drama by some variant of the struggle-of-brothers theme. This has several Biblical archetypes – Cain and Abel, Esau and Jacob, Ishmael and Isaac – which become important in its development. In the conventional interpretation of the Bible, the figures of the social establishment, Isaac and Jacob, are the accepted ones; with Romanticism, there comes a transfer of sympathy to their exiled brethren. The so-called Byronic hero is often a Romantic version of the natural man, who, like Esau and Ishmael, is an outcast, a solitary much given to communing with untamed nature, and who thus represents the potentially expanding and liberating elements in that nature.[11]

De Haldimar and Wacousta, certainly, are struggling brothers in Frye's sense. So, too, are Manvers and Haverfield in the earlier *Frascati's*. In particular, the fratricide of the first 'Canadian Brothers' – unlike the marriage of American Adams in their forest Edens – ominously recalls the tragic crime of our first brothers. The figures of Cain and Abel may be more relevant to the Canadian experience than that of Adam, as Richardson and later writers suggest. In *The Secular Scripture*, Frye links Cain and Abel with the theme of the demonic double.[12] His further comments on the Byronic hero in his study of romanticism help focus this theme: 'He has great energy, often great powers of leadership, and even his vices are dignified enough to have some aesthetic attraction. He is often aristocratic in birth or behaviour, with a sense that, like Esau, he is the dispossessed rightful heir – here the theme combines with the sense of nostalgia for a vanished aristocracy. When he is evil, there is often the feeling that, as with Byron's Cain, his evil is comprehensible, that he is not wholly evil any more than his evil is a force that society has to reckon with.' For Frye, the greatest of all his incarnations in English literature is Brontë's Heathcliff, an embodiment of the wildness of Yorkshire moors and heath as Wacousta is of Canadian bush and rivers. The hideous Heathcliff, appearing fifteen years after the dark Wacousta, 'has in full the sense of a natural man who eludes all moral categories just as nature itself does, and who cannot be simply condemned or accepted. In contrast, the Jacob-figure, the defender of the establishment, often seems unheroic and spoiled by a soft or decadent civilization.'[13]

The theme of brotherhood or friendship and their betrayal is of paramount importance in all of Richardson's writing, fictional, historical, and autobiographical. It informs his inquiries into what constitutes authentic community and his portrayals of North American garrisons. In the flashback in which Wacousta recounts to Clara de Haldimar the history of his family and her own, the betrayed and once very naive outcast blind to the dark side of others bewails the 'intimacy [which] suddenly sprang up between' himself and her father: 'this incongruous friendship – friendship! no, I will not so far sully the sacred name as thus to term the unnatural union that subsisted between us.' 'Fire and ice,' he exclaims, 'are not more opposite than were the elements of which our natures were composed' (III, 194; 447).

In a key passage, Wacousta, once a romantic idealist, describes his 'partly antithetical and partly complementary' relationship with De Haldimar, the cautious law-and-order figure: 'He, all coldness, prudence, obsequiousness, and forethought. I, all enthusiasm, carelessness, impetuosity, and independence' (III, 194; 447). Here is the 'original' pattern of opposites in tension. This paradigmatic relationship is boldly stated in order to establish that the ideal bond between 'brothers' implies balance and complementarity. What later appear to be warring opposites are actually two component parts of a complex psychological entity. Their friendship conforms to that outlined by Jean Paul Richter, the coiner of the word 'doppelgänger':

> Jean Paul's characteristic *Doppelgangers* are pairs of friends (in the original sense of 'fellows, two of a pair'), who together form a unit, but individually appear as a 'half,' dependent on the *alter ego* ... they are like contrasting, but complementary, sides within one complex nature ... The divergences seem, in fact, to emphasize the mutual need for completion and support, in the sense of Friedrich Schlegel's definition of intimate friendship: 'A wondrous symmetry of essential characteristics, as if it had been pre-ordained that one should complete the other on every point.' These symmetrical pairs feel as instinctive an impulse towards one another as the urge which impels the Platonic twin-souls to seek out their respective partner and restore the original unity between them.[14]

'Opposition is true friendship,' writes Blake.[15] Wacousta speculates that 'my wild spirit was soothed by the bland amenity of his manners' (III, 195; 447). Ideally, impulse and intellect, feeling and reason, wild daring and caution, body and head are harmonized, just as, on a larger scale, Indian and European, wilderness and civilization are brought into balance. Such seems to be the case, for a brief moment, only in the Old World. What is dramatized in the New World borderland in peculiarly Canadian terms is a tragic dissociation of sensibility, a separation of thought and feeling, head and heart, which seems to have widened into an unbridgeable gulf. In the Wacousta–De Haldimar struggle, I suggest, Richardson dramatizes what he sees as the conflicting opposites that keep the Canadian psyche in tension, developing them with the fugues and arabesques so dear to the Canadian double vision. One aspect of this vision relevant to Richardson's work is discussed by Robertson Davies in his essay 'The Canada of Myth and Reality.' Davies cites a line from Douglas Le Pan's poem *Coureurs de bois* which encapsulates what he terms the dual nature of the Canadian soul: 'Wild Hamlet with the features of Horatio.'[16] Inside the cautious, prudent Horatio, there lies a dark, fiery brooder. Similarly, in Davies's *The Manticore*, Dunstan Ramsay, the dull Canadian schoolmaster from Southwestern Ontario who is also a vigorous spiritual seeker, avers that 'Mackenzie King rules Canada because he himself is the embodiment of Canada – cold and cautious on the outside, dowdy and pussy in every overt action, but inside a mass of intuition and dark intimations.'[17]

The wild Wacousta's struggle with his staid double is highlighted in his 'Eden' flashback, chapters 7–11, volume 3 of the 1832 edition. Coming as it does towards the end of the romance, revealing the betrayed idealist, the accomplished artist, and man of sensibility behind the shadowy monster, it is literally and figuratively 'the inside story.' It is also the untold story, displaced in the novel's myriad doubles and triangles, and one which the silent Governor de Haldimar would keep the voluble Wacousta from telling. Those qualities which receive the most emphasis as Wacousta tells his story are the aristocratic Morton's 'exiled brethren' qualities: his impassioned communing with the rugged, untamed nature of the Scottish Highlands and the sea, romantic sensibility and intuition, boundless energy and animal boisterousness, athletic prowess and thirst for adventure. Above all, Richardson stresses the young man's aesthetic and mystical strivings and his intense imagination which enshrines the mountain-top maiden Clara Beverley as the embodiment of 'ideal beauty,' 'the being of my fancy's creation' (III, 210; 455). At the same time, Wacousta himself is presented as a story-teller, a voice, narrating himself into existence and out of the silence in which the tight-lipped Governor has confined him.

'Years of passionate imagining,' (III, 214; 458) exclaims Wacousta to the second Clara, daughter of the woman he loves and the man he hates, had left his vision unrealized. Edited out of most editions is a crucial scene indebted to the Narcissus myth so familiar in Romantic literature and repeated with variations throughout *Wacousta*: 'How often, too, while bending over some dark and threatening precipice, or standing on the utmost verge of some tall projecting cliff, my aching head (aching with the intenseness of its own conceptions) bared to the angry storm, and my eye fixed unshrinkingly on the boiling ocean far beneath my feet, has my whole soul – my every faculty, been bent on that ideal beauty which controlled every sense! Oh, imagination, how tyrannical is thy sway – how exclusive thy power – how insatiable thy thirst' (III, 210; 455–6).

Addressing the imagination, Morton/Wacousta proclaims Clara Beverley as its creation: 'no sooner didst thou, with magic wand, conjure up one of thy embodiments, than my heart became a sea of flame, and was consumed in the vastness of its own fires' (III, 210; 456). The 'master passion' (III, 209; 455) of Reginald Morton is the spiritual or mystical pursuit of an elusive yet consuming vision of the soul's other half. His is a rage for beauty and transcendence as fierce as that of Le Pan's Rusty in *The Deserter*, Cohen's F. in *Beautiful Losers*, or Symons's multiple protagonist in *Combat Journal for Place D'Armes*. By his very nature, he stands in opposition to established society and its official representatives; humourless, practical, unimaginative soldiers preoccupied with the matter-of-fact, utilitarian concerns of a materialistic and puritanical culture, they misunderstand, patronize, ridicule, persecute, and finally forcibly reject him.

It is highly significant that Morton, as representative of 'the imaginative man' (I, 179; 100) devalued and exiled by the garrison, is an artist. Again, this important aspect of his identity is omitted in most editions. Morton speaks of his devotion to painting, an art 'in which I had attained considerable excellence; being enabled, from memory alone, to give a most correct representation of any object that particularly fixed my attention' (III, 236; 469–70). Such a 'photographic' memory is not out of place in a romance marked by duplication, water- and mirror-reflection. Given 'the talent of so perfect an artist ... there could be no question that the painting' of Clara's portrait by Morton 'was exquisite'; 'The likeness was perfect, even to the minutest shading of her costume.' Indeed, she mistakes it for a 'mirror that reflected back her living image' (III, 239; 471–2). This portrait is itself 'doubled,' the painter making an exact copy of it.

Like other romantic questers in search of reintegration and wholeness, Morton is alternately restored and torn apart by the 'influencing agency of that Unseen Power' that claims him for its own: 'Why did my evil genius so will it ... that I should have heard those sounds and seen that face [Clara's]? But for these ... my life might have been the life – the plodding life – of the multitude; things that are born merely to crawl through existence and die, knowing not at the moment of death why or how they have lived at all. But who may resist the destiny that presides over him from the cradle to the grave?' (III, 205–6; 453). Mystic and artist, lover and explorer, Morton is odd man out in a regimented garrison society which places little value on individuals following the uncertain inner promptings of an Unseen Power. His reflections appear to be shared, in part, by the narrator: 'It is in solitude, our thoughts, taking their colouring from our feelings, invest themselves with the power of multiplying ideal beauty, until we become in a measure tenants of a world of our own creation, from which we never descend, without loathing and disgust, into the dull and matter-of-fact routine of actual existence. Hence the misery of the imaginative man! – hence his little sympathy with the mass, who, tame and soulless, look upon life and the things of life, not through the refining medium of ideality, but through the grossly magnifying optics of mere sense and materialism' (I, 179; 100).

The Eden flashback reveals a Morton/Wacousta who represents what D.G. Jones, describing F., the mystic, madman, and terrorist in *Beautiful Losers*, terms 'the two poles of the irrational, the world of the flesh and the world of the spirit.'[18] 'All enthusiasm, carelessness, impetuosity, and independence,' the athletic Morton, unlike the cautious, sedentary De Haldimar, is animated by a 'spirit of adventure,' playfulness and 'wild daring' (III, 199; 449–50). An experienced mountain climber, he scales the precipitous crags for the pleasure of overcoming the difficulties they present. Danger, chance, the unpredictable, the tumultuous, the unexpected – everything the garrison worries about and plans against – he delights in encountering. Abjuring the closed-in garrison, he exultingly 'rides' the whirlwind, the vast open spaces of sea and mountain-top, of heights and depths.

Whether in the Highlands or the vast Canadian space, Morton/Wacousta gives himself up to the flux and flow of the cosmos. All is energy, a dynamic interplay of elemental forces as in Gibson's *Perpetual Motion* or the storm-tossed universe of D.C. Scott and Lampman. Morton embraces both the beauty of terror and the beauty of peace. Unlike the static De Haldimar, he is always moving. Moving across continents and oceans, he aligns himself with the fluid realm of wilderness and nomadic Indian, a world constantly in movement; to the garrison soldiers, Wacousta is little more than a blur. His descendants in *The Canadian Brothers* are roving American frontiersmen associated with the turbulent border river. His literary progeny also include Reaney's endlessly spinning Donnellys, Callaghan's whirling, changing Peggy Sanderson, Kroetsch's restless Michael Hornyak in *But We Are Exiles*, – a dynamic figure in love with motion, racing crazily across Canada with his reserved Ontario law-student double – and perhaps even Aritha Van Herk's perpetually moving adventuress Arachne Manteia in the parodic, postmodernist *No Fixed Address: An Amorous Journey*.

Wacousta's extremely mobile face – such a contrast to De Haldimar's rigid mask – receives repeated emphasis. 'The constant play of his features betrayed each passing thought with the same rapidity with which it was conceived' (I, 242; 134), not unlike the strange swift whiteness of Judith West's face, symbolically linking this outcast with the swirling wind blowing across the prairie in Ross's *As For Me and My House*. Associated with the realm of water and the fluctuation of the seasons in the new land, Wacousta can be passionately violent at one moment and tranquil and reflective the next, a paradoxical characteristic he shares with Reaney's Donnellys, Mitchell's Bens, Callaghan's Peggy Sanderson, and Wiebe's Riel.[19] In contrast, the secretive De Haldimar, a stiff 'martial-looking man,' possesses 'stern, haughty, and inflexible features' (I, 61; 35). A mask concealing his real thoughts, his face denotes his aversion to change, movement, and metamorphosis which disturb De Haldimar as much as they do Ondaatje's Billy and Pat Garrett, because they resist control.

Morton's animal vitality and boisterousness are constantly in evidence throughout the flashback. While the soaring, high-spirited youth is associated here with a stag and an eagle, his Canadian incarnation as Wacousta evokes comparisons with a wide range of animals, ferocious or swift-moving, predatory or hunted: a tiger, a wolf, antelope, deer, and a wounded lion at bay. Dressed in deerskin, Wacousta as wild man is adorned with porcupine quills, wild deer hooves, bird feathers, and a buffalo horn inscribed with pictures of birds, beasts, and fish. Like other impetuous, energetic idealists and passionate outcasts associated with animals and the landscape or seascape, Wacousta symbolizes the life of the body; one thinks of MacLennan's Jerome Martell, Le Pan's Rusty, Cohen's F., Crawford's Max, Reaney's Will Donnelly, Ross's Judith West, and O'Hagan's Tay John. Morton places his confidence in himself – in imaginative vision and love – and in nature and its spontaneous processes rather than in the law, the rules, and regulations of the garrison world which only frustrate and, he feels, unnecessarily limit him.

His is a romantic zest for life, a recklessness and devil-may-care attitude that attends a surrender to one's instincts. In contrast with a society caught up in memories of the past or in anticipating the future, Morton manifests an absorption in the present moment; at times, his is the childlike wonder and awe before nature and the mysteries of a forbidding yet inspiring landscape which characterizes Mitchell's Brian and the Young Ben, Buckler's David, or Grove in *Over Prairie Trails*. 'Obeying, as I ever did, the first impulse of my heart' (III, 207; 453), the artist-idealist–lover takes delight in and draws strength from the irrational, the devastating, and the savage in nature. At home in 'the raging elements' (III, 210; 455), he comes to embody their inexhaustible power and variety. Rather than make nature over, he takes it as it is. Morton enters into ecstatic, sensuous communion with the stormy Highlands even as he merges into the more forbidding Canadian environment; in contrast, De Haldimar tries to conquer and consolidate his power over it.

The sailor and mountain climber accepts, even affirms, the violence of an uncontrollable nature. Immersing himself in the destructive element of life, he finds it buoys him up. Morton's energies are rooted in the irrational vitality of nature, not in the rational activity of the intellect, the domain of his prudent friend Ensign de Haldimar. Guided by 'presentiment' (III, 206; 453), he follows his intuition and the promptings of the unconscious while De Haldimar, going by the rule-book, demonstrates what many observers, discussing our cultural climate, see as an overreliance on the arguing intellect and an insistence that reality be absolutely rational. As a result, Richardson's outcast comes to represent all that is wayward, wanton, mysterious, unpremeditated, overwhelming, illegal, and lusty in life – a Lord of Misrule, a carnivalesque figure of Riot and Dionysian revel.

Wacousta: Poseidon and The Wild Man

Riding his chariot of horses across the sea, Poseidon, god of the oceans and god of horses, embodies the two age-old symbols of ... our fluid unconscious. With no predetermined shape of its own, [water] is constantly in movement ... Poseidon was the most primitive of the gods, the earthshaker, the god of storms and earthquakes, of the sudden devastation of tidal waves – the dangers unleashed when the forces slumbering under the surface of consciousness erupt.

ARIANNA STASSINOPOULOS, *The Gods of Greece*

Poseidon is also a metaphor for the man or woman who can go deeply into the realm of feeling and emotions, and gain access to what is down there: soul and sorrow, great beauty and monsters of the deep ... Poseidon's sphere is the realm of emotions, and the man for whom Poseidon is the archetype is directly in touch with his instincts and feelings, which he expresses spontaneously and immediately if he's extroverted, and may harbour within if he's introverted. And he grows up in a culture that prefers boys and men to be unemotional.

JEAN SHINODA BOLEN, *Gods in Everyman*[20]

The struggle between Wacousta and the Governor is a Canadian version of an ancient conflict whose mythological context is the antagonistic yet complementary relationship of the two brothers Poseidon and Zeus who divided the world between themselves (and Hades). Its dimensions are best gauged by an appeal to recent feminist scholarship and commentary by members of the 'mythopoetic' wing of the contemporary men's movement. Both explore the fascinating link between Greek myths – allusions to which abound in Richardson's writings – and the psyche. Jungian analyst Jean Bolen in *Gods in Everyman* (1989) suggests that the pattern of male Greek deities represents different qualities in the male psyche; they exist both as archetypes that predispose certain types of behaviour and response and as cultural stereotypes of masculinity. In her chapter on Poseidon, Bolen delineates an archetypal configuration of which Wacousta seems a nineteenth-century manifestation.

Poseidon's mythology as she elucidates it encompasses patterns we have been attentive to in Richardson's work and will find greatly elaborated in *The Canadian Brothers*. As in *Wacousta*, the emotionality and spontaneity that the sometimes turbulent, sometimes reflective Poseidon personifies is conveyed through imagery of the powerful, ever-changing moods of the sea which can be both a beautiful and a terrifying realm; like the indistinct border region of wavy curves and circles, the realm of watery depths is another blurred world 'so deep and so dark that clear vision is no longer possible and one can only dimly sense what is there.' Poseidon enjoys a double identity as sea god and as 'husband of the earth' (the meaning of his name), a pre-Olympian consort of the great goddess known for his intense sexuality and fertility. As is the case with Wacousta and De Haldimar, Poseidon contrasts with the impersonal Zeus who submerges feeling to maintain control; Zeus has much to learn from this god, notes Bolen, even as Poseidon might counter a susceptibility to being overwhelmed by rage by developing abilities to plan, reflect, focus, and think objectively. Like Wacousta, Poseidon in his negative or shadow aspect is the ultimate grudge holder; the depths he sinks to in an irrational revenge which drowns all rationality are evident in his relentless ten-year pursuit of a treacherous Odysseus. Like Wacousta, Poseidon reacts emotionally to betrayal, loss, and public humiliation by opening the floodgates to rage and grief. And like Wacousta, Poseidon is father of destructive monsters and savage giants who inherit his own worst nature.[21]

'Poseidon is Zeus's shadow,' states Bolen. This 'lookalike of Zeus' in his positive aspect mediates 'access to emotional depths' which 'is an unappreciated aspect of men's psyches ... devalued and repressed in patriarchal cultures.'[22] In a section of her study entitled 'Poseidon as Archetype of The Wild Man,' Bolen identifies the rejected god with 'the wild man at the bottom of the pool' in the story of Iron John in *Grimm's Fairy Tales*, the commentary on which forms the basis of poet Robert Bly's *Iron John: A Book about Men* (1990) – perhaps *the* text of the men's movement. As the personification of that vibrant, instinctive masculinity that men must reclaim or be in touch with to be whole, the dishonoured wild man of the forest Bly describes so well is, for Bolen, Poseidon known by another name.

Richardson seems to have been familiar with some variant of this ancient story 'called "Iron John" or "Iron Hans" ... first set down by the Grimm brothers around 1820' (Bly).[23] In his non-fictional exposé of the garrison mentality *The Guards in Canada*, Richardson wittily confides to us that such is the apprehension he seems to have inspired in his detractors on one occasion that they, as well as 'the *Militaires*, already felt in anticipation the iron grasp of a Hans of Iceland, a Rob Roy, or a Wacousta himself.'[24] The explicit connection Richardson makes between himself, Wacousta, and Iron Hans is too tantalizing to ignore and invites comment. As the story of Iron John opens, we find out that when travellers or hunters leave the comfortable, familiar surroundings of the king's castle and venture 'beyond the boundaries ... outside the enclosure' into the strange depths of the nearby wilderness, they never return.[25] One day, a young man risks going into the forest dreamscape alone, and as he passes by a pond, a gigantic hand suddenly reaches up to him from deep down in the water, not unlike that of the spectral Wacousta seizing Frederick at the bottom of the border river abyss. The hand succeeds only in pulling under the dog the man has wisely brought with him. Eventually, with several other companions, he bravely and laboriously buckets out the pond to discover lying at its bottom a huge, wild-looking man covered from head to foot with flowing, rusty-red hair.

This frightening being 'lives in the water, under the water,' comments Bly. Not unlike Poseidon and Wacousta, 'he also lives wholeheartedly on earth; his wildness and hairiness in fact belong to earth and its animals.' The primitive giant is brought back to the castle where the rather security-conscious and judgmental king imprisons him in an iron cage in the sunlight and pronounces him 'Iron John.' Like Wacousta, Iron John or The Wild Man is perceived as dangerous, and labelled as such, especially by those whose goal is to achieve position, keep power, look good, and control emotion. 'Contact with Iron John requires a willingness to descend into the male psyche and accept what's dark down there, including the *nourishing* dark.' What Bly suggests at more length 'is that every modern male has, lying at the bottom of his psyche' under layers of cultural conditioning, just such a 'deep male' being of true strength, exuberance, joyous sexuality, deep feeling, and compassion, one whom Bly is careful to distinguish from the savage or macho male men – and women – already know too well.[26]

Just as Frederick de Haldimar disobeys his father's direct order and journeys into the forest, the king's son sets Iron John free and goes into the dark forest with his unlikely mentor. 'As the boy leaves for the forest, he has to overcome, at least for the moment, his fear of wildness, irrationality, hairiness, intuition, emotion, the body, and nature' – everything De Haldimar's garrison walls out. 'Iron John is not as primitive as the boy imagines,' nor Wacousta as primitive as the soldiers believe, 'but the boy – or the mind – does not know that yet.' Indeed, the Wild Man is actually a baronial king just as within Wacousta there resides the chivalric Sir Reginald Morton. Before the end of the story, the king's son under Iron John's influence grows into an authentic masculinity issuing in genuine community with other men and women and communion with the earth. Contrary to the conventional wisdom of the king's domesticated enclave no less than the Governor's, he learns from 'the instinctive one' what Morton/Wacousta, the Monk Knight, and his companions the Baron, Zuleima, and Ernestina know, that ' sexual energy is good ... that animal heat, fierceness, passionate spontaneity is good; and that excess, extravagance, and going with Pan out beyond the castle boundaries is good too.'[27]

Wacousta is a wild man, but he is not the Wild Man Bly delineates far more evocatively than I can suggest here. Though Wacousta the lover, the risk-taker, the instinctive one, the wounded grieving one rings true, Wacousta the killer and rapist is the opposite of Iron John who nurtures and gives life rather than takes it and who enters into equal partnership with the feminine. The Wild Man is not opposed to civilization, but he is not completely contained by it either, notes Bly. Perhaps we see in him that 'good double energy,' a balance of 'both Apollo and Dionysus,' that fascinated but eluded Richardson in his doubles from Wacousta/De Haldimar to the Monk Knight/the Baron.[28]

Governor de Haldimar: 'Moral Monster' and Establishment Manticore

The double hook. The total ambiguity that is so essentially Canadian: be it in terms of two solitudes, the bush garden, Jungian opposites, or the raw and the cooked binary structures of Levi-Strauss. Behind the multiplying theories of Canadian literature is always the pattern of equally matched opposites.

ROBERT KROETSCH[29]

Structurally, Wacousta's flashback is juxtaposed to chapter 6, volume 3 of the original 1832 edition. This key chapter, focused exclusively on Colonel de Haldimar, is entirely missing from most editions, transforming the story into the type of black/white melodrama of Manichean opposites favoured by American editors operating out of another literary tradition. As a result, both De Haldimar and Wacousta are thinly rendered as villains, although Richardson has created characters who are an ambiguous mixture of 'positive' and 'negative' traits. Intent on balancing the attractiveness and repulsiveness of these twin figures for the Canadian psyche, Richardson does not resolve the paradoxes and contradictions inherent in the troubled relationship of these equally matched opposites. The original work is characterized by a disturbing ambivalence in the conflict between authority and rebellion – here linked with the clash of disparate cultures and of modes of being – that we now identify as highly distinctive of our literature. American editors have blurred this issue by creating a totally despicable law-and-order figure consonant with the 'biases' of their own literary tradition. In so doing, they subvert Richardson's intentions by eradicating the ambivalent double response the reader of the original work is obliged to make. They distort the qualified acceptance of the need for boundaries, limits, and some form of societal order, ideally one protective of community and fostering its growth while at the same time allowing for the maximum degree of individual freedom and personal self-realization.

De Haldimar and Wacousta are figured forth as archetypal forces vying for possession of the New World. Together, they explicate the nature of the national psyche as Richardson knew it, the conflicting opposites that keep it in tension. As in Wiebe's *The Temptations of Big Bear* and Scott's *Antichthon*, 'reality' is a double-edged affair in Richardson, and the divergent or multiple perspectives which are generated are part of a system of balances designed to counter the reader's (and author's?) own leanings and prejudices. There is a temptation to side with one or the other at different times in the story, either with De Haldimar, whom Robin Mathews calls 'the perverse expression of law and order,' or with Wacousta, 'the perverse expression of romantic individualism.'[30] To do so is to get caught in defending one extreme without seeing what the author is intent on us seeing: that they are interdependent and, in themselves, tragically incomplete. In this sense, *Wacousta* is a litmus test of the Canadian sensibility.

As often happens, we are pulled both ways at once. The reader's sympathies shift constantly as the text discloses more essential aspects of each figure; their claims on our approval or sanction are alternately supported and undercut. *Wacousta*'s balanced appeal to our romantic sympathies and our sober judgment is nowhere more apparent than in the juxtaposition of the outcast's flashback and the chapter reviewing De Haldimar's past. Just as the Eden chapters mitigate Wacousta's ferocity by disclosing his ardent idealism and romantic imagination, chapter 6 of volume 3 establishes the 'survival' value of De Haldimar's prudence and forethought; it shows his previously repressed emotions beginning to thaw his reserve, explains his extremely harsh behaviour towards Halloway, and qualifies his severity, locating the roots of his inhumanity in the tyrannical, patriarchal ideal of order enshrined by the British military institution he so single-mindedly serves. The tragic and inescapable imperfection of the imported garrison social order in the New World is the source of *Wacousta*'s endless tragic dilemmas. The most dramatic assimilate themselves to the conflict of group versus individual, of the herd sacrificing a *pharmakos*. Besides the antagonism between civilization and nature, the romance delineates a parallel opposition of order and violence within the garrison enclave itself. As in Kroetsch, Callaghan, Findley, Reaney, and Davies, the romantic energies of the individual battle with the traditional, unquestioned restraints of the garrison. Both sides, Richardson insists, have their creative and destructive aspects.

What is indicted in Richardson's tale is not so much De Haldi-

mar, however culpable and morally obtuse, but the entire imported military/social system of the British Empire which he represents. His are not just personal defects but cultural ones. As the
narrator informs us, 'the stern peculiarities of his character ...
originated in an education purely military' (III, 161; 428). The
zealous empire builder is governed by a strict, unquestioning
adherence to a militant ideal that is being transplanted to a New
World milieu which resists the imposition of an order foreign to
it. It is a vision of imperial order rather than one of freedom that
he serves.

Sober, industrious, distrustful of emotion, De Haldimar is a
strong-willed, self-righteous exponent – and an unconscious
victim – of the old European order and what today would be
called the patriarchy. His sensibilities have been irremediably
skewed and locked into the fixed posture dictated by the army,
and a culture that privileges the head over the heart.

> Without ever having possessed any thing like acute feeling, his
> heart, as nature had formed it, was moulded to receive the ordi-
> nary impressions of humanity; and had he been doomed to move
> in the sphere of private life, if he had not been distinguished by
> any remarkable sensibilities, he would not, in all probability, have
> been conspicuous for any extraordinary cruelties. Sent into the
> army, however, at an early age, and with a blood not remarkable
> for its mercurial aptitudes, he had calmly and deliberately imbibed
> all the starched theories and standard prejudices which a mind by
> no means naturally gifted was but too well predisposed to receive.
> (III, 140–41; 417)

Addiction to Perfection

De Haldimar is an extreme expression of the garrison's either/or
mentality, which is a Procrustean bed carving recalcitrant individuals to fit the ideal of a homogenized society. '[H]e was a severe
and a haughty man, – one whose military education had been
based on the principles of the old school – and to whom the
command of a regiment afforded a field for the exercise of an

orthodox despotism, that could not be passed over without the immolation of many a victim on its rugged surface' (III, 140; 417). Both Reginald Mortons may be numbered among such 'victims,' prey to what in *The Studhorse Man* is called 'the eternal violence of law and order.'[31] Both fall foul of what D.G. Jones in *Butterfly on Rock* identifies throughout our literature as an overly exclusive, arid, and militant ideal that would reduce life to a purely rational and mechanical system. And addiction to perfection, as Marion Woodman reminds us in her book of that title, leads to the waste-land. Richardson is our first novelist to inveigh in both fiction and non-fiction against 'the sterile self-destructive character of that ideal,' that 'arrogant and aggressive masculine logos' (Jones) so perceptively assessed by figures associated with the men's movement such as Robert Bly, Robert Moore, James Hillman, Michael Kaufman, and Ray Jones, and feminist writers such as Riane Eisler, Jean Bolen, Charlene Spretnak, and Carol Christ.[32]

Unlike Wacousta who chooses emotion and intuition over practicality and calculation, 'Colonel de Haldimar was not one given to indulge in the mysterious or to believe in the romantic. Everything was plain matter of fact' (III, 152; 423). A stolid exemplar of the daylight consciousness that Davies and Kroetsch speak of, armed with a sharp, penetrating intellect, the reader first sees this Zeus figure – perhaps symbolically – 'bearing a lamp in one hand and a naked sword in the other' (I, 32; 19–20). 'A caution and vigilance of no common kind were unceasingly exercised by the prudent governor' (I, 25; 16), we are told on the first page of the story; De Haldimar's last words urge the officers dutifully to 'pay every attention to the security of the garrison' (III, 358; 535). Indeed, the opening chapters are choked with the repetition of such garrison watchwords as 'prudence,' 'caution,' 'discipline,' 'vigilance,' and 'precaution.' De Haldimar's first sentence is the now classic opening question of all 'westerns,' one posed by the lawman in baffled pursuit of an elusive outlaw: 'which way did he go?' (I, 32; 20).

De Haldimar opposes to nature and the instinctual side of human beings the world of the mind. Such is his over-emphasis on the intellect and on will-power that he strives to effect what

Grove's Edmund Clark, a tyrant likewise motivated by pride and fear, calls an order that represents a dictatorship of mind over matter. As Jones notes in Grove's works, the arid and militant ideal De Haldimar devotes himself to implementing in the New World invariably incurs the destruction of human life and constitutes an assault upon the human spirit. What is gained in security and stability is lost in terms of vital energy and heartfelt passion.

Other establishment or law-and-order figures in Canadian literature have inherited Colonel de Haldimar's perverse, virulent strain of rationality. The cool, detached, intellectual streak that makes him an 'inhuman murderer' (I, 278; 154) renders Mitchell's Mrs Abercrombie 'the town assassin,' Ondaatje's Sheriff Pat Garrett 'a sane assassin' and 'an academic murderer,' and Grove's Edmund Clark 'an almost insane schemer' prepared 'to assume the most absolute power, as a dictator ... to maintain law and order' and to 'eliminate' dissenters through 'Police and soldiery ... machine guns and tanks ... for the good of the masses themselves.'[33] Although Wacousta seems to be mad, perhaps, as Perry Nodelman notes in an article on Ondaatje's *The Collected Works of Billy the Kid*, 'the real madmen are those who believe that sanity is total control and total lack of emotion.'[34]

Perhaps the most important clue to De Haldimar's ambitious, patriarchal behaviour and the betrayal of his best friend comes right at the beginning of the romance before the full extent of its significance can be gauged. In a work in which so many things are doubled, it is not surprising that there are two curses. '"Ah!" observed Captain Blessington, "this is indeed the greatest curse attached to the profession of a soldier. Even among those who most esteem, and are drawn towards each other as well by fellowship in pleasure as companionship in danger, this vile and debasing principle – this insatiable desire for personal advancement – is certain to intrude itself; since we feel that over the mangled bodies of our dearest friends and companions, we can alone hope to attain preferment and distinction"' (I, 43; 26). If De Haldimar is the victim of Ellen's curse, Wacousta has been the innocent victim of this, 'the greatest curse.' Richardson chooses to emphasize this first curse at length in the opening chapters. He deems it important enough to detract from the surface action of tight suspense and mystery, reiterating it twice. For all the fear of the wilderness, this selfish, divisive desire for personal advancement is the real law of the jungle. Garrison life lived according to this 'debasing principle' is analogous to contemporary business life which for Bly 'allows competitive relationships only, in which the major emotions are anxiety, tension, loneliness, rivalry, and fear ... Having no soul union with other men can be the most damaging wound of all.'[35]

Here an expression of the Cain and Abel motif, the scramble for preferment 'over the mangled bodies of our dearest friends' is a particularly fertile theme in Canadian literature; it informs works from Heavysege's *The Advocate* to Richler's *The Apprenticeship of Duddy Kravitz* to Davies's Deptford trilogy. The story opens and closes in an enactment of this curse. Blessington, Charles, and Everard speak out against promotion obtained through the misfortune of others. Delme and Murphy, like the young Ensign de Haldimar, indulge in 'such selfish anticipations.' It is dramatically appropriate, therefore, that Wacousta's first stray shot kills the ambitious Murphy, that 'eternal echo of the opinions of those who look forward to promotion' (I, 43; 25), while his last shot kills the calculating Ensign Delme, Ensign de Haldimar's mirror-image. Both unfeeling men are shot through the heart, their deaths as symbolic as that of Grove's Edmund Clark, likewise killed by a bullet through the heart whilst defending the mill that now resembles a beleaguered fortress.

Richardson's poignant description of Governor de Haldimar in chapter 6 is a classic portrait of a type now all too familiar to readers of Canadian and feminist writings and the literature of the men's movement. It demands quotation at length.

> As a subaltern, M. de Haldimar had ever been considered a pattern of rigid propriety and decorum of conduct. Not the shadow of military crime had ever been laid to his charge. He was punctual at all parades and drills; kept the company to which he was attached in a perfect hot water of discipline; never missed his distance in marching past, or failed in a military manoeuvre; paid

his mess-bill regularly to the hour, nay, minute, of the settling day ... and, to crown all, he had never asked, consequently never obtained, a day's leave from his regiment ... With all these qualities, Ensign de Haldimar promised to make an excellent soldier; and, as such, was encouraged by the field-officers of the corps, who unhesitatingly pronounced him a lad of discernment and talent, who would one day rival them in all the glorious privileges of martinetism. (III, 141–2; 418)

De Haldimar's quest to have and to hold power and position has become his life and has cost him his human features, as Wacousta's quest has cost him his. The Governor resembles an efficient, merciless machine exacting unquestioning obedience and grinding out robot-like conformity – a machine that works incessantly and works at keeping everything under control. Yet despite all his weaknesses, De Haldimar is presented with the same teasing ambiguity, understanding, and sympathy as is Wacousta. In that very important chapter 6, the narrator maintains that

Whatever might be the stern peculiarities of his character, – and these had originated in an education purely military, – Colonel de Haldimar was an officer well calculated to the important trust reposed in him; for, combining experience with judgement in all matters relating to the diplomacy of war, and being fully conversant with the character and habits of the enemy opposed to him, he possessed singular aptitude to seize whatever advantages might present themselves. The prudence and caution of his policy have already been made manifest in the two several council scenes with the chiefs. (III, 161; 428)

L.R. Early argues that 'a case can be made for De Haldimar as an exemplar of competence and responsibility.'[36] The Governor is an able administrator and a shrewd organizer. Like the practical business men in *Five Legs*, he knows how to get things done; in both cases, this is part of their Puritan heritage. 'Scrupulously exact in the arrangement of his papers' (III, 75; 381), the fastidious bureaucrat is efficient, orderly, organized, pragmatic, analytical. Under his prudent supervision, the fledgling British colony does survive and endure, despite hardship and disaster and in the face of what strikes them as cosmic indifference and perhaps hostility. While his actions often end up sacrificing lives, they also preserve them; as Foucault's works testify, power is an ambivalent force. In some matters, De Haldimar does display a very Canadian genius for compromise. His policy of conciliation with regard to Ponteac and the three tribes he commands receives approbation. When the Indians are trapped inside the fort, De Haldimar cleverly uses the occasion to impress upon them the benevolent intentions of the empire he represents, to declaim against the French and to castigate Wacousta as a treacherous French spy unworthy of associating with a people he only misleads. So impressed is Ponteac by this show of forbearance and good will that he later concludes a peace with the British. Fort Détroit survives, in part then, through De Haldimar's competent deployment of well-disciplined troops who defeat Ponteac's plans to capture it.

Neither De Haldimar nor Wacousta is a one-dimensional character. They may have a symbolic or iconic dimension, but they are also well-defined individuals alive with contradictions. The Governor is as capable of feeling as Wacousta is of systematically formulating a 'feasible and rational plan' (III, 249; 477) to effect Clara Beverley's descent down the mountain. Both men display leadership capabilities, although Wacousta is certainly a more spell-binding orator. At the same time, the excessive severity of De Haldimar's treatment of Halloway, Ellen, Everard, and others proves divisive and increasingly alienates him from his troops; so, too, the extent of Wacousta's revenge estranges Oucanasta and stirs up his nemesis in the person of her brother. Both leaders are capable of change. Chapter 6 reveals a lonely, isolated De Haldimar who is beginning – albeit too late – to moderate his extreme behaviour.

He, too, becomes, in Wacousta's phrase for himself, an 'altered being' (III, 288; 497).

Whether it was that he secretly acknowledged the too excessive sternness of his justice in regard to Halloway (who still, in the true acceptation of facts, had been guilty of a crime that entailed the penalty he had paid), or that the apprehensions that arose to his heart in regard to her on whom he yearned with all a father's fondness governed his conduct, certain it is, that, from the hour of the disclosure made by his son, Colonel de Haldimar became an altered man. Without losing any thing of that dignity of manner, which had hitherto been confounded with the most repellent haughtiness of bearing, his demeanour towards his officers became more courteous; and although, as heretofore, he kept himself entirely aloof ... there was more of conciliation in his manner, and less of austerity in his speech. (III, 159–60; 427–8)

This change parallels that mellowing which the ferocious Wacousta undergoes in Clara de Haldimar's company, the captive beauty, in turn, feeling compassion for the savage beast. Growth begins only after the Governor experiences humility, vulnerability – and grief. Grief is the door to feeling in De Haldimar as Bly maintains it is for most men. Charles's death helps free the loving father long buried within the physically and emotionally undemonstrative Governor. The Governor's coldness and cruelty become painfully apparent to him – and to the garrison. The formerly insensitive man of the head 'goes out of his mind with grief' and comes to his senses. Descending from his summit, De Haldimar begins to regain some humanity through 'learning to shudder' (Bly), a phrase Davies also uses to describe a similiar process in David Staunton, his aloof manticore. Explains Bly in a section of *Iron John* entitled 'The Road of Ashes, Descent, and Grief,' 'Gaining the ability to shudder means feeling how frail human beings are, and how awful it is to be a Titan. When one is shuddering, the shudder helps to take away the numbness we spoke of. When a man possesses empathy, it does not mean that he has developed the feminine feeling only; of course he has, and it is good to develop the feminine. But when he learns to shudder, he is developing a part of the masculine emotional body as well.'[37]

As in the fiction of Grove, Davies, Atwood, Laurence, Kroetsch, and Callaghan, it requires a costly irruption of irrational forces to change or moderate the ways of characters like De Haldimar. The Governor appears to be at the very beginning of that painful journey toward the reintegration of undeveloped feelings later undertaken by law-and-order figures like Davies's Justice Staunton or Callaghan's 'Commander' Ira Groome.

Of Shadow Kings, Dark Fathers, and Father-Hungry Sons: Zeus and the Patriarchy

Zeus is the archetype of the dynastic father ... Zeus is emotionally distant, does not have an earthy nature, doesn't try to please women, and isn't passionate. Because the Zeus man may focus on achieving power, other aspects of his personality become stunted ... Zeus's realm was the sky, and the Zeus archetype predisposes a man to live in his head ... The message that something is wrong needs to get through to the Zeus man.

JEAN BOLEN, *Gods in Everyman*[38]

The sterile and self-destructive character of De Haldimar's ideal of mechanical perfection is tragically manifest in his severe conduct towards members of his own family. Such behaviour forecasts that of Gibson's Robert Fraser in *Perpetual Motion*, Grove's wilful, domineering patriarchs, Hagar Shipley's father in Laurence's *The Stone Angel*, Ostenso's Caleb Gare, Maggie's tyrannical parents in Reaney's *The St. Nicholas Hotel*, Kroetsch's William Dawe in *Badlands*, and countless others. De Haldimar not only pits his will against the new land but also against anyone who dares question his pronouncements, including his children.

> Much of the despotic military character of Colonel de Haldimar had been communicated to his private life; so much, indeed, that his sons, – both of whom ... were of natures that belied their origin from so stern a stock, – were kept at nearly as great a distance from him as any other subordinates of his regiment. But although he seldom indulged in manifestations of parental regard towards those whom he looked upon rather as inferiors in military rank,

than as beings connected with him by the ties of blood, Colonel de Haldimar was not without the instinctive love for his children which every animal in the creation feels for its offspring. (III, 147–8; 421)

The father-son bond is treated with great importance in *Wacousta* and *The Canadian Brothers*. The emotionally distant De Haldimar possesses the lineaments of 'The Remote Father' or 'The Darkened Father' whose literary manifestations Bly traces in stories about the Titans Uranus and Cronos through to the contemporary figures of the Emperor and his deadly servant, Darth Vader (whose name is a pun on dark father).[39] Like the suspicious and uneasy Governor, such men tend to compete as rivals even with their own sons. De Haldimar considers his son Charles – a Poseidon 'feeling' type who openly talks about and shares his feelings – embarrassingly inferior and effeminate because he reacts emotionally rather than rationally in a culture that regards such behaviour as negative. Although the father in his dynastic urge has named this son after himself, hoping he will mirror or replicate his ideal of manliness, the gentle, sensitive, and receptive Charles is a 'soft male' (Bly) who recalls the Governor's emotionally expressive wife whom he seems to have single-mindedly pursued only to neglect and let quickly suffocate in his passionless presence.

Charles, in turn, experiences grief due to the remoteness and secretiveness of his workaholic father. Rather than reject his punitive parent outright as an American son might do, the introspective Charles becomes a 'Father-Hungry Son' bent on suppressing his nature and – like 'The Canadian Brothers' – living up to his father's expectations by excelling as a soldier under his command. He also gives himself over to taking care of others at the expense of his own well-being. All such reactions are familiar attempts of emotionally abandoned and shamed sons to 'ascend above their wound,' as Bly would say. Harshly and coldly critical, De Haldimar is unable to give his blessing to his son, who seeks this elsewhere in a male mentor aptly named Blessington. In *Iron John* we read, 'Not receiving any blessing from your father is an injury.

Robert Moore said, "If you're a young man and you're not being admired by an older man, you're being hurt."'[40]

As the foregoing quotation from *Wacousta* suggests, in a text that emphasizes relationship and the interconnectedness of all characters, Governor de Haldimar and the culture he tries to establish through force in North America privilege a model of human relationships – whether in personal or professional spheres – based on the principle of ranking and rivalry rather than linking or affiliation. Feminist scholar Riane Eisler in *The Chalice and the Blade* (1987) and *The Partnership Way* (1990) refers to the former as 'dominator model' societies which tend to be authoritarian, hierarchial, competitive, aggressive, frequently patriarchal, and defiantly set apart from nature, and to the latter as 'partnership model' societies which constellate 'feminine' values like egalitarian linking and bonding, non-violence, active caring and nurturance, and connection with the earth. Partnership or 'the power of affiliation' – what Canadian educator Mac Freeman calls 'duetting' – is the hallmark of cultures opposed to dominator modes. It reflects a sense of the interconnectedness of human beings that Richardson surely appreciated and of the interwoven texture of all life which feminist writers like Jean Bolen, Merlin Stone, Charlene Spretnak, Carol Gilligan, Luisah Teish, Starhawk, and Mary Daly discern in goddess cultures. While partnership societies conceptualize the powers governing the universe in the female form of the goddess, dominator ones – of which De Haldimar's garrison is typical – often worship and pattern relationships after a sternly divine Father who wields a thunderbolt or a weapon, devalue the feminine, and equate true masculinity with the power urge, dominance, total control, and rational thinking.[41]

Eisler's historical study of Western civilization helps to clarify some of the male-male and male-female relationships in Richardson's work, throwing light on the Governor's plans to establish a patriarchal dynasty, to rule over the wilderness, his children, and his own instinctual nature. It is a plan shared by his symbolic descendants, the haughty, ambitious, and autocratic empire-builder Abe Spalding in Grove's *Fruits of the Earth*, an Ontarian determined to 'conquer this wilderness,' to force the land to take 'the impress of his mind and will,' and the dogmatic John Elliot senior in *Our Daily Bread*, 'a thinker' 'proud of the preponderance, in him, of brain over impulse' and 'appraising reason above all else.' Interestingly, both men are paired with their opposites. Abe's best friend is the philosophical Nicoll whose words seem the 'utterance of that very landscape itself; as though Nicoll were the true son of the prairie, and he, Abe, a mere interloper.' John Elliot senior is balanced harmoniously with 'his complement,' his wife Martha who 'seemed to do instinctively, action coming from the heart, what he chose to do after mature deliberation, his action being dictated by the brain.'[42]

Like Grove's empire-builders or Atwood's Commander of the Republic of Gilead in *The Handmaid's Tale*, Governor de Haldimar is a 'Shadow King,' a term coined by psychoanalyst and theologian Robert Moore, author (with Douglas Gilette) of *King, Warrior, Magician, Lover: Rediscovering the Archetypes of the Mature Masculine* (1990). In contrast to the firm but kindly King (or Sacred King) who is powerful and 'uses power to empower,' nurture, validate, and bless others, the Shadow King exercises abusive power over others, and does not foster creativity, facilitate growth or enhance potential.[43] As the shadow part of the father archetype, whether in the individual male psyche or in society at large, he is visible in the Governor's paranoiac suspicion of motives and loyalties and in his capacity to remain unmoved in the face of the suffering of others. It is this very lack of empathy which calls down Ellen's curse on him and his family, thus animating the plot of the epic. In a mythological context, both the King and the Shadow King are manifestations of the Zeus archetype, for Moore, Bly, and Bolen the presiding 'god' of Western culture. Governor de Haldimar possesses positive Zeus energy to some extent; he is not without leadership qualities, an overview perspective, and a capacity for quick, decisive action taken to sustain the community. He also manifests the dark side of this distant, authoritarian, power-seeking sky god who, as Arianna Stassinopoulos puts it, 'becomes in his darkness an enemy of the life-force, locked in his structures and laws, fearing and resisting change and any threat to the status quo.'[44]

Jean Bolen's insightful analysis of the central Olympian god 'who excels ... at determining boundaries' and of his psychological resonance as an archetype of the male psyche will help draw together my comments on the personality traits of Governor de Haldimar and his symbolic descendants in Canadian literature. 'Like all successful rulers, Zeus was adept at strategy, forming alliances ... Zeus has the ambition and the ability to establish a realm over which he was the chief god, and the urge to preside over one's own territory is a major drive of this archetype, which shapes men (and women) to be and behave like Zeus ... He exalts control, reason and will above all other qualities ... To sit at the summit, with power, authority, and dominion over a chosen realm is the Zeus position ... The driving force is the urge to extend the boundaries of the kingdom.'[45]

Where the Governor/Zeus establishes, defends, extends borders, Wacousta/Poseidon leaps over them or finds himself unable to recognize or set them. And unlike his counterpart, 'For Zeus, finding a suitable wife is not a matter of heart or soul connection, but a matter of state ... He went after women with the singleness of purpose that is characteristic of his "eagle" nature. Seeing who he wants, he does whatever is necessary to get close to her ... Once he has succeeded, his attention most likely again focuses on his work realm.' Bolen's description of Zeus as 'the archetype of the dynastic father' succinctly clarifies the Governor's attitude towards his children: 'His expectation of them is similiar to what he expects of his subordinates: to be obedient and carry out his will. His favourite children replicate his ideal of himself as a fairminded, superior person who does not let emotions ever get "out of control" ... He considers showing vulnerability or neediness or being emotional signs of stupidity or weakness.'[46]

Such is the 'god' of the man Richardson depicts as the mythic founder of the Canadas. He is a man whose distant descendants – respectable sons of the patriarchy manning the bastions of Zeus power – are doomed through the curse of the marginalized Ellen to struggle with the offspring of his outlaw double in the sequel to *Wacousta*, *The Canadian Brothers*.

CHAPTER FOUR

The Canadian Brothers: Narcissus and Circe on the Border River

The more I experience this part of Ontario with its mysterious border islands – Walpole and St. Anne's, Tecumseh is buried on the former – its Indian traditions, its great marshes and a rich folklore lode that runs from Lake St. Clair right over to Long Point ... I have the feeling that it's a place rather like Circe's island, Aiaia, an isle of the dead where you go to be reborn. Marshy country breeds fen-ghosts and jack o'lanterns?

JAMES REANEY, *Halloween* 2

The divided landscape is within as much as without, one loses oneself in it, drowns in it, in order to reappear whole ...

W.H. NEW, *Articulating West*

I feel I am acting out America's relationship to the Canadas. Martin is the imperial ogre while I play the role of genteel mate who believes that if everyone is well-mannered, we can inhabit a peaceable kingdom. That is the national dream of the Canadas, isn't it? A civilized garden where lions lie down with doves. I did not see the difference until I married Martin. We possess no fantasies of conquest and domination. Indeed, to be from the Canadas is to feel as women feel – cut off from the base of power.

SUSAN SWAN, *The Biggest Modern Woman of the World*[1]

The special features of Richardson's sensibility – an ironic double vision and voice, ambiguity, a strong tragic sense, and an intuitive feeling for the spirit of place – are again apparent in *The Canadian Brothers*. As the sequel to *Wacousta; or, The Prophecy*, it takes up family history about fifty years later. As its subtitle indicates, *The Prophecy Fulfilled* dramatizes the future woes summarized by Ellen Halloway's oracular pronouncement. The pattern of action takes the form of a cyclical descent into and ascent out of the demonic realm. In this chapter, I trace Gerald Grantham's descent into the nightworld of romance with its emphasis on growing confusion of identity, labyrinths or prisons, cruelty and horror, metamorphosis, mirrors, doubles, and twins.

In so doing, I hope we will become attuned to Richardson's attempts to explore and explain the assumptions of two cultures which are in collision. Again, he uses the mirror-like border river as a metaphor for a double focus. Like *Wacousta, The Canadian Brothers* is structured via break boundaries, an intermingling of contrarieties which is the hallmark of his nightmarish borderland. The motifs of the struggle of brothers and the demon-lover are once more interwoven with the doppelgänger theme, the latter given one of its familiar variants as the narcissistic mirror-reflection. What results is an imaginative retelling of the myths of Narcissus and Circe in North American terms.

A brief plot summary may help recall the salient features of the story. *The Canadian Brothers*, as the subtitle denotes, is at once *The Prophecy Fulfilled* and *A Tale of the Late American War*. Richardson deftly interweaves the working out of Ellen's curse of 1763 prophesying the horrible deaths of all De Haldimars with the military events of the War of 1812 between the Canadas and the United States. As such, it anticipates the mixture of the fictive and the historical, of myth and documentary, to be found in Reaney and the 'historiographic metafiction' (Hutcheon) of Findley, Ondaatje, Wiebe, Chris Scott, and others. The conflict between the two families surfaces after several generations in the clash between the two Canadian brothers Gerald and Henry Grantham (descendants of Colonel de Haldimar) who are officers in the British fortress at Amherstburg and Jeremiah Desborough (descendant of Wacousta) who is an American settler and spy residing in the bush fronting the Detroit River. Though their true identity is long concealed from each other and the reader, their antagonism assumes the imaginative pattern of the struggle in *Wacousta*.

The unprincipled Desborough, 'prince of traitors,' has secretly assassinated Major Grantham, the father of Gerald and Henry, out of a 'hatred ... for the stern magistrate' (II, 42). His inextinguishable desire for revenge manifests itself in continued hostilities to the Canadian brothers who are as much esteemed as he is loathed. The opening scene dramatically reveals how these personal animosities have expanded into historical ones. Desborough's plan to facilitate the secret passage of an American gunboat past Fort Detroit is designed to cast suspicion upon Gerald's allegiance. Gerald, however, captures the gunboat and becomes a war hero. Yet this initial victory ironically heralds the fall of 'the once high, generous and noble minded Gerald' (II, 193). Aboard the ship is another descendant of Wacousta/Poseidon, Desborough's daughter Matilda, who is known only as Miss Montgomery, the niece of the captured American naval officer.

Gerald is captivated by her but is thrown into despair because Matilda's love is contingent upon the cold-blooded assassination of a lover who once wronged her. Any such deed would violate the brothers' pledge to their dying father never 'to swerve from those principles of virtue and honor, which had been so sedulously inculcated' (II, 44) in them. Once again, Richardson emphasizes the dynamics of the father-son relationship. Matilda becomes 'the agent of Fate in effecting his destruction' (II, 206); his passionate oath to her supersedes the pledge to his father (ironically given by Henry in his absence), thus linking him to the murderer of his father. Just as the brotherly bond between Wacousta and De Haldimar is split over Clara, Matilda severs that linking Gerald and Henry.

The border conflict is developed in terms of the struggle-of-brothers motif. Richardson presents a classic confrontation between those two doubles the disciplined, law-abiding Canadian garrison officer and 'the half-civilized backwoodsman' and outlaw from the United States whose 'cunning alone could serve his purpose in a country, the laws of which were not openly to be defied' (I, 83). It is of the utmost significance that Colonel de Haldimar's descendants are Canadians and Wacousta's Americans. Richardson uses the two family trees to reflect the differences between the two nations which are 'diametrically opposed in their interests, their principles, their habits, and their attachments' (I, 83). Interestingly, the Granthams seem purged of the worst traits of De Haldimar while the Desboroughs appear to have retained those of Wacousta.

While the Governor was 'all coldness, prudence, obsequiousness, and forethought' (III, 194; 447), the Canadian brothers are distinguished only by prudence and forethought. 'Inheriting the martial spirit of their family' (II, 41) and something of Major Grantham's 'rigid notions of right' (II, 33), the young Granthams try to live up to the expectations of the unblemished magistrate who enjoys a high position in the social scale. The orthodox Henry is a dutiful and obedient son; generous-hearted, conscientious, circumspect, and reserved, he follows the dictates of his reason. He is unswayed by those passionate impulses which will soon engulf his brother who plunges into Poseidon's realm of emotion and instinct. Like the passive Charles de Haldimar, Henry is the one who remains rooted at home on 'unrepublican soil' (I, 82) while his roving brother, like Frederick de Haldimar, becomes involved in adventurous journeys which take him across the border into a strange and terrifying world.

'Gerald, whose reputation for vigilance, in all matters of duty, was universally acknowledged' (II, 25), is as bold and daring a man of action as his grandfather Frederick in *Wacousta*. Both are war heroes whose initial acts save the garrisons they serve; ironically, this is accomplished by breaking the law. Frederick leaves Fort Détroit disobeying a direct order not to do so and travels with Oucanasta to the Indian encampment where he overhears the scheme to capture the British stronghold. Although not strictly justified to do so, Gerald leaves the gunboat he commands and travels with Sambo, the old and faithful family servant, to Desborough's hut; there they overhear the traitor and his son devising a similar stratagem to further the American war effort.

The Canadian brothers' father is a loyalist who has married the melancholy daughter of Frederick and Madeline de Haldimar. Major Grantham is explicitly compared to De Haldimar, yet although austere in manner, severe in his administration of justice, he is not a shadow king tyrant or a desiccated *senex*. Neither is he unduly proud, unjust, or intolerant. No hypocrite, the magistrate is a benevolent and temperate man whose exemplary behaviour wins the respect, if not the love, of the garrison community. While not cold and unfeeling, he has a marked 'reservedness of disposition' (II, 33) and is slow to show affection.

The American Desboroughs have inherited Wacousta's/Poseidon's affinity for water, passion for revenge, independence, ferocious energy, and recklessness. They have not inherited Sir Reginald Morton's romantic idealism or his heroic spirit. Like Wacousta, they are marginal members of society, outcasts, and outlaws. Disdainful of authority, insolent, and irreverent, they insist on following their own individual bent. Amoral and ruthless, cunning and resourceful, Desborough and Matilda are associated with an untamed nature. 'That monster Desborough' (II, 117) is a restless, mobile American frontiersman, the 'most unruly and disorderly of the worthless set' (I, 42) who have settled along the border. An uncertain compound of Kentuckian and Yankee, he is usually designated by the latter appellation. Tall, robust, swift-footed, tricky, and sinister, the black-browed backwoodsman recalls his father Wacousta and, in his curses and imprecations against the Granthams, his mother Ellen Halloway.

Like his Jacobite rebel ancestor, the notorious renegade is associated with various wild animals: bears, tigers, and wildcats. He, too, possesses 'a thunderin' voice that made the woods ring' (II, 141). He also dupes others and is duped in turn. Unlike Wacousta, he is given to slander; he tries to blacken Gerald's reputation by raising doubts about the officer's fidelity to the crown. As Gerald notes of his adversary, 'the strictness of my father, during his magistracy, in compelling him to choose between taking the oaths of allegiance and quitting the country, had inspired him with deep hatred to himself and disaffection to the Government' (I, 122).

Matilda and Arnoldi, Desborough's daughter and son by an unnamed woman, are equally dangerous. The latter, now a soldier in the Michigan militia, is denounced by the garrison as a deserter and a traitor. The Desboroughs compose no family unit in the conventional sense of commitment and mutual love and respect; like many an American outlaw, Matilda has no real family at all, Desborough having abandoned her as an orphan on Major Montgomery's doorstep. Her immunity from parental behest is in direct contrast to the family-oriented Canadian brothers. Like Wacousta, the beautiful but repellent Matilda is fearless and single-minded in her inhuman revenge against her betrayer. Her mobile features, mercurial nature, and wild, scornful laugh also proclaim her heritage. As her father is 'The Yankee,' Matilda is often referred to as 'The American.' Like the Desboroughs, the Americans in general are fiercely independent, undisciplined, and enterprising; unlike the highly organized, uniformly costumed, and obedient Canadian and British soldiers of whom the Granthams are exemplars, 'when checked ... they looked not for a remedy in the resumption of order, but in the exercise each of his own individual exertions ... his own personal resources' (II, 47).

In volume 1 of *The Canadian Brothers*, Richardson is intent on describing the differences between his twin families and the two nations with which they are aligned. But as in *Wacousta*, the border region is one of bizarre metamorphosis. The sequel is likewise organized around break boundaries, those points of reversal where opposites run into one another and merge. The most pronounced paradoxical inversion of identity is the grotesque transformation of Gerald Grantham, the magistrate's son, into his opposite or double, the American outlaw. Under Matilda's malign influence, the Canadian brother loses his Grantham/De Haldimar traits and takes on those of the Desboroughs. In him, the dual worlds of civilization and rude nature, order and lawlessness, life and death, begin to overlap and interpenetrate. This border struggle of Canadian and American brothers with its attendant exchange of identity opens up the work's thematic meaning and structural design.

The 'border blur' phenomenon is at once a characteristic of the nightmarish borderline area and of the nightworld in the descent narratives of romance. Again, I appeal to Campbell, McLuhan, and Frye in elucidating its complexities. In the latter's account of the Romantic myth and Campbell's exposition of the stages of the adventure of the mythological hero, there are two orders of nature, one the world of ordinary social human experience, the other a world connected with uncultivated nature. The heroes and villains of romance exist primarily to symbolize the contrast between the two.[2] Here the symbolic 'bridge' between these two domains – between the idyllic childhood world of Amherstburg, 'one of the loveliest spots that ever issued from the will of a beneficent and gorgeous nature' (I, 1), and the violent nightworld of the American wilderness – is a mysterious border island in the middle of the Detroit River.

Significantly, it is at Matilda's request that the Canadian brothers and their companions voyage by boat to the forested Hog Island half-way between Upper Canada and the States. To reach it, it is necessary to pass by the 'Bloody Bridge' which linked the two domains of European and Indian in *Wacousta*. For the first time in his life, Gerald becomes angry with his brother because of Henry's obvious aversion to Matilda and his warning against pursuing such a cold and unsettling woman. On the island, during a hunt for fowl, the two brothers 'thread the mazes of the wood' (I, 208) in a sullen mood. In a symbolic scene conveying his destructive infatuation, Gerald 'beheld a remarkably fine bird, which ... had its neck outstretched and its gaze intently fixed on some objects below. Tempted by the size and beauty of the bird Gerald fired and it fell to the earth. He ... was in the act of picking it up, when a sharp and well known rattle was heard ... The warning was sufficient to save him had he consented even for an instant to forego his prize ... Before he could again raise himself an enormous rattlesnake had darted upon him, and stung with rage perhaps at being deprived of its victim, had severely bitten him' (I, 216).

This key episode in 'The Crossing of the First Threshold' (Campbell) implicitly recalls an earlier one in which Gerald, having crossed the border river on a reconnaissance mission, is driven by a fatal curiosity to pursue a wraith-like figure to a graveyard and then to a cottage near the 'Bloody Bridge.' Through a window, Gerald watches the fascinating being who is 'gazing intently on the features of the sleeper' (I, 169) within. Suddenly, the figure draws a dagger and is about to stab the unsuspecting victim when Gerald blindly fires his pistol. Fearing capture, he departs before he knows the identity of the two individuals. During the trip to Hog Island, he is moved to recount the adventure; when he tells of the shooting, Matilda pales, clutching her side. The reader later learns, of course, that the midnight assassin is indeed Matilda, her intended victim Colonel Forrester, her betrayer. Yet despite Henry's warnings and indications of Matilda's cold-bloodedness, Gerald does not forgo his 'prize' (also Wacousta's term for his spiritual treasure) which he has taken from the captured American schooner.

Gorgons and Vampires

As the foregoing scene suggests, the ambiguous Matilda no less than Wacousta is both victim and agent of destruction, both 'bird' and 'snake.' Stung with rage at being deprived of her victim, she infects Gerald with the venom of her revenge, eventually enticing him to become her avenger; indeed, it is in terms of *Wacousta*'s imagery of poison, disease, and paralysis that Gerald's tragic infatuation is conveyed. Like Arnoldi who is associated with 'the Gorgon' (I, 145) or Wacousta with his 'power to paralyse' (II, 31; 175), Matilda, whose 'look ... almost petrified where it fell' (I, 23) benumbs Gerald on the enchanted border isle; by the end of the story, he is 'turned to stone' (II, 199), recalling our last glimpse of Governor de Haldimar. The island episode is a dramatic enactment of the epigraph to *Wacousta* from Young's *The Revenge*: 'Vengeance is still alive; from her dark covert, With all her snakes erect upon her crest, She stalks in view, and fires me with her charms.'[3]

We should not be surprised to find the figure of the gorgon at this bridge between worlds. Such a monster, as J.E. Cirlot explains in *A Dictionary of Symbols*, 'is a symbol of the fusion of opposites,' 'of conditions beyond the endurance of the conscious mind, slaying him who contemplates it.'[4] As an almost unconscious Gerald succumbs to the snake bite, Matilda's demonic identity as a composite of witch, gorgon, Circe, and vampire-queen of the dead becomes readily apparent. Although only the Indians are said to know the remedy for Gerald's condition, the American vows to restore his life. A figure of occult wisdom, Matilda is 'busily employed in stirring certain herbs which she was boiling over the fire that had been kindled' (I, 217). Then, 'to the surprise and consternation of all around, she applied her own lips to the wound ... Her countenance and figure, as she stood in the midst of the forest, preparing the embrocation, so well harmonizing with the scene and occupation; the avidity with which she sucked the open wound of the sufferer, and the fearless manner in which she imbibed that which was considered death to others; all this ... threw over the actor and the action, an air of the preternatural ... [Henry] scarcely could persuade himself she was not the almost vampire and sorceress that his excited imagination had represented' (I, 218–20).

The witch-like Matilda is the demonic mirror inversion of the innocent Clara Beverley in *Wacousta* who is 'in classic harmony with the surrounding scenery' (III, 213; 457) of her Eden. Clara applies a dressing of herbs to Fidelity, the wild deer she has tamed and which Sir Reginald Morton has just wounded during a hunt with Gerald's great-grandfather. In Matilda and Clara, we see what the perceptive Richardson critic Jay Macpherson calls in another context the tendency for landscape to become a mirror which generates 'spectres and soul-mates, images of horror and desire' and what Campbell terms the Temptress and the Meeting with the Goddess.[5] Wacousta's soulmate is associated with Diana and ascent to a mountain-top Eden in the Highlands which is bathed in light; Gerald's spectre is associated with the gorgons and Circe and descent into a dark, hellish valley in the American South. One is a muse, the other a Medusa.

Thus begins, towards the close of volume 1, Gerald's metamorphosis and his descent into the nightmarish border world of romance. Just as his father is killed by Desborough while out hunting, he is psychologically and spiritually slain by the backwoodsman's daughter during a hunt. As Frye observes, 'We are often reminded of this type of descent by the imagery of the hunt. A knight rides off into a forest in pursuit of an animal and as he disappears the dream atmosphere closes around him ... In this threshold symbol of entering a world of sleep all images begin to take on an erotic quality ... There seems to be an increasing identity between the forest and a shrouding female body, of a rather sinister kind ... the hunter is seeking a false identity which is the same thing as his own destruction. The consummation of the hunt ... is the turning of the pursuer into the victim.'[6]

Volume 1 of *Wacousta* ends by emphasizing the gulf between an immigrant and an indigenous mentality in the image of Ellen standing over a casket in the centre of the fatal bridge, screaming her curse of death on the race of De Haldimar. Volume 1 of *The Canadian Brothers* ends with the tragic split between Canadian and American sensibility symbolized by another coffin and another Morton; the prophetess' granddaughter, the sorceress of Hog Island, is in Henry's words, 'a beautiful casket, which, on opening is found to contain not a gem of price, but a subtle poison, contact with which is fatal' (I, 190). The mysterious woman who is identified with graveyards, caskets, and vampires saves Gerald's life, but only to keep it for herself. From this point on, he is never quite sure of his identity, and the narrative movement keeps sinking into anxiety and nightmare.

Gerald is now in Matilda's possession, infected with a spiritual poison that renders him one of the living dead. The bewitched sailor begins to look like the cold and ghostly Matilda; he gradually becomes as violent and uncontrollable as Desborough and the savage backwoodsmen. Gerald's metamorphosis recalls that of the De Haldimars who have crossed over the border river into the lower world of the Indian. Hog Island, we remember, was the spot where Wacousta temporarily imprisoned Gerald's ancestors; the sorceress' fire summons up the image of the Indians dancing around their fire in a 'devilish throng' (III, 112–3; 402). The De Haldimars are infected by the wendigo-like Wacousta with the same disease of despair and death-in-life weariness which Gerald succumbs to. The 'almost utter unconsciousness' (III, 169; 433) into which these *mort-vivants* descend also makes them somnambulists staggering wildly through the bush or aboard the schooner; bedevilled by Wacousta, these newly arrived shades in Hades come to resemble the wild, spectre-like Wacousta and the Indians.

The vampire and *mort-vivants* motifs in both works (and in *The Monk Knight of St. John*) are clarified in this passage from the unedited *Wacousta*: 'The vampire of despair had banqueted on their hearts. Their vitality had been sucked, as it were, by its cold and bloodless lips; and little more than the withered rind that had contained the seeds of so many affections, had been left' (III, 26; 354). Once bitten, Gerald and the De Haldimars take on the extraordinary pallor, the wild eyes, the nocturnal aspect, and other corpse-like features of vampires from Goethe's Bride of Corinth to Stoker's Dracula. In *Wacousta*, Madeline's 'pale and spectral face' features 'a row of white and apparently lipless teeth' (III, 10; 345). Reduced to infantile despair, Charles's cheek 'pale as marble, and his lips bloodless and parted,' present a 'deathlike image' (III, 125; 408). In *The Canadian Brothers*, believing he is seeing Wacousta's ghost, Sambo 'beheld two glaring eyes magnified by his fear into thrice their natural size' and 'a mouth open, and a row of large and ragged teeth display themselves in a grin of derision' (II, 99). Characterized by 'the savage grin of the wild cat' (I, 93), Desborough is a cannibal whose hatred for the Indian makes him 'thirst for the blood of the heathens as a child for mother's milk' (II, 141). 'When Wacousta drinks the blood of his enemy,' the warrior informs Oucanasta's brother, 'it is the blood next his heart' (II, 161–2; 246). Wacousta explains to Frederick that the fearful howling of his wolf-dog is due to his lust for the blood of the De Haldimars. Like the wolf-dog, both Wacousta and Desborough lunge for the throats of their victims.

Exchanging his first kiss with the blood-soaked Ellen on the 'Bloody Bridge,' Wacousta 'bent his face over that of the pale and inanimate woman, and pressed his lips to hers, yet red and moist with blood spots from the wounds of her husband' (I, 179; 154). The erotic undercurrents in the vampire legend become more pronounced in the eerie figure of the voluptuous Matilda. Her terrible vampire-like feeding on Gerald anticipates that of the wolfish Eisengrim on Sir John in Davies's *World of Wonders*. She is repeatedly described as cold, bloodless, and deathly pale. Under her 'deadly spell' (II, 91), Gerald grows just as white and rigid as the demon-lover who encompasses his ruin. Their relationship echoes that of Coleridge's cold, snake-like Geraldine, the creature of the midnight wood, and the spellbound Christabel, a dweller in chambers; *Christabel* also concerns itself with a struggle of brothers, gothic metamorphosis, and a dream in which a man sees a bird languishing on the forest floor, bends down to pick it up, and is surprised to find a serpent coiled round it.

Matilda is as spectral as her grandparents Ellen and Wacousta. At the beginning of *Wacousta*, the latter enters De Haldimar's fort so silently that the soldiers conclude the intruder must be a ghost and 'Not a living soul' (I, 33; 20). In the first volume of the sequel, on another midnight in Detroit almost fifty years later, Matilda enters Forrester's cottage which is surrounded by a 'fence of palisades' (I, 165). Seeing this 'spirit of another world' gliding noiselessly along, Sambo declares 'dat no a livin' ting ... e ghost' (I, 165). In each instance, the midnight wanderers from Hades's realm deposit miniatures and love letters at the bedside of the betrayer whom they awaken with threats of death.

Volume 2 of *The Canadian Brothers* is a descent narrative which combines two themes Northrop Frye finds in Thomas Lovell Beddoes's *Death's Jest Book* (1849): 'the demon-lover whose love is death and the two brothers who symbolize the two orders of nature, the living and the dead worlds.' Richardson's is a cast of mind which reminds us of this fascinating writer; he may well be the Canadian Beddoes. Richardson's exploration of the 'Romantic Macabre' here and in *The Monk Knight of St. John* is clarified by a work like *The Bride's Tragedy* (1822). As Frye comments, 'The demon-lover theme is ... the symbol of a life-death identity. This identity can manifest itself only in the form of an antithesis ... Its main thematic symbol in Beddoes, as so often elsewhere in Romanticism, is that of the struggle of brothers, of which one represents ordinary life driving toward death, the other death seeping back into life.'7

As in *Wacousta*, the border river is central to the exposition of both themes. Here it is a historic as well as a symbolic dividing line between Canadian and American 'brothers,' the living and the dead. Standing in the centre of the 'Bloody Bridge' at midnight are the fierce guardians to the entrance of the land of the dead, Wacousta and his familiar, Onondato the wolf-dog. In the sequel, the counterpart of this Byronic fatal man, the fatal woman, performs the same symbolic function; the realm of the dead is reached by crossing the border river into the States. The revolution Matilda effects in Gerald's nature finds its field of metaphor in the border river. The scene of *The Canadian Brothers* is a world overwhelmed by water, beneath which the hero descends into deepening crises of identity. This is a development of the water imagery in *Wacousta*, especially the final volume. 'The world of waters' (II, 73) is the unruly or unpredictable element, the element of transition, of transformation, which I have associated with Poseidon and the realm of instinct and emotion in chapter 3. Key events transpire on water or close to it. Through his telescope, Gerald first sees the veiled Matilda aboard the American ship in the middle of the border river even as Colonel de Haldimar, through his telescope, sees Wacousta in the middle of the fatal bridge. Their encounter is as fateful as that of 'Commander' Groome and his secret sharer whom he pulls out of the ocean depths in Callaghan's *Close to the Sun Again*. For the smuggler Desborough, the river is a highway, an escape route upon which he and his son can light out for the American territory when pursued by the garrison.

The historical Hog Island (like the historical 'Bloody Bridge') becomes an apt location for the transformation of Gerald, who is often designated simply as 'the sailor,' by this American Circe. She soon turns him into a self-confessed slave, a brute ready to commit murder. It is not until the end of the second volume, however, that the total symbolic import of the border island is felt. The sailor is entranced; he has 'gazed upon her whose beauty was the rock on which his happiness had been wrecked' (II, 154). 'He had gazed on the witching beauty of the syren' (II, 158) and finds himself plunged into a 'Romantic Agony.' The Circe-like Matilda is an elusive, sinister *femme fatale*, the Romantic embodiment of the cruel mistress of courtly love. 'The dead and shipwrecked lovers in the world of Circe's malignity remind us of the traditional Courtly Love convention, the cruel mistress gloating over her collection of slain lovers ... Closest to the Courtly Love convention ... are the victims whom La Belle Dame Sans Merci has in "thrall" in a barren landscape of late autumn ... Like all hells, it is not a world of death but of life in death, where the repose of death is unattainable.'[8]

As an irresistible lover who sucks away energy, ambition, and even love for selfish reasons, Matilda belongs to a large Romantic family. One thinks of Keats's icy cold, deadly white Lamia, the snake-woman with 'her Circean head'; despite warnings from a very rational friend, Lycius becomes 'serpent's prey' on the forested island of Crete. 'The hell-born Circe' in Keats's *Endymion* is a cruel enchantress and an 'angry witch.' Endymion, who has also known 'love's madness' in his quest for ideal beauty, is imprisoned by the cold, pale Circe in a labyrinthine marine world. Under her spell, like Gerald he becomes one of the living dead; 'Stung / And poison'd,' his is also a 'slain spirit' which succumbs to a secret grief. The palsied Endymion likewise enters into a trance and becomes 'as dead-still as a marble man.'[9] Richardson may also be indebted to *La Belle Dame Sans Merci* which Miyoshi describes as 'a very Gothic poem with its vampire theme and use of the double identity.'[10] Matilda also resembles 'The Spectre-Woman' aboard the skeleton ship in Coleridge's *The Rime of the Ancient Mariner*: 'Her skin was as white as leprosy, / The Night-mare LIFE-IN-DEATH was she, / Who thicks man's blood with cold.'[11]

Through the Looking-Glass

Gerald's descent into a subterranean or submarine world is conveyed through the recurrent image of the vortex or whirlpool.

With Kyd's relish for Stygian gloom, Richardson mythologizes the St Clair River in *Wacousta* by reference to Scylla and Charybdis. Volume 2 of *The Canadian Brothers* begins in autumn with Gerald's voyage, without his brother, across the border to the American port of Buffalo. Through Desborough's treachery, the schooner the newly promoted war hero commands is captured. As a POW, he learns to his despair the one condition on which Matilda will consent to become his: the murder of her seducer. Such an act, of course, offends his strong moral sense and directly conflicts with the brothers' pledge to uphold their parents' principles of honour and virtue. When we next encounter the sailor two chapters later, he and Sambo are adrift in a frail canoe on the border river outside the Amherstburg garrison; a howling tempest mirrors his inner state. Like Frederick and Madeline de Haldimar who have perished at sea in a hurricane, the Canadian sailor ironically has not 'subdued the world of waters, and chained them in subservience to the will of man' (II, 73). The descendants of Zeus do not fare well in Poseidon's world.

Gerald is swallowed up by a whirlpool. 'Drawn into the boiling vortex,' he disappears in 'the very heart of the raging eddy.' 'The element whose brawling they appeared to brave with an indifference bordering on madness' (II, 74–5) proves a destructive one; yet it does not bring immediate death as Gerald had hoped. Like Byron's Manfred who similarly tries to drown himself, he is cursed to live until it pleases fate to terminate his wretched life. The whirlpool and the vortex are apt images for Gerald's suicidal state of mind as the now self-absorbed sailor enters the night world. They also ironically connect his passion with Sir Reginald Morton's which, 'like the whirlwind of the desert, sudden and devastating' (III, 220; 46), plunged him into a similar inverted world. At the bottom of the vortex's whirling, coiling circles, of course, is Circe's circular temple: Matilda's Kentucky residence is located in a narrow valley surrounded by a circular ridge of hills. In this antithesis to the square fort, Matilda finally turns the garrison officer into an outlaw, 'a being sunk in crime' (II, 203).

The 'altered' (II, 84) Gerald has suffered a negative sea-change. He has, indeed, drowned psychologically. Like Shelley's withered, spectral Alastor in his storm-tossed bark, Gerald has descended into a fluid world of labyrinths and whirlpools. His death-in-life condition is horribly apparent to Henry who has, ominously, taken his brother to recuperate in 'the chamber of death' of their 'sainted parents' (II, 86–7). 'An extraordinary alteration was perceptible in his whole appearance. Instead of the blooming cheek, and rounded and elegant form ... he now offered to the eye of his anxious brother an emaciated figure, and a countenance pale even unto wanness – while evidence of much care, and inward suffering, might be traced in the stern contraction of his hitherto open brow' (II, 78).

'Degenerated so far as to border on the character of the drunkard and the suicide' (II, 86), Gerald experiences that profound loss of identity which overcomes all of Richardson's border-crossers. Volume 2 reveals Richardson's interest in 'boundary' states of consciousness, the realm of the submerged or the underside of consciousness which is the peculiar province of the romance. Henry fears his brother is the victim of 'the partial overthrow of intellect' (II, 78). Gerald's last words before his capture are 'This is ambiguous' (II, 30); having escaped and recrossed the border, he now 'speaks in riddles' (II, 88). Inhabiting that strange borderland between sleeping and waking, he is cold, uncommunicative, and unaffectionate. 'I did seek oblivion of my wretchedness in that whirlpool,' he confesses before passing out, 'as the only means of destroying the worm that feeds incessantly upon my heart' (II, 86). Such recurrent imagery of devouring is characteristic of romances from *The Odyssey* to *The Hobbit* and here harks back to Gerald's snake bite and is paralleled by the attempts of a wily and aggressive United States to incorporate its weaker neighbour.

Once past the break boundary, the continuity with his previous life is broken. 'Formerly as remarkable for sobriety, as for every honourable principle' (II, 79), Gerald demands wine upon being pulled out of the water. Besides reflecting a desire to drown his sorrows, the request also marks an increasing withdrawal from his brother and a detachment from the moral tenets of his parents, especially Major Grantham who, like the abstemious Tecumseh, abhors drunkenness. It does align him, however, with Desborough who eagerly imbibes 'the poisonous distillation of the country, miscalled whiskey' (II, 93–4); the whiskey-poison equation also links up with the image of Matilda as a fatal poison.

Such an alteration, a recurrent feature of Richardson's world of break boundaries, is typical of romance. Frye speaks of 'some kind of break in consciousness ... involving a change so drastic as to give the sense of becoming someone else altogether.' Sir Reginald Morton is transformed into the gigantic Wacousta, Gerald into a potential murderer. This 'break' may be externalized as a change in social context or in fortune such as capture by pirates. Gerald's ship is captured by the outlaw and smuggler Desborough just as Wacousta seizes the schooner bearing Gerald's ancestors. Such a break 'is really an obliteration of memory'; it may be connected with 'a curse or demonic possession,' 'the collapse of the rightful order in the mind,' or 'a sinking from a waking world into a dream world.' 'Drunkenness is also a projection of the theme of the break in consciousness' as are 'outlawed societies' like the Highland clans of *Rob Roy* or the smugglers of *Guy Mannering*.[12]

Narcissus

The structural core of romance, according to Joseph Campbell and to Frye in *The Secular Scripture*, is the individual loss or confusion or break in the continuity of identity. 'Almost a stranger to himself' (II, 133), Gerald 'seemed but the shadow of his former self, while the melancholy of his countenance had in it something wild and fierce.' Totally self-preoccupied, he is caught up in 'the indulgence of some secret and all absorbing reflection' (II, 81). Ever since his fall into the mirror-like border river, he has been 'an altered being – too much rapt up in himself to give heed to others' (II, 101). This recalls 'the standard romance pattern of a double identity': A figure 'changes his identity' and his second self 'may be said to be the shadow or dreaming counterpart of the one he had before.' For Frye, this exchange of original identity for its shadow or reflection is exemplified by the story of

Narcissus who drowns, 'passing into a lower or submarine world. The reflecting pool is a mirror, and disappearing into one's own mirror image, or entering a world of reversed or reduced dimensions, is a central symbol of descent.'[13]

The myth of Narcissus lies behind Richardson's depiction of both Sir Reginald Morton/Wacousta and Gerald Grantham. It helps to explain why the confusion of identity in romance is so often associated with the struggle of brothers and twins and doppelgängers who are so prominent in descent imagery.[14] James Reaney and Jay Macpherson have commented astutely on what we may provisionally call 'the Narcissus archetype' in *Wacousta*, noting the great number of characters who gaze down from and/or fall from heights into mirror-like bodies of water. Much of this occurs on the bridge over the border river; however, the paradigmatic instance is detailed in Wacousta's flashback of his days as a solitary youth roaming the precipitous crags which overhang the sea in the neighbourhood of Morton Castle: 'How often ... have I madly wished to press to my bounding bosom the being of my fancy's creation ... How often, too, while bending over some dark and threatening precipice, or standing on the utmost verge of some tall projecting cliff, my aching head (aching with the intenseness of its own conceptions) bared to the angry storm, and my eye fixed unshrinking on the boiling ocean far beneath my feet, has my whole soul – my every faculty, been bent on that ideal beauty which controlled every sense! Oh, imagination, how tyrannical is thy sway' (III, 210;45).

Like Narcissus who rejected all suitors for his love, Morton's 'heart had never once throbbed for created woman'; instead, 'to this phantom I had already yielded up all the manlier energies of my nature' (III, 212; 456). To keep himself balanced, Morton needs to be on friendly terms with the pragmatic De Haldimar side of his nature. As Jungian psychotherapist E.F. Edinger urges us to remember, the myth of Narcissus implies something quite different from an excess of indulgent self-love. It alerts us to a split or divided state of being. 'Narcissus yearns to unite with himself just because he is alienated from his own being ... we love and yearn for what we lack. Narcissism in its original mythological implications is ... a frustrated state of yearning for a self-possession which does not yet exist ... union with the image in the depths requires a descent into the unconscious, a *nekyia* or symbolic death.'[15]

In *The Canadian Brothers*, both Granthams and Desboroughs fall into the border river. Locked in one another's arms, the last members of each family, as well as other Canadians and Americans, plunge to their death in the Niagara River gorge. As in *Wacousta*, we find motifs which Macpherson associates with the Narcissus myth, most notably the lament for a lost paradise, a fall from a pastoral idyllic landscape into a desolate wilderness.[16] Gerald also rejects conventional lovers for the phantom that has captured his romantic imagination and has begun to drain him of his vitality; however, the actual Matilda falls far short of 'the faultless image,' the ideal of 'womanly perfection' his imagination has conjured up. The 'fearful blemish' which marks 'the symmetry of the whole' is her murderous hatred of her former lover. As is usually the case with the tragic hero or lover of Romanticism, what begins as love ends in frustration, torment, or suicide.[17] While Gerald's 'imagination had drawn and lingered on such pictures ... assured as he was they could never be realized, he finally resolved to court death' (II, 161).

In her article on the Narcissus myth in *Alphabet*, Macpherson refers to Frazer's explanation of Narcissus's death in *The Golden Bough* as due 'to one of those water-fairies who drag your reflection under water, leaving you to die without it.' Matilda as 'syren' (II, 158) resembles these figures. Her later incarnations in our literature include the withdrawn Greta and the spell-binding Mrs Potter who is associated with the waters of death in Sheila Watson's *The Double Hook*; as D.G. Jones notes, they also 'appear in the guise of Ondine, the Lorelei or destructive water nymph, who provides one of the archetypes of life turned in upon itself, narcissistic, frozen in its own reflection or caught in the grip of its own past.'[18] The Gerald-Matilda-Forrester relationship and that of Morton-Clara-De Haldimar are examples of what Macpherson terms 'the Narcissus triangle': 'The Narcissus motif is characterized by a tendency toward triangular groups of persons, roughly corresponding to Narcissus, the other self, and Echo, or in Blake's convenient terms, "subject," "spectre" and "emanation." [19] Translating this triangle into the terms I have used elsewhere in this study, we have Gerald/Narcissus; his other self, or double-by-division, the spectral Matilda; and Echo, or his double-by-duplication, Forrester. The dynamics of this triangle will soon become apparent. This last comment by Macpherson must suffice to illuminate the workings of this myth which I have already traced in *Wacousta* and whose appearance in the sequel will concern us in the rest of this chapter.

> Narcissus as the gloomy egoist left over from a desolated world of Sensibility has two obvious, though not always discreet, choices. All he needs is an author with some vague notion of the appropriate related 'matters' – Psyche's house, Prospero's island, perhaps the Old Man of the Mountain and his fraudulent paradise. He then can become the hero of an adventure-romance, a Wacousta or Captain Nemo or Count of Monte Cristo. Or he can depart into a horror story, where his situation may be elaborated into a whole complex of mirrors, portraits, doppelgangers, automata, complementary personalities, spirit-maidens or hypnotist's dummies, beastmen or Calibans, possessing forms of 'otherness,' and similar vehicles of soul-fragments.[20]

There is a veritable spectrum of such doubles and complementary personalities in *The Canadian Brothers*, ranging from the obvious to the well-nigh barely discernible. There are two Granthams, two Forresters, even two Indian brothers: the noble savage Tecumseh and the wily Prophet. In word and action, Gerald summons up the figures of his ancestors as Matilda does hers. Desborough and Sampson Gattrie, two American frontiersmen who had to choose sides in the border war, are exact opposites. One becomes a loyalist, the other a spy for the Americans. They live back-to-back near Amherstburg as do the conflicting Forrester and Matilda in Frankfort, Kentucky, yet Gattrie's place is neat, well-cultivated, and fertile while Desborough's is smothered by wild forest. 'The old man's truly excellent and exemplary son'

(I, 112) is the moral opposite of 'the scoundrel son of a yet more scoundrel father' (I, 126). Both Americans are unpredictable, anarchic, and half-civilized creatures whose problematical individualism is thrown into high relief in confrontation with the (Canadian) law. But where Gattrie's wild spirits are tamed by the censorious Major Grantham, Desborough's are driven underground into a desire for revenge.

Gerald's and Forrester's lives interpenetrate and duplicate one another. Both are war heroes, publicly celebrated and privately scarred. Their relationships with Matilda almost lead to the death of both. They save each other's lives on numerous occasions, usually without being aware of the other's identity. In Frankfort, they share the same hotel. Both have black servants, Forrester's recalling Sambo. Forrester is betrothed to Gerald's cousin Julia; their marriage would unite American and Canadian as would Matilda's and Gerald's. Julia's retiring and respectable sister Gertrude nurses an unrequited love for Gerald; although she is in nature poles apart from her rival Matilda, there is some blurring of identity between them, Gertrude vowing that she could have loved Major Montgomery almost as her own father. Both Gerald and Forrester are engaged in that 'dualism of simultaneity' which reveals Richardson's fascination with synchronicity. As Gerald sails up the border river to deliver a demand that the American forces at Detroit surrender, Forrester at the same time sails down it to deliver a similar message to the Canadians at Amherstburg; they pass each other on opposite sides of an island, inexplicably unable to see one another either going or returning. Gerald's comrades mistake Forrester's boat for his and Forrester's figure for his own.

As in *Wacousta*, virtually every action and character is reflected over and over again as if caught in two facing mirrors. Such cases of duplication involve balanced symmetry and the active equipoise of opposite forces. So interwoven are the families along the border, so used are they to gathering together for reunions and parties, that in the actual siege of Detroit it seems 'that a fête, not a battle, was intended' 'between two brave and friendly powers' (I, 172). In Dennis Lee's terms, Americans and Canadians are presented as 'coinciding like two fields of force in a single space, rather than standing over against each other like two armies on a battlefield.' In Richardson's mosaic borderland world of implosion, interrelatedness, and equilibrium, even incidental detail manifests 'the dualism of savage fields' or 'the coincidence of opposites'[21]: in this uncannily festive (carnivalesque?) air of the siege, 'the volumes of smoke, vomited from the opposing batteries, met and wreathed themselves together in the centre of the stream' (I, 172).

The 'submarine mirror world' of romance is one of 'reversed or reduced dimensions.'[22] It is full of unexpected reflections, echoes, and correspondences. As we recall from the first chapters on *Wacousta*, Richard Chase calls romance a kind of 'border fiction' where the actual and the imaginary intermingle. Such a form is perfectly adapted to Richardson's content – border-crossings. Again, the mirror-like borderland of *The Canadian Brothers* as of *Wacousta* is best described in McLuhanesque terms as an 'area of spiralling repetition and replay ... of both interlace and interface, an area of "double ends joined," of rebirth and metamorphosis.'[23] Volume 2 certainly presents Gerald as imprisoned within such a mirror world. Some time after being retrieved from the border river, he and Sambo again cross the border into Detroit. They retrace their steps to Forrester's cabin, the site of the thwarted assassination in the first volume.

On this second midnight, disguised in dark cloaks as was Matilda, they in turn are watched by an equally curious American 'tanner': ' ... as if expecting at each moment to encounter some dread inhabitant of the tomb, he at length contrived to place himself in the very position in which Gerald had formerly been a witness of the attempt at assassination. From the same window now flashed a strong light ... the astonished tanner ... scarcely knowing whether he gazed upon the living or the dead, would have fled, had he not ... been rooted by fear, and a species of fascination, to the spot' (II, 95–6). With his 'pale, attenuated, sunken countenance' (II, 96), Gerald strikes the frightened American as one of the living dead. Ironically, Sambo likewise mistakes the tanner for a ghost, that of 'the once terrible Wacousta.' The aged Sambo believes it is 'the same face which had presented itself ... at the window of the Canadian's hut, on the night of the departure of his master, Sir Everard Valletort, and Captain De Haldimar, for Michillimackinac in 1763' (II, 99–100).

This boxes-within-boxes structure becomes more pronounced after Gerald, saying farewell to his brother, again crosses the border into the States a few hours after this episode. Fighting recklessly in the battle of Fort Sandusky, his is the suicidal urge 'of a man who courts not victory but death' (II, 112). We catch yet another reflection of Lieutenant Grantham in the tragic figure of Lieutenant Raymond, his fellow soldier, who had also 'determined from the outset to court his death' (II, 65) in an earlier conflict. Raymond's honour and courage had also been unjustly impugned by the very soldiers who had attacked Gerald's reputation in the story's opening episode; like Gerald, Raymond is an individual psychologically separated from the group with which he once identified.

With the deaths of Captain Cranston, another 'alienation figure,' and the jester Middlemore, Gerald is increasingly isolated from the familiar world of his past. Sambo, 'a sort of connecting link' (II, 101) between the brothers and their departed parents, remains with Henry on the Canadian side of the border; he has gone mad after seeing Wacousta's ghost. This lower world is one of 'increasing alienation and loneliness: the hero is not only separated from the heroine or his friends, but is often further isolated by being falsely accused of major crimes.'[24] After he is captured for the second time, Gerald is accused of being a spy, although the charges are dismissed. Besides aligning him more closely with those master spies Desborough and Arnoldi, the accusation ensures that Gerald's descent into the South begins with an ironic reversal in social status: as the sailor ruminates, 'the hero of one hour might be looked upon and hanged as the spy of the next' (II, 121).

Appropriately enough, Gerald is captured by the Americans under Colonel Ernest Forrester, his double, just as Forrester's cousin, Captain Edward Forrester, had taken him captive aboard the schooner in Buffalo. Since Gerald refuses to divulge his rank and has, indeed, tried to remain anonymous, he is to be detained in Frankfort pending a confirmation of his identity. Since crossing the border, that identity has become very slippery, the officer and gentleman deliberately obscured in the uniform of the private grenadier and now further distorted after Gerald's double has him dress in his own clothes in order 'to transform him into a backwoodsman' (II, 124). As in Scott (and later in Atwood, Kroetsch, and Reaney), such clothing changes indicate that abrupt change in social status and identity so characteristic of descent narrative. The Canadian loses all his civilized distinctions one by one.

Polyphemus

'Journeying into the interior' (II, 121) with Forrester's aide-de-camp, Captain Jackson, an uncouth Tennessee frontiersman, the POW descends deeper into a heart of darkness along 'The Road of Trials' (Campbell). Winding their way through dense forest, 'moving over some extensive plain where nothing beyond themselves told of the existence of man' (II, 127), both travellers 'presented an appearance quite as wild as the waste they traversed' (II, 139). 'The alteration in his dress was calculated to deceive into a belief of his being an American' (II, 137), yet Gerald's metamorphosis is psychological as well as physical. The Canadian's open, confiding nature that delighted in social or group activities has soured; like a reclusive and independent woodsman, he prefers to be left alone. Despite Jackson's attempts to 'thaw his companion's tongue into sociability' (II, 134), the pensive Gerald 'neither spoke himself nor appeared to enjoy speech in another' (II, 128).

The extent of his transformation into an American backwoodsman is signalled in an unexpected twilight encounter with the only other person they meet in their 'curst long ride through the wood' (II, 140) – the backwoodsman par excellence, Desborough. Having crossed the border to Buffalo as Gerald's prisoner and escaped by jumping into the water, 'the surly and inhospitable woodsman' (II, 134) has sought to avoid imprisonment in the

Canadas by temporarily residing in a rude log hut on the skirt of the forest forming one of the boundaries of the vast savannah they had traversed. 'This apology for a human dwelling' (II, 130) is a mirror reflection of his hut on the forest's edge near the border river and is described in the same phrases. Indeed, the entire episode mirrors the initial encounter in volume 1 between Gerald's brother, Middlemore, and the wily Yankee. As elsewhere, similar phrasing helps establish the parallels. As Desborough contemplates his chances of victory in a fight with Henry and Middlemore, 'His eye rolled rapidly from one to the other of the officers' (I, 92); before Desborough allows Gerald and Jackson (who shares Middlemore's penchant for puns) into his hut, 'he glanced rapidly from one to the other ... until he seemed to have mentally decided that the odds of two to one were somewhat unequal' (II, 131).

Faced by Henry and Middlemore, the huge son of the gigantic Wacousta 'drew himself to the full height of his bony and muscular frame' (I, 93–4). Desborough likewise attempts to intimidate Jackson and his prisoner by 'stretching his tall and muscular form to its utmost height' (II, 137). In each case, a fight eventually ensues. The youthful Canadian brothers are no match for the vengeful American whose exuberant physical strength, a common attribute of lower-world denizens, has increased ten fold since crossing the border onto 'republican soil' (I, 82); this recalls Wacousta who grows taller and stronger in the course of his revenge. And just as Wacousta sees through Frederick's duck-hunter disguise at François's inn, Desborough discovers Gerald's identity. Nor do the echoes end here. Already doubled, the passage also resonates with the scene in which Gerald and Sambo spy on Arnoldi and Desborough at the latter's hut on the border river (I, 121–30); this episode occurs prior in time to Henry's and Middlemore's spying mission on Desborough, but later in terms of the narrative. The 'watchfulness' of the Canadian brothers is inherited from the visually oriented De Haldimar who spies on Morton.

Jackson keeps Desborough from strangling Gerald. The renegade is tied to one of the logs of his hut, now become his prison.

During the night, Jackson awakes to discover 'Gerald stooping over the sleeping Desborough, one hand reposing upon his chest, the other holding a knife.' This scene conjures up two others: that of Matilda hovering over the sleeping Forrester and one just related by Desborough in which he kills two Indians just as he wakes them from their sleep. Gerald denies Jackson's charge that he was about to 'assassinate a sleeping drunken man' (II, 147). He has, in truth, only cut loose a miniature of Matilda which Desborough wears around his neck; this confirms his suspicions that the Yankee, his father's assassin, is the real father of Matilda, herself guilty of assassination.

Yet the Canadian is becoming more assassin-like, more Desborough-like, all the time. Indeed, while fighting the savage woodsman, the once disciplined officer 'became uncontrollable, until his anxiety to inflict a mortal injury upon his enemy became in the end as intense as that of the settler.' Grabbing the knife with which Desborough killed the Indians, the wild Gerald raised it 'to avenge his father's murder, but the idea that there was something assassin-like in the act as suddenly arrested him' (II, 144). Before long, however, he will become a reluctant agent of death, raising Matilda's knife against the unsuspecting Forrester.

The episode at Desborough's hut underscores the overlapping of identity between the Canadian brother and the Yankee. Gerald has become almost as antisocial, selfish, and morbidly self-absorbed as the misanthropic woodsman who deliberately 'made tracks through the swamps ... for this here hut, which I know'd no livin' soul had been nigh for many a long year' (II, 142). 'I *have* no friends – I *wish* to have no friends' (II, 136) vociferates the loner to his unwelcome visitors. The tragic reversal in Gerald's character comes when the representative of Canadian civil society voices the same 'desire of concealment' (II, 133), to insist upon a similar frontier seclusion and withdrawal from civilization. He has already come to share Desborough's drunkenness, his 'savage and diseased spirit' and 'the bitter tempest raging in his soul' (II, 149–50). Like Gerald, the outlaw is also severely altered since his border crossing: 'A great change had taken place in the manner of Desborough. Ferocious he still was,' but like those Byronic brooders Wacousta, Matilda, and now Gerald, 'He had evidently suffered much, and there was a stamp of thought on the heavy countenance that Gerald had never remarked there before' (I, 137). Given such resemblances knitting them together, it is not surprising that the Canadian's former hostility toward Desborough undergoes a sudden overnight reversal: discovering his connection with the man who is the father of the woman who obsesses him, he swears that 'death from my hand, under any circumstances, is the last thing he has now to apprehend' (I, 148).

Another prominent aspect of this wasteland confrontation is clarified by Frye's mapping of romance motifs. In a labyrinthine world where the forest has turned subterranean, most of what goes on is 'cruelty and horror, yet what is essential is not cruelty as such but the presence of some kind of ritual.'[25] This is as true of Matilda's rites in her temple as of Desborough's ritual meal which he offers to serve up to his guests. His 'history of the dried meat' (II, 142) has the same nauseating impact as does the mention of those mysterious grey 'lumps' in Conrad's *Heart of Darkness*. Desborough's 'ogre-like repast' (II, 140) consists of human flesh from the corpses of the Indians he murdered in revenge for his son's death.

Amused by the horrified looks of his visitors, 'this self-confessed anthropophagos' 'burst into a laugh that sounded more like that of some wild beast than a human being' (II, 137). At the bottom of the nightworld is the most concentrated symbol of the grotesque, the cannibal feast; this locates us in 'a Hieronymous Bosch landscape in which men turn into animals and animals into men.'[26] We are still in Circe's realm. This motif 'is important not for its horrific frisson, but as the image which causes that frisson, the identifying of human and animal natures ... Such a theme merges with the theme of human sacrifice in its most undisplaced form, which is the swallowing of a youth or maiden by a subterranean or submarine monster.'[27] Here these monsters are Desborough and Matilda. They are as inclined to human sacrifice as the giant Wacousta. Again, the savagery of the white man far exceeds that attributed to the Indian.

The Temple of Doom: Circles and Squares Revisited

Having escaped from the clutches of the American Polyphemus, Gerald and Jackson leave the cannibal's den behind to descend further into Kentucky and into the very heart of the labyrinth where Matilda's temple is situated. The Southern state whose crude, savage inhabitants are 'Half horse, half alligator' and 'little removed from ... the native Indian' (I, 78) is the symbolic equivalent of the wilderness domain of the Ottawas in *Wacousta*. It, too, is developed via circle and curve imagery. On parole in Frankfort, Gerald abjures human contact. 'Rambling through the wild passes of the chain of wooded hills which almost encircles the Kentuckian capital' becomes his 'only distraction.' Feeling 'the dense gloom of these narrow vallies ... more in unison with his sick mind than the hum and bustle of a city,' Gerald's days are spent 'threading their mazes' (II, 152), this last phrase an echo of his fateful border island wanderings.

At twilight on one occasion, having 'utterly lost his way' and despairing of retracing his steps 'by the circuitous route he had originally taken,' he spies in 'the wild scene' 'a small valley completely hemmed in by the circular ridge on which he stood.' Descending noiselessly 'into the centre of the little plain,' he comes upon 'a small circular building ... resembling a temple ... so closely bordering upon the forest ridge ... as to be almost confounded with it.' Peering through a window, Gerald is rivetted to the spot by the sight of a black-robed female whose eyes are fixed upon a portrait which he fails to recognize as that of his double Forrester. In an ironic reversal, Gerald meets his fate by running away from it; the voluptuous woman is Matilda, whom 'he believed to be still far distant, whom he had only a few moments previously fled from, as from a pestilence, and whom he had continued to love with a passion that defied every effort of his judgement to subdue, making his life a wilderness' (II, 153–4).

In this inverted world, the climactic temple scene is a replay of a medley of previous 'hidden observer' scenes. It mirrors the midnight scene in volume 1 when Gerald, having crossed the border river to the American shore to watch the movements of the enemy, peers through a boat window. He watches a dark, cloaked figure seated at a table reading a letter by candlelight; in the temple, Matilda also peruses a letter – Gerald's own – by candlelight. The first 'window scene' is immediately followed by another at Forrester's cabin with its square rooms. The temple episode is also interwoven via direct verbal echoes with Gerald's midnight spying on Desborough and Arnoldi in volume 1 to which I have already alluded. At the window of Desborough's hut striving to get a better view of its occupants, Gerald accidently makes a noise; Desborough yells 'Who the hell's there?' (I, 125), and his voice echoes through the silent forest. At the temple window trying to obtain a fuller glimpse of its tenant, Gerald again makes a slight noise; Matilda's 'Who is there?' is similarly 'repeated in echo from the surrounding woods' (II, 157). While Gerald interrupts Desborough and Arnoldi who are planning revenge on 'the curst race of Granthams' (I, 131), he disturbs Matilda who is devising her revenge on Forrester. Again, while watching Gerald and Sambo through the window at Forrester's cabin, the American tanner makes a sound that alerts the officer.

Thus, Richardson creates boxes within boxes within boxes, mirrors mirroring mirrors ad infinitum. Such spiralling repetition is indeed dizzying. As in *Wacousta* and *The Monk Knight of St. John,* a paradoxical fusion of events and characters is played out within a wholesale pattern of recurrence, coincidence, and analogy. Such compulsive circling of the same point approximates the nature of dreams, in which various seemingly autonomous scenes can best be understood as varying ways to describe the same central idea. The myriad interweaving and interlocking parallels of this spiral dance span two large volumes. Only once does Richardson explicitly make the connection for the reader, and that is to link the sequel to *Wacousta* in the scene detailing Sambo's ghostly vision. Such 'amplification by analogy' creates a web of correspondences, large-scale echoes, and rhythms which, far from being a heavy-handed creation, is so subtle as to have gone critically unremarked in *The Canadian Brothers, The Monk Knight of St. John,* and to a large extent in *Wacousta.* Perhaps James

Reaney is correct when, commenting on these 'endlessly absorbing romances,' he avers that 'Richardson's work is not just "good in parts." The problem is, as usual, that there are parts of us unable as yet to deal with this writer's complex vision.'[28]

As in the preceding episode at the cannibal's lair, the temple-of-doom chapters present the eerie convergence of identity between Grantham and Desborough. Cold and 'deadly pale' (II, 160), Matilda Desborough, as she is now known, devours Gerald psychologically, swallowing his identity in both its personal and national dimensions. The siren practises what Mario Praz in *The Romantic Agony* terms 'sexual cannibalism,' cannibalism itself, of course, a grotesque parody of merging of identity.[29] In her temple as 'wholly secluded from society' (II, 160) as her father's hut, Gerald is moved to worship the white goddess and 'confess his idolatry' (II, 157). The spellbound sailor mechanically calls himself her 'slave' and invites her to 'mould me to your will' (II, 158–64).

These last chapters afford a more undisplaced glimpse of that figure whom Frye identifies in Rider Haggard's *She* as 'a beautiful and sinister female ruler, buried in the depths of a dark continent, who is much involved with various archetypes of death and rebirth.' This 'earth-mother at the bottom of the world,' whom Robert Graves calls the white goddess, presides over a false paradise like Circe's isle or Acrasia's Bower of Bliss; like Matilda's circular temple, these imprisoning lower worlds have marine associations.[30] Nautical metaphors abound. The whole irrational sea, Poseidon's subconscious world, seems to rise up against him, and he is overwhelmed by the flood-waters of passion. 'Virtue, honour, religion, all the nobler principles in which my youth has been nurtured,' laments Gerald, 'have proved too weak to stem the tide of guilty passion' (II, 164). 'The utter sinking of his sad and broken spirit' (II, 152) bespeaks 'the abstraction and melancholy in which he was usually plunged' (II, 127).

While the emphasis in Clara's mountain-top Eden is on the recovery of identity, in Matilda's submarine world it is on false identity. What the drowning Narcissus really does, according to Frye, 'is exchange his original self for the reflection that he falls in love with, becoming, as Blake says, "idolatrous to his own shadow." '[31] In trying to embrace Matilda, Gerald is attempting to embrace his own false identity as assassin and outlaw, as 'a being sunk in crime' (II, 203). While Matilda encourages the magistrate's son to see himself thus, it is the same thing as his own destruction. 'Fallen from his high estate of honor,' like Desborough he conceals himself in 'the forest, where he wandered during the day without other aim or purpose than to hide the brand of guilt, which he almost felt upon his brow' (II, 195–6).

To transform the Canadian from his brother's keeper into Cain, Matilda turns Gerald's values and perspectives upside down. She has argued that while he thought he was the preserver of life he is really the assassin, firing on one who may have been avenging a crime. Speaking in riddles and paradoxes, the sphinx-like Matilda effects other such ironic reversals. Gerald's very Canadian sense of duty, which the sardonic woman has earlier scorned (II, 9), is inverted to the point where, 'yielding to the sophistry of Matilda's arguments, he was sometimes led to imagine the avenging of her injuries an imperative duty' (II, 195).

The American outlaw also redefines the Canadian's concepts of law and order. 'Crime is a word too indiscriminately bestowed,' she asserts; 'What the weak in mind class with crime, the strong term virtue' (II, 164). To eradicate the martial spirit of the Granthams, she sets out to expose the military ethos, identifying soldiers as hired assassins. 'Worldly policy and social interests alone have drawn the distinction' (II, 166) argues Matilda. Through a shift in perspective, military combat becomes murder, the heroes villains. All the opposites begin to run into one another. Like the trickster Wacousta, Matilda is also 'an enemy of boundaries,' challenging the conventional boundaries between the civilized and the savage and upsetting hierarchies. Such reversals are consistent with Matilda's vampire aspect; the vampire, as Cirlot notes, is associated with inversions and metamorphoses, ambivalence, duality, paradox, and the *coincidentia oppositorum*.[32]

To the Grantham's 'rigid notions of right' (II, 33), Matilda opposes her own shifting, multiple perspective. She assaults his sense of rectitude, his hallowed social and moral principles.

Fiercely independent, a law unto herself, she is scornful of customary patterns of behaviour and subject to no influence but her own will. She chafes against the bonds of decorum, defying the established code and denying the social contract as fraud and illusion. Consistent with her role as an extreme example of American individuality, the solitary Matilda rejects the claims of the social dimension of identity upheld by Gerald's family and his nation. She ignores community. She endeavours to strip him of all ties to groups and collectivities, to sever all bonds and translate him out of the garrison matrix.

Her apologia of crime and her verbal sparring with Gerald echo the debate on things Canadian and American between her 'uncle,' Major Montgomery, and Gerald's hero General Brock in volume 1. Both Brock and Gerald repeat the same phrases in defence of their principles, insisting on 'the difference of the motive' (I, 67; II, 166). While 'Major Montgomery has the happy talent of making the worse appear the better cause' (I, 66), Gerald remarks to Matilda, 'with what subtlety of argument do you seek to familiarize my soul with crime' (II,167).

At this crucial point in the tale, Matilda tells 'The story of my wrongs' (II, 170). It echoes Wacousta's flashback and seems intended to render her almost as ambiguous as her ancestor. The parallels set up help secure the reader's sympathy, but to nowhere near the same degree as that felt for Wacousta. Matilda and Wacousta are doubles-by-duplication, the former's life reduplicating the latter's, thus consolidating the revenge motif which unifies both works. Appropriately, the accounts of both outcasts reverse the thrust of the imagery used to characterize themselves. De Haldimar and Forrester are labelled fiends, monsters, reptiles, and villains. Confiding in friend and lover, Wacousta and Matilda are played false and betrayed by those society deems respectable. The key word in both works is 'fidelity,' the name of Clara Beverley's animal companion, the integrating force of the human community. Both stories present a world in which human ideals and loyalties are constantly betrayed, in which Cain has just broken faith with Abel; in Bly's terms already referred to, it is 'The Road of Ashes, Descent, and Grief.'

Just before their wedding is to take place, Forrester (what better name for an American on the frontier) comes to doubt Matilda's fidelity. He discovers her in the arms of a black man who is Desborough in disguise extorting money from her. (Wacousta also disguises himself as a black man on occasion.) Biased by first impressions as much as De Haldimar, Forrester refuses to listen to Matilda's explanation. Like her grandmother begging at the feet of the hard-hearted De Haldimar, she throws herself before Forrester. Yet 'neither mercy nor justice dwelt in that heart' (II, 174). Matilda raises some doubt about Forrester's own fidelity, suggesting his affections may lie elsewhere; we recall in volume 1 that he lies to his new love Julia when asked about his connection with Matilda. The latter soon becomes unjustly accused by 'the vulgar crowd' of 'vile passion for a slave' (II, 176-8), the South's greatest fear. Matilda paints her slanderer as proud, ambitious, and prudent as Wacousta does De Haldimar, another 'remorseless seducer' (III, 243). The Blatant Beast is the most dangerous creature roaming Richardson's wilds.

Presenting herself as a victim, 'a woman whose only fault was loving too well,' Matilda echoes Wacousta's allusion to the trusting Othello. The perfidy of another has prompted her revenge and 'turned my love into gall' (II, 176), a phrase that both Wacousta and Gerald use to describe their tragic metamorphoses. Gerald is confounded by her ambiguous combination of attractive and repulsive traits, her split character as both 'Venus' (I, 57) and ice goddess: she is 'eminently calculated to inspire passion, but seemingly incapable of feeling it' (I, 58). Still, he remembers when 'the voluptuous beauty of Matilda shone paramount' (II, 156); it is this glory that Gerald would like to catch, but he ends up hooking the dark water-nymph instead.

Matilda's avowals of love for the sailor remain suspect, just as the reader is never sure of the extent of Forrester's culpability. Her injunction not to judge by appearances – surely a hazardous enterprise in such a hall of mirrors – while self-serving is also one that receives auctorial sanction in Wacousta. Despite a final declaration that Gerald has been her dupe, Matilda remains a shadowy, elusive, ambiguous figure. As in Beddoes, the interpenetration of life and death is not quite the same thing as that of good and evil; at any rate, the latter might better be approached, as D.G. Jones suggests, in its Canadian formulation as 'the problem of Job. What shall we make of Leviathan?'[33]

Gerald's awareness of himself as exile and outsider comes during the romance's final 'window' scene the night before the assassination. As in *Wuthering Heights*, the window is a symbolic barrier or border separating/linking two contrasting realms, the conventional and the alien. Up to this point, most of these episodes have featured law-abiding citizens peering into the shadowy depths where lurk the outlaws. Significantly, this pattern is now reversed. Gerald, the assassin, stares through the window into the lighted rooms where his victim, still unknown to him, is being celebrated by the townsfolk. He who has attempted to ignore the past is about to murder its visible emblem, Colonel Forrester, his old self. By the time of the assassination itself, it is impossible to distinguish Gerald from Matilda. They wear identical disguises. Both appear more like animated corpses than living beings.

The site chosen for the killing is the symbolic equivalent of the fatal bridge joining the two domains of civilized and primitive in *Wacousta*. Here we have another ravine, one of those wild passes or fissures in the hills linking Matilda's and Forrester's private residences, 'two dwellings which lay as it were back to back, on either side of the formidable barrier' (II, 194). As in the Desborough-Gattrie conflict, again Richardson presents that paradoxical relation of civilization and rude nature, a relation partly antithetical and partly complementary, which Frye sees expressed by some variant of the struggle-of-brothers theme.

Just as Gerald is about to stab his double, the light from the full moon reveals the features of 'the preserver of his life.' 'As the eyes of the murderer and his intended victim met, their recognition was mutual and perfect.' It is at once a moment of recognition and of reversal. Although Matilda urges him on, 'the spell had lost its power, and Gerald continued immoveable – apparently fixed to the spot.' In abject shame, he tells Matilda to leave him and begs Forrester's forgiveness. The nadir of his descent has been reached. 'Turned into stone' (II, 199–200) by the American gorgon, he is imprisoned within a world of paralysed life-in-death like similar figures in Keats and Beddoes.

Ascent

Ascent themes for Campbell, Frye, and Bolen involve the growing of identity through the casting off of whatever conceals or frustrates it. With the removal of enchantment, Matilda's beauty loses its subjugating influence. 'The snapped wire' leaves the 'puppet' (II, 205) dangling. Gerald is now involved in what Frye describes as the 'separation of the demonic principle from its opposite, when the two closely resemble each other.'[34] Imprisoned within 'the fatal temple' (II, 202) along with Matilda who herself has once more attempted to stab Forrester, Gerald gains insight into the cunning and craft of the white goddess at whose altar he has sacrificed his honour. He becomes conscious of what his double terms 'the arts of the woman who seems to have lured you into the depths of crime.' In this world of fatality, the sailor sees himself as Circe's dupe; but, as compassion supplants passion, he also realizes Circe is equally as fated a victim as himself, one who has been 'wrecked on the same shore' (II, 206), a very Canadian twist to this traditional motif.

In the profound darkness of the temple, he whose only 'object was to stupefy recollection to the uttermost' (II, 151) begins 'for the first time ... to reflect on the past' (II, 204). He guiltily recalls the pledge not to dishonour his family; he calls to mind the warnings of his brother, that 'unsparing monitor' (II, 85) who has embodied his conscience. That role is now taken up by Forrester who accuses him of disgracing family, country, and profession but who, like a good secret sharer, promises to keep the assassination attempt his secret.

Just as romance begins with a break in consciousness or loss of memory, in ascent imagery, following the recognition of the demonic and its separation from the progressive or surviving elements, there ensues the restoring of the broken current of memory. Gerald begins to acknowledge and possess his own past, the roots of his identity, in a quest for genealogy, one which characterizes much of our literature, as Kroetsch and others aver. The descent theme, Frye reminds us, 'often has a great deal to do with one's descent in the genealogical sense, where the crucial event is the discovery of the real relation between the chief characters and their parents.'[35] At this point, Gerald's 'imagination recurred to the traditions connected with his family and with the dreadful curse.' 'In the intenseness of his new desire to satisfy his doubts' (II, 204) concerning Matilda's family connection with Ellen Halloway, he asks her a series of questions which clarify the fatal relationship between the Desboroughs and the Granthams, the Mortons and the De Haldimars. Such questions of identity now resolved, it is dramatically opportune for Matilda to commit suicide; she does so, appropriately enough, by poisoning herself, surely an anticlimactic gesture for one who seems to have long since crossed the border between life and death.

The Canadian Brothers is about the loss and regaining of identity. 'Balancing between the possession of Matilda at the price of crime, and his abandonment of her at that of happiness' (II, 212), Gerald is rendered monstrous by this love-and-honour conflict. Dubbed a 'changeling' by Matilda, in him the two domains of the civilized and the savage intersect, until he becomes 'a chaos of contending passions' (II, 206–7). The consequence of having been bitten by the border serpent is the awareness of opposites, and this means being thrown into a state of conflict. The inability of the Canadian to decide what he is or what he wants to be reflects a larger national identity crisis. Gerald does gain some wisdom in the lower world, however, that promises release from this double-bind. In the penultimate chapter, he recalls the seminal observation of Captain Jackson's that has often recurred to him, 'that he "was never born to be an assassin" ' (II, 212). The magistrate's son was never born to be an outlaw, to take the law into his own hands and defy social and moral standards. The criminal grandeur of the American will not hallow such defiant behaviour. Like Rusty in Le Pan's *The Deserter*, one of the things the Canadian brother discovers in his descent into the underworld is that he is Canadian.

As with Rusty, Watson's James Potter, the narrator of Atwood's *Surfacing*, and other characters in Canadian literature who have experienced the stripping away of all ties and bonds, Gerald's ascent is an ascent out of a narrow concern with himself and back into society. It is a return to the conventional world of his parents, of his boyhood. For him as for Callaghan's Kip Caley, Reaney's James Donnelly, and even the unconventional narrator of Cohen's *Beautiful Losers* and other reluctant or repentant Canadian outlaws, the greatest feeling is that of belonging to a family. Gerald wants to join the ranks again, literally and psychologically. With the martial spirit of his family in the ascendant once more, he sees it as his duty to die for his country, fighting alongside his selfless brother and national heroes like General Brock.

Longing to engage the human community once again, Gerald rejects the seductive but in the last analysis self-destructive siren call of a fierce individualism. The American way of life as it is exemplified by the Desboroughs does not amplify, it distorts and threatens his sense of himself, eroding his inner core; this is the 'demonic' element which he must realize as such. Instead of the narcissistic withdrawal from life of the American, he must reaffirm the great survival value of the principles of commitment, responsibility, and participation to which his countrymen are dedicated. 'Too much rapt in himself to give heed to others' (II, 101), he has shared the Desboroughs' appetite for isolation and independence; in Matilda's temple, he has sanctioned their championing of the primacy of the solitary self, of independence rather than interdependence. Vowing to become a murderer, to become Cain, Gerald has sounded like an American outlaw who wants to light out for the territory to pursue his lawless life, like a frontiersman for whom hell is other people: ' " ... with you even crime may sit lightly on my soul. But we will fly far from the habitations of man. The forest shall be our home ... Yes," he pursued, and with a fierce excitement snatching up the holy book and again carrying it to his lip – "once more I repeat my oath"' (II, 178).

Although not born to be assassins, like Callaghan's heroes and lovers, Richardson's Gerald, Morton, and the Baron in *The Monk*

Knight of St. John are all potential murderers, Shadow Warriors. Gerald's 'fierce excitement' echoes Matilda's and forecasts the 'fiercely exultant' mood of Callaghan's Sam Raymond (*A Passion in Rome*) or John Hughes (*It's Never Over*). 'Such exultation,' as Ina Ferris observes, 'contains a kind of ruthlessness ... and its heady sensation of freedom in isolation is profoundly dangerous.'[36] Richardson, no less than Callaghan in these early works, dramatizes the destructiveness of the exultant self. Surely the array of doubles, twins, etc., throughout *The Canadian Brothers* and *Wacousta* underscores the illusion of the isolated self. The social or communal aspect of identity is undeniable and inescapable. Richardson's stories assert both the fact and the obligation of interdependence; we are members one of another.

The implosive character of the borderland, manifested in such coiled relationships and overlapping identities, compels commitment and participation in depth. There are no separate identities; one cannot avoid a certain complicity even with one's opposite. Indeed, in terms of the Narcissus myth, there is only one character, so any murderous conflict is bound to be suicidal. Characters and settings twist and spiral around one another in double strands replicating themselves ad infinitum. Perhaps Richardson's interest in synchronicity may best be understood in terms of both the Hermes and Narcissus archetypes. In a world which is structured through an interaction and an interlacing that bespeaks the essential kinship of everyone, it is sheer folly for Gerald to want to bury himself in the American forest.

The theme of human sacrifice which symbolizes the nightworld of romance is inherent in the struggle-of-brothers conflict which finds its archetype in Cain and Abel. If, as Jay Macpherson suggests, the highest human virtue is self-sacrifice and the blindest evil the urge to sacrifice others, then Henry manifests the former, Matilda the latter.[37] Henry, whose fraternal love is spurned after his brother's contact with Matilda, vows to help Gerald 'even to the very sacrifice of life' (II, 87). Aligned with Zeus, Henry would extend the self, not withdraw or descend into it. Though there is a sense in which his virtues are untried, Henry embodies aspects of what Bly calls positive Zeus energy and what Frye calls 'a more creative side of the garrison mentality, one that has had positive effects on our intellectual life.'[38] His fortitude and prudence are family qualities which Gerald comes to value during his ascent.

A selfish withdrawal into self such as characterizes the Desboroughs is the sign of an unbridled ego that – like Kurtz's – knows no restraint, goes beyond reasonable human limits, and generates murderous or barbaric excess. Matilda's temple no less than Desborough's hut is the site of human sacrifice; the fact that both become prisons for their monstrous owners suggests the ultimate outcome of an excessive fascination with the self. Without the civilizing restraints, limits, and containment of a Canadian social structure, American energy proves wild and anarchic, undisciplined and meaningless; without the vitality of the latter, however, the former is in danger of becoming calcified, as is the case in *Wacousta*. A working alliance of the two is demanded, not a bloody conflict that is suicidal for both parties.

Gerald's physical ascent out of the dark temple, now Matilda's tomb, begins at dawn. This is appropriate for one who is associated with the sun (II, 122) and daylight consciousness and who is imprisoned by a vampire woman associated with the full moon and night-time consciousness. Restrictions on Gerald's action are resolved through his double; Forrester, 'his benefactor' (II, 209), effects both a 'Rescue from Without' and 'The Magic Flight' (Campbell), ensuring Gerald's escape on one of his horses. *The Canadian Brothers* to this point has been a descending spiral, whirling into ever narrowing closed circles. In the last two chapters as Gerald emerges out of the submarine world, there is a progressive bursting of these closed circles. In his spiral ascent, he makes the circuit of the circular ridge of hills, winding his way out of the labyrinth of the South. Moving further up north, he recrosses the border river (recalling Campbell's 'The Crossing of the Return Threshold') and ascends the Heights of Queenston.

In the final chapter, the connections between the Gerald-Matilda conflict and the larger international one become more apparent. While the irresolute Gerald had been balancing between forsaking and embracing Matilda, 'the success of the British and

American armies had been alternating' (II, 214). Gerald's descent had been paralleled by the British and Canadian defeat at Fort Sandusky. The chapter after that detailing the spellbound Gerald's pledge to commit murder presents Tecumseh's fears concerning the annihilation of the identity of the Indian people caught in 'the hated thraldom of American tyranny and American usurpation' (II, 186), the defeat of the British, and Tecumseh's death. While Gerald is regaining his identity, the British and the Canadians, though overpowered by the sheer size of their gigantic opponent, have also escaped death in the 'Cul-de-Sac' in which they were trapped. The 'confidence in themselves, which had been weakened by a series of reverses' is regained. Just as the passive Gerald again becomes a man of action, the military's 'bold and active offensive operations' are instrumental in 'restoring ... to the victors that moral confidence which was necessary to the honor of the army, and the preservation of the country' (II, 215). It is skilful interweaving of documentary and myth, the historical and the fictive.

The closing scene describes Brock's ascent of the heights which the Canadians and British recapture from the invading Americans. It is a deliberate anachronism, the events described having occurred in 1812 not in 1813; yet setting and conflict are consistent with the imaginative demands of Richardson's tragic romance. Richardson does not subscribe to Scott's or Cooper's providential view of history in which a benevolent deity often stage-manages a secure and glorious national destiny. Ellen's curse is more durable than Matilda's spell: before the brotherly bond between Gerald and Henry can be restored, it is totally severed in 'the fratricidal act' (II, 220). Given Gerald's exchange of identity with the American, it is ironically appropriate that he be mistaken by Henry for the American rifleman who has just killed Brock, the hero of Upper Canada. Gerald dies in the arms of his brother who has shot him with 'the deepest desire of vengeance' (II, 219). The Canadian brothers remind us of our first brothers, Cain and Abel.

Henry now becomes Cain, 'a fratricide' (II, 220), switching identity with the Americanized Gerald who guiltily harbours an image of himself as Cain. The entire scene in the Canadian South is a 'reshooting' of the assassination attempt in the American South. The musket falls from Henry's hand just as the knife raised against Forrester had from Gerald's. There is the same moment of recognition between 'brothers,' the same exclamations of dismay and appeals to God. The cycle of despair and descent played out south of the border is begun again north of it in a much more telescoped version. The imagery of that descent is retraced in concentrated form; there is the same emphasis on disease, unconsciousness, a death-in-life weariness, and self-absorption (II, 220–3). Nautical metaphors are repeated as Henry is 'plunged' into a 'stupor' (II, 220).

As Gerald dies in Henry's arms, Brock expires in those of Henry's close friend. Burning with revenge, the British and Canadian soldiers chase the Americans 'to the verge of the terrific precipices which descend abruptly from the Heights of Queenston. Here their confusion was the highest.' Those who chose to 'perish to the last' 'precipitated themselves down the abyss' into the hell that yawned beneath.' Another rifleman who has also journeyed up from the South – Desborough – leaps upon Henry, uttering 'a terrific scream in which all the most infernal of human passions were wildly blended.' While this emblematic scene is being enacted, 'As if by tacit consent, both parties discontinued the struggle, and became mere spectators of the scene' (II, 224–6). While the Canadians and Americans look on, Desborough raises Henry from the ground as easily as had Wacousta Clara de Haldimar on the border bridge; like his ancestor, Desborough utters an exulting laugh and throws himself and his victim backward into the abyss. This last struggle duplicates their first in volume 1 when Desborough had similarly thrown Henry over backward, this emphasis part of the imagery of inversion.

The prophecy is fulfilled. The last of the De Haldimars and of the Mortons are dead. The Canadians and Americans share their apocalyptic fate, plummeting into the ravine of the border river, their mangled bodies blurring into one another, inseparable in death as in life. Richardson here undermines, even parodies, the nation-building mythology of Scott and Cooper. The border river abyss becomes a mass graveyard as it had in *Wacousta*. That work begins with a single funeral and ends with a quadruple interment. *The Canadian Brothers* begins with Henry standing in an Indian graveyard; Matilda, herself described as a coffin, is seen later outstretched on 'Mad Ellen's' grave and Desborough sorrowing over the rotting corpse of his son. Deathbed scenes proliferate. Each work is informed by 'a descent into a lower world of graves and caves,' into 'the land of death and burial,'[39] not unlike the submerged battle-scarred world of Findley's *The Wars*.

Wacousta and *The Canadian Brothers* are complementary in a variety of ways. Defiant individualism, that anarchic assertion of the ego seen in Matilda's desire for revenge and Gerald's irrational passion for her, may be just as unbending and death-dealing as the robot-conformity encouraged by the garrison mentality. One breeds monsters of vengeance, the other monsters of 'virtue.' Again, opposites run into one another: Matilda is described in the same terms as Colonel de Haldimar. Both are rigid, cold, unfeeling, severe, and given to human sacrifice. Both succumb to a kind of paralysis or living death. Circular temple or square fort, outlaw code or garrison mentality, each represents a dehumanizing extreme which is enclosed and barren. Both figures are tyrants with steely, inflexible wills, whether the victims they dominate allow themselves to be slaves or robots.

De Haldimar's garrison is likened to a prison. Matilda's temple has bars on its one window; boundless intemperance in nature, as Macduff says to Malcolm, is a tyranny. Set for the most part inside the fortress walls, *Wacousta* addresses itself to an exposure of the garrison or herd mentality; each Reginald Morton is pitted against what is often an indifferent or hostile society. Set for the most part beyond the pale of civilization, *The Canadian Brothers* exposes the dangers of the American credo of individualism; society is for the most part just and nurturing, the limitations placed on individuals acceptable ones, the law a necessary counterweight to those who pursue anarchic self-assertion. As such, both books comprising Richardson's five-volume, 1,430-page epic of the founding (and premature death?) of this country nicely balance one another. Neither the inflexible British philosophy of the Old Order nor the American style of New World individualism is appropriate to Canada. Some elusive synthesis is required if tragedy is to be averted.

Constructing and Deconstructing National Epics: Scott, Cooper, and Richardson

Richardson's *Wacousta* is at the centre of the Canadian tradition. Judged against Walter Scott's historical romances or James Fenimore Cooper's frontier romances, *Wacousta* is wondrously complex and enigmatic. Judged from a present perspective, within the tradition it so roundly represents, it is of major importance.

JOHN MOSS, *A Reader's Guide to the Canadian Novel*

American literature is above the ground or on top of the water ... but Canadian literature is under the ground ...

GEORGE BOWERING, *A Short Sad Book*[40]

Richardson's dark, tragic vision of North America, informed by descents across borders into underworlds, can only with difficulty be expressed in the optimistic type of historical romance expressing a glorious national destiny, as originated by Sir Walter Scott. With its discontinuities, gaps, and frightening double-hook ironies, Richardson's epic invokes and questions the myths of nation building and at times seems to parody what numerous critics consider the naive optimism and cultural security of Scott and Cooper. Yet Richardson, no less than Cooper, seems to have learned some of the traditional principles, conventions, and tactics of story-telling from this entertaining writer, one of the most popular and influential figures of his age. In *The Secular Scripture*, Frye begins his discussion of the uniformity of romance formulas over the centuries with a salute to the formulaic techniques employed by the versatile Scott; he considers 'The Wizard of the North' critically misunderstood today, underrated, and sometimes patronized.

Scott is, especially in Richardson, simultaneously acknowledged and challenged. Spurred on by the example of Scott's national approach, each in his own way is engaged in historical myth-making, telling his own culture what it is and how it came to be. The Waverley Novels, The Leatherstocking Tales, and *Wacousta* and *The Canadian Brothers* play the role of national epics. Yet Scott's ordered social world and Cooper's harmonious frontier and forest worlds are ruled by the conventions of comic or historical romance, whereas Richardson's ironic overlapping of garrison and wilderness domains obeys the laws of romantic tragedy. Such a form strikes him as more appropriate to the Canadian situation. The plots of *Écarté* and *Frascati's* feature English heroes who return to England after imprudent adventures abroad to inherit those rewards consistent with the happy ending of comic romances à la Scott. Yet those works set in British North America – *Wacousta, The Canadian Brothers, Westbrook* – are very different. They are tragedies whose dark, gothic atmosphere and problematic vision bespeak a gloomy individual and national fate charged with uncertainty and apprehension. This change of mode is highly telling. It underlines the immense gulf separating 'The Father of Canadian Literature' and the two writers with whom he is often associated.

Such comparisons have, on occasion, been hasty and ill-considered. Riddled with paradox and ambiguity, Richardson's fiction confronts us with the disturbing inhabitants, many of them doubles, of a monstrous nightworld. The distinction between the civilized and the primitive, light and dark, hero and villain, so zealously maintained in Scott and Cooper, is increasingly blurred in Richardson's echoing and deconstruction of British and American national mythologies. His writings work to contest the traditional closure of Scott and Cooper: they provide no satisfying ordering or resolving. At the end of *Wacousta*, one line is allotted to tell of the marriage of Frederick and Madeline, rather than one or two chapters. Like the final sentence of the sequel, the last line, like the first, sounds an ominous note: Ellen Halloway's disappearance into the wilderness, like Wacousta's initial appearance inside the fort, signals that irrational element which is finally beyond the control of the garrison and again combats, disrupts, and subverts any conceptions of a reassuringly ordered and coherent scheme of things.

For Richardson, it is dramatically and mythically necessary that, at the very beginning of our history, the 'lost' causes if such there be, appear to be both that of the Indian and the European one of the conquest of a forbidding and wild continent. Indeed, as at the end of *The Canadian Brothers*, we have the feeling that both sides lose. The Europeans are as doomed as the Indians, a point the sequel underlines. Both are victims and tormentors. Both feel threatened and nearly extinct. The tribe and the regiment are equally preoccupied with survival. Scott and Cooper confidently reminisce about past conflicts from the vantage point of an established and well-defined society that has overcome obstacles to its growth. They can afford to indulge in a safe and cozy armchair nostalgia, in confident conceptions of a strong, optimistic national destiny and a benevolent deity.

Richardson writes at a time when the future of his homeland is in doubt (has there ever been any other time?), when its identity is undefined, when the history of the emergent nation, which he sought to write, is ignored by that country itself. *Wacousta's* focus is not on the last of the Mohicans or the Jacobites, the last of the Ponteacs or the Oucanastas (who live on); it is on the last of the De Haldimars and Mortons, the twin founding families of a precarious culture. Both perish in the War of 1812, a battle which Richardson, to his lasting dismay as veteran, historian, and artist, realized should have catalysed, but did not, a sense of separate national identity. The historical situation dictates that he not work within the mode of comic romance. A deep-seated cultural fear and an intolerable anxiety demand expression. Richardson writes from out of the perspective offered by 'the deep gloom that envelopes every part of the abyss' (II, 227) that swallows everyone and everything at the end of *The Canadian Brothers*.

As his introduction indicates, Richardson knew he was breaking new ground with *Wacousta*, just as Cooper realized *The Last of the Mohicans* was a new kind of romance. In each case, it seems to have taken some readers a little longer to appreciate this. But, as D.H. Lawrence remarks in a piece entitled 'The Spirit of Place,' 'It is hard to hear a new voice, as hard as it is to listen to an unknown language. We just don't listen.'[41]

CHAPTER FIVE

The Shadow Cast by Southern Ontario Gothic

... the part of the country I come from is absolutely Gothic: You can't get it all down.

ALICE MUNRO

... as Nathan Cohen pointed out, sure it's Southern Gothic: Southern *Ontario* Gothic. And that exists.

TIMOTHY FINDLEY

Canada needs ghosts, as a dietary supplement, a vitamin taken to stave off that most dreadful of modern ailments, the Rational Rickets.

ROBERTSON DAVIES[1]

Richardson's is the dark vision of a nightmarish border world haunted by the horrors of both wilderness and garrison. Such an eerie nightworld as he creates is faithful to the nineteenth-century Canadian experience and illustrates the impact of the environment on story-telling. As the quotations which preface this chapter and the following four sections suggest, it is especially true to the spirit of place of Southwestern Ontario. Concealed beneath the orderly, brisk surface of daily life in Richardson's garrisons no less than in Alice Munro's small towns are hidden depths comprising what the latter 'Souwesto' writer calls 'the other side of dailiness'; in both authors as in Reaney, Davies, Engel, Knister, and Gibson, there is a disturbing break-boundary recognition of, and insistence upon, gothic discontinuities and contradictions, a prevalent one being that the familiar is the grotesque and the grotesque the familiar. A double discourse is set up in which the realistic and the fantastic blur and invade or break one another's boundaries.

In her *History of Ontario*, Margaret Avison speaks of that 'very eerie feeling' which this region has inspired in its settlers; twice moved to emphasize the howling of wolves, she observes that 'For many years Baldoon' – located near the spot where Wacousta captures the schooner from Michillimackinac and memorialized in Reaney's play *Baldoon* – 'was rumoured to be a haunted place.'[2] Richardson initiates a literature of 'incubus and *cauchemar*' 'full of ghosts' and 'deep terror,' the source of which, Frye argues in an oft-quoted passage, is the unusually exposed contact of the writer with a consistently sinister and menacing nature which Canada provides. Tragic 'Visions ... of a riddle of inexplicable death ... of inexplicable evil' proliferate as do 'monsters' from Richardson's Wacousta through Pratt's dragon to Drew's wendigo. And, we are reminded, 'Whatever sinister lurks in nature lurks also in us'; a frontier doppelgänger emerges whose lineaments have been described earlier.[3]

Apposite here also are D.H. Lawrence's reflections in *Studies in Classic American Literature* on how a writer and a culture come to terms with the New World. Cooper's denial of the dark gothic realm of incubus and *cauchemar*, his escape into the daylight dream world of 'wish-fulfillment,' elicits a telling comment which provides a context for assessing the differences between him and Richardson, for perceiving what each looked for in past authors, and for evaluating the unique achievement of each: 'When you are actually *in* America, America hurts, because it has a powerful disintegrative influence upon the white psyche. It is full of grinning, unappeased aboriginal demons, too, ghosts, and it persecutes the white man like some Eumenides, until the white men give up their absolute whiteness. America is tense with latent violence and resistance. The very common sense of white Americans has a tinge of helplessness in it, and deep fear of what might be if they were not common-sensical. Yet one day the demons of America must be placated, the ghosts must be appeased, the Spirit of Place atoned for.'[4]

Like all poetic environments, Richardson's is a mixture of memory and literary convention.[5] In Wacousta and The Canadian Brothers, the blend is a most felicitous and inextricable one. Perhaps the most obvious literary influence, besides Byron's narrative verse, is the tradition of the gothic novel. In Cooper, it is the most insignificant. Scott, who welcomes the orderly and rational organization of bourgeois society, also regards as unwholesome the gothic's disturbing claims for the irreducible reality of evil and mindless cruelty, of the inexplicable, the irrational, and the monstrously terrifying – in short, all the powers of chaotic nihilism which find utterance in Richardson's world and throughout our literature. As a literary strategy, the gothic mode must have impressed Richardson as a particularly congenial vehicle for expressing both his own memories of border incidents as a soldier and a POW as well as his countrymen's response to a strange and unpredictable new land. For Carl Klinck, 'Wacousta is a "Gothic tale" which is poetic and a romance in a sense which does not belong to Cooper, for Wacousta is essentially a complex of vivid external equivalents (shrieks, surprises, terrors) for the outrages of mind and heart experienced by Richardson when he was a boy at war in the forests of the Canadian border.' Wacousta's and The Canadian Brothers's claims on our critical attention are strengthened if we give them a historical perspective. As Klinck observes, at the time of 'Pontiac's Rebellion' and 'the War of 1812, reality on the Niagara and Detroit borders offered literature some Indian-frontier imagery exceeding romantic fancies. Canadian writers (except Major John Richardson) and British readers generally have neglected this surfeit of the spectacular, this almost incredible profusion of New World "Gothic" material.'[6]

Klinck speaks of 'the storybook lustre' surrounding the major figures of both historical crises, the strong sense of 'history verging on romance.'[7] Fascinated by blurring the borders between the fictive and the documentary, Richardson introduces historical documents of various kinds into his fiction, and historical works such as *War of 1812* are indebted to the constructive powers of the novelist, an interplay characteristic of Canadian postmodernism as Linda Hutcheon reads it.[8] Richardson's historical sources themselves reflect this persistent and intriguing overlapping of history and romance. In the entry entitled 'Exploration Literature' in *The Oxford Companion to Canadian Literature*, Germaine Warkentin refers to an eyewitness account of the fall of Fort Michillimackinac which is acknowledged in *Wacousta*: Alexander Henry the Elder's *Travels and Adventures in Canada and the Indian Territories* (New York 1809). 'It relates in the first part a classic captivity narrative, the centrepiece of which is a brilliant recounting of the massacre ... The result is a Gothic atmosphere of tension and mystery ... *Travels and Adventures* divides itself ... sharply between the conventions of Gothic and chronicle.'[9]

In Henry and in Richardson, one can find confirmation of Frye's belief that, after crazing the explorers, the New World incubus moves on to haunt the artists. It glares through the gorgons, centaurs, and cyclops of the literature which follows the Greek colonies no less than through the gigantic wolf-men, hellhounds, and spectres of that following the British colonies in North America. This stranger-in-a-strange land motif informs *Wacousta* and other nineteenth-century works as much as it does those tales of 'a world of mystery outside the Greek clearing.'[10] In *Freaks: Myths and Images of the Secret Self*, Leslie Fiedler like Joseph Campbell before him notes that the traditions which have most deeply influenced the post-Renaissance West – the Greek, the Hebrew, and the Norse – all represent human culture as beginning after a tribe of monstrous giants has been killed off.[11] In Richardson's epic account of our origins, Canadian culture begins only after a monstrous giant, a veritable 'spirit of darkness presiding over his terrible legions' (II, 125; 227), is slain.

Like 'an Old English poet, with his head full of ancient battles and myths of dragon-fights, in the position of having to write for the sophisticated audience of Rome and Byzantium,' Richardson had to face disconcerting technical problems in his quest for a form that would express his imaginative vision.[12] The conventions of the gothic novel offered a convenient means of registering the deep fear and placating the New World ghosts Lawrence and Frye speak of. Fiedler stresses that the gothic's 'half-playful, half-pathological evocation of half-believed in monsters remained for almost a hundred years the West's chief method of dealing with the night-time impulses of the psyche.'[13] That Richardson is painstakingly selective in the sources he borrows from and adapts to the Canadian experience soon becomes evident through surveying what in the tradition and in particular authors he chose to develop, play down, alter, or omit.

'The assumptions that underlie the Gothic and its sister genres, the mystery and the horror story,' begins an entry on Margaret Atwood in *The Oxford Companion to Canadian Literature*, 'are indeed the real sources of Atwood's conceptual framework.' So it is with Richardson. Indeed, he anticipates Atwood's 'notion that the important images, archetypes, and genres in Canadian literature are tied to concepts of monsters, ghosts, and the Gothic.'[14] Both share what Eli Mandel in his essay 'Atwood Gothic' calls 'a physiological imagination,' something he also attributes to Michael Ondaatje. Mandel's comments, cued by a chapter in Ellen Moers's *Literary Women* entitled 'The Female Gothic,' provide us with a working definition of the genre: 'Gothic, says Moers, is writing that "has to do with fear," writing in which "fantasy predominates over reality, the strange over the commonplace, and the supernatural over the natural, with one definite auctorial intent: to scare ... to get to the body itself, its glands, muscles, epidermis, and circulatory system, quickly arousing and quickly allaying the physiological reactions to fear." '[15] While I emphasize this aspect of gothic here, the next section of this chapter focuses on another salient one: the sense of entrapment in an antiquated, decaying social order from Richardson to contemporary writers from Southwestern Ontario.

The atmosphere of tense expectancy, mystery, and brooding terror in strange and horrifying locales which Richardson sought to evoke was long the province of the gothic, as Reaney, Macpherson, and Northey have noted. Here was a dramatic, and often sensational, abandonment of the sober daylight world.

Inaugurated in 1764 with the publication of Horace Walpole's *The Castle of Otranto*, it attained great popularity in the 1790s with Anne Radcliffe's five romances. With Charles Robert Maturin's *Melmoth the Wanderer* (1820), it reached its apogee. The gothic novel with its nightmare symbolism 'was part of the movement away from neoclassic ideals of order, restraint, and reason toward an admiration for the picturesque, the sublime, and the emotional in art. As the century drew toward its revolutionary conclusion, its former faith in a rationally ordered universe and in the validity of human reason as a cognitive instrument was undermined; at the same time the growing respect for intuitive, imaginative insight resulted in the exultation of irrational mental activities as the supreme mode of knowing.'[16]

Several critics have discussed the relationship between the gothic, the grotesque, and the fantastic and periods of cultural disorder or upheaval, a relationship also informing Canadian postmodernism. Symbols and motifs adequate to express the anguished Canadian psyche during the two historical crises Richardson describes appear throughout gothic literature. Graphic scenes of the blood-curdling terrors of the Inquisition, sometimes involving cases of unjust condemnation, are much favoured by the gothicists (and postmodernists like Chris Scott in the trial and execution of the heretic/visionary Giordano Bruno in *Antichthon*, or in similar scenes in Atwood's *The Handmaid's Tale*); they are but one example of the savage restraints of the despotic old order which parallel those acts of civilized barbarity enacted in the name of justice by 'one whose military education had been based on the principles of the old school' (III, 140; 417), the tyrannical Colonel de Haldimar.

Wacousta presents a border world that is doubly restrictive. A repressive and claustrophobic garrison is mirrored by a forest which 'formed, as it were, the gloomy and impenetrable walls of the prison-house' (II, 237; 286). This sense of confinement echoes 'the nightmare symbolism of Gothic fiction' of which, for W.F. Axton, 'the characteristic metaphors are those of imprisonment (usually with overtones of horror or death) and its resultant paranoia. The figurative texture of the Gothic novel is a projection of the romantic mind's sense of entrapment in an antiquated culture, its struggle to break from it, and its guilty consciousness of both its participation in obsolete attitudes and its transgressions against traditional standards.'[17]

The tension and anxiety inherent in this split state of mind find expression, according to Axton, in the divided nature of the gothic hero-villain. That conflicting play between rational judgment and intuitive sympathy so characteristic of the original *Wacousta* may hark back to the ambiguities of the tale of terror. The depiction of Wacousta as a dark outlaw and wanderer incorporates features from three types of gothic figures as catalogued by D.P. Varma.[18] These are the robust, moody tyrant-usurper motivated by ambition and unbridled passion; second, the disillusioned and passionate victim of destiny who is a lonely, despairing being enmeshed in circumstances both beyond his control and of his own making; and third, the mysterious and terrible superman, offshoot of Milton's Satan, the latter, along with Hamlet, standing at the head of the family tree of gothic and Romantic hero-villains. In effect, Richardson seems to be sewing together bits and pieces of different gothic hero-villains, from Manfred in *The Castle of Otranto* to Frankenstein's creature, to create his own monster with a Canadian stamp. Anne Radcliffe's Schedoni, the ruthless murderer in *The Italian*, is a possible avatar. Yet, unlike Wacousta, Schedoni is not sensitive and imaginative. Like Maturin's Melmoth and Charlotte Dacre's Zofloya, however, Schedoni has those piercing eyes and that hypnotic glance which Wacousta eventually inherits, as do Wiebe's Riel and Davies's Eisengrim and Parlabane. But De Haldimar also possesses eyes which seem to penetrate the observer and read her or his inmost thoughts. Richardson's borderland features twin tyrants because both garrison and wilderness are menacing.

Richardson's lifelong interest in the struggle-of-brothers motif may have been sustained by a variety of works revolving around fratricide and/or usurpation: Lewis's *Alonso the Brave* and *The Castle Spectre*, Radcliffe's *The Romance of the Forest* and *The Italian*, Maturin's *The Fatal Revenge*, Beddoes's *The Second Brother* and *Death's Jest Book*, P.B. Shelley's *Zastrozzi, A Romance* and *St. Irvyne;*

or, The Rosicrucian, Wordsworth's *The Brothers* and *The Borderers,* Coleridge's *Remorse* and *Zapolya,* Godwin's *Caleb Williams,* Hogg's *The Confessions of a Justified Sinner,* and, of course, Mary Shelley's *Frankenstein.* As the last entries in my list suggest, the struggle-of-brothers motif easily modulates into that of the double or doppelgänger. This is a device eminently suitable for probing the dark side of existence and the divided self. Preoccupied by the notions of duality or opposites held in tension, Richardson advances the double as a significant motif in Canadian literature. It does not attract Scott or Cooper, both of whom are not committed to penetrating too far into the shadows.[19] The gothic's concern with problems of the divided self offers several points of departure for one as fascinated as Richardson is with the myriad interwoven affinities between complementary pairs and groups of people.

The motif of mysterious doubles becomes, of course, a vital theme of terror in romantic literature. This is particularly true of German Romantic writing – Goethe, Richter, Hoffmann – to which Richardson may have been exposed during his European travels. Whether German or British, they write 'to shake the philistines out of their self-satisfied torpor. *Épater la bourgeoisie*: this is the secret slogan of the tale of terror ... the gothic is ... perhaps the first avant-garde art in the modern sense of the term ... The popular success of *Frankenstein* ... has obscured the fact that it was launched as an advanced book; and that it belongs to a kind, one of whose functions was to shock the bourgeoisie into an awareness of what a chamber of horrors its own smugly regarded world really was.'[20]

Richardson's dramatization of a fractured Canadian psyche, his creation of an ironic and ambivalent voice and vision, of a multiple, shifting perspective, and even of particular scenes may reveal a debt to Mary Shelley's *Frankenstein, or The Modern Prometheus* (1817). The antithesis between De Haldimar and his enemy is a very complex one and can be described more fully in the larger context of Romantic literature and its characteristic mythology. In a very real sense, the Colonel creates the ferocious Wacousta out of the loving and chivalric Sir Reginald Morton. 'If I am that altered being,' asks Wacousta, 'to whom is the change to be ascribed?' (III, 288; 497); Frankenstein considers his monster 'my own vampire, my own spirit let loose from the grave, and forced to destroy all that was dear to me.'[21] The irony of De Haldimar's fate approximates that of Frankenstein's: he, too, is a Cain, involuntarily murdering all his loved ones through the agency of his creature. Once again, the figure of Cain draws this Canadian author, while that of Adam attracts Americans like Cooper, Hawthorne, and Melville.

Wacousta and De Haldimar possess attributes in common with the demon and his maker. Cut to the same pattern as Robert Louis Stevenson's Dr Jekyll, Frankenstein and De Haldimar are emotionally stifled, unmarried, joyless, and obsessed with proprieties. Hideous and deformed, Wacousta shares the gigantic monster's gliding, spectre-like presence. Both strike others as demons or animals even as 'Mr Hyde,' also associated with the body and its energies, seems troglodytic. 'A horrid apparition' with 'the shape of a man,' Shelley's monster is likewise endowed with remarkable agility and 'superhuman speed.' It, too, utters 'fearful howlings' and possesses a 'loud and fiendish laugh' that echoes throughout the landscape until Frankenstein feels 'as if all hell surrounded me with mockery and laughter.'[22] Swearing inextinguishable hatred for their arch-enemies, both monsters become solitary wanderers; they seek refuge in a wild nature, abhorring themselves and cursing the barbarity and eloquently lamenting the hypocrisy and injustice of society.

Both Wacousta and the monster refuse to kill their adversaries outright, preferring instead to torment them by slaying innocent members of their families. Heathcliff, Hyde, and Hogg's devilish double in *The Confessions of a Justified Sinner* pursue a similar course. Such revenge assuages to some degree what Harold Bloom calls 'the great desolation of love rejected' from which there is no release.[23] As in Byron's *The Giaour*, 'The heart once thus left desolate / Must fly at last for ease – to hate.'[24] Wacousta's flashback in which he narrates the development of his sensibility, his betrayal by De Haldimar, and the reasons for his revenge parallels the monster's tale-within-a-tale which is similar in content. Both are accounts of the tragic fall of a noble being of great potential.

More sinned against than sinning, these monsters which society rejects prove a source of energy and vitality in harmony with nature capable of rejuvenating the old order. Ironically, the creature is 'more human,' 'more imaginative ... more intellectual and more emotional than his maker.' Like Wacousta, Frankenstein's monster is also 'more lovable than his creator and more hateful, more to be pitied and more to be feared.'[25] This split response is due to their ambiguous dual nature which Byron's band of noble outlaws also share. Consider this passage from *Lara*: 'In him inexplicably mix'd appear'd / Much to be loved and hated, sought and fear'd ... / So much he soar'd beyond, or sunk beneath.'[26] For all of these figures, this air of the fallen angel, of satanic defiance, derives from that archetype of revenge and revolt, Milton's Satan:

> he above the rest
> In shape and gesture proudly eminent
> Stood like a Tow'r; his form had yet not lost
> All her Original brightness ...
>   Dark'n'd so, yet shone
> Above them all th' Arch-Angel: but his face
> Deep scars of Thunder had intrencht, and care
> Sat on his faded cheek, but under Brows
> Of dauntless courage, and considerate Pride
> Waiting revenge: cruel his eye ... [27]

Such is the figure celebrated by P.B. Shelley for his energy, defiance, and magnificence in contrast to the cold security and hypocritical vengeance of his oppressor. Thus, in Richardson, a gigantic, dark-skinned Wacousta 'whose enmity to our colonel seems almost devilish' (III, 317; 513) attacks the fortress of the calculating Governor: 'His face was painted black as death; and as he stood under the arch of the gateway, with his white turbaned head towering far above those of his companions, this formidable and mysterious enemy might have been likened to the spirit of darkness presiding over his terrible legions' (II, 125; 227).[28]

The Ungrateful Dead: Southwestern Ontario *Senex* and *Mort-Vivants* Figures

The Wild Man's qualities, among them love of spontaneity, association with wilderness, honoring of grief, and respect for riskiness, frightens many people. Some men, as soon as they receive the first impulses to riskiness and recognize its link with what we've called the Wild Man, become frightened, stop all wildness, and recommend timidity and collective behavior to others. Some of these men become high school principals, some sociologists, some businessmen, Protestant ministers, bureaucrats, therapists; some become poets and artists.

ROBERT BLY, *Iron John*

The geographical frontier was not simply pushed further away ... It was, instead, metamorphosed. Writers, fortified by the iconoclasm of admitting their 'pagan' attraction to a life force rather than a 'Protestant' adherence to social conventions, overtly transformed the frontier from a physical to a metaphysical 'place.'

W.H. NEW, *Articulating West*[29]

Certain preoccupations of Canadian experience awaited projection in the gothic form. One such is the ambiguous conflict between abiding by and striding over 'the laws of man.' In *Wacousta*, this is dramatized in the struggle-of-brothers relationship between De Haldimar and Wacousta, in *The Canadian Brothers* by the tortured relationship between their descendants, the Canadian Gerald Grantham and the American Matilda Montgomery. Well aware of an oppressive garrison mentality bent on perpetuating moribund Old World customs and institutions in the New World, Richardson seems drawn to a genre that, as Axton realizes, vividly registers 'the human spirit's sense of its imprisonment and perversion by an old, tyrannical order: its awareness that it had been bound from without by absolutist institutions, and twisted within by the attitudes these same institutions engendered.'[30]

This antiquated, decaying social order, I suggest, is personified in *senex* and related *mort-vivants* figures. Colonel de Haldimar's character conforms especially to that of the unbending *senex*, Wacousta's to that of the flowing, mercurial Trickster. In *The Shaman's Doorway: Opening the Mythic Imagination to Contemporary Consciousness*, psychotherapist Stephen Larsen examines the *senex* archetype (primarily in its negative or dark aspect) under the heading of 'The Myth of the Crippled Tyrant.' A beleaguered country is ruled by an aging, impotent king; the infirmities in the land correspond to a deficiency in the king. Most often his malady is 'rigidity, combined with a tyrannical or authoritarian enforcement of his petrifying will.'[31] For Larsen as for Bly, Woodman, Eisler, and Bolen, such a figure is a symbol of a tyrannical severity and power urge that has outlived its usefulness; he is, in Joseph Campbell's phrase, 'the monster of the status quo: Holdfast, the keeper of the past.'[32]

As the Old World man, De Haldimar with his family compact faithfully expresses this pattern. A stolid defender of the old order, his imported ideal codifies the values of limitation, firm boundaries, definition, and tradition. Such values, of course, have an important place in a culture as in the psyche, yet the inflexible Governor has retreated into a rigid posture in which all definitions and frames of reference have become finally established and no longer subject to debate: the psychological procrustean bed of the patriarchal and garrison mentality. He is an insecure *senex* figure who has petrified into a narrowly judgmental role. Paradoxically, notes Larsen, 'the precise and deliberate defense mechanisms which had been instituted to ward off the unforeseen ... *themselves become the symptoms.*'[33] In Richardson's terms, the garrison betrays itself: the ideal order is the curse. Throughout the course of his revenge, as Wacousta grows larger, taller, and darker, De Haldimar becomes progressively paler, stooped, and attenuated. Emotionally if not literally stunted and paralysed, the man at the top is finally 'Bowed down to the dust' (III, 367; 541)

– a crippled tyrant indeed. Yet Holdfast must die before a more humane leader can emerge.

Larsen, like Bly and Moore, often refers to a study of the *senex* figure by Jungian analyst Marie-Louise von Franz who writes: 'His deficiency consists mainly in an exaggerated egocentricity and hardening of the heart.' Such are De Haldimar's weaknesses. Von Franz states that the *senex* is always paired with his opposite, the *puer aeternus*, a good term to describe the adolescent idealist Reginald Morton. Explains Larsen, emphasizing the *puer's* positive characteristics rather than his naiveté and immature grandiosity, 'His antagonist, the symbol of the spirit of life, is the eternal child, the *puer aeternus*. The *puer* represents everything the *senex* has become cut off from: youth, beauty, feeling, sexuality, change. And the *senex* in turn represents what to the youth seems unattainable or repugnant: stability, power, responsibility, and worldly wisdom. As in any dynamism, these pairs of opposites are forever in conflict yet inextricably bound together, the presence of one evoking the other.'[34] Such is De Haldimar's relationship to both Reginald Mortons.

Once again, Richardson may best be understood by comparison with those writers who follow him. The same mythic quality invests an analogous situation in MacLennan's *Barometer Rising*. The narrator sees 'the generous ones' like Neil Macrae and Penny Wain victimized by Colonel Wain, 'the descendant of military colonists who had remained essentially a colonist himself,' a man who seems to have been born old; while 'the old men' who rule Canada persist in holding onto the power structure of the old order, the young men 'who had believed the myth that this was a young man's country, were being killed like fools thousands of miles away in a foreign world.' As in *Wacousta*, there is a suggestion of the magic complicity between killer and killed, hunter and hunted: at one point it seems to Neil 'that he had become two persons, himself and his uncle Geoffrey Wain.'[35]

The dismembered *senex's* complementary redeeming figures are the eternal youth and the feminine. Both represent, in different inflections, what the incomplete *senex* lacks: rejuvenation, love, creativity, authentic linkage to others. 'If the *senex* is awake to his deficiency, even a little, he may be spared dismemberment. In fairy tales the wise old man is often accompanied by a beautiful young woman.'[36] By ridding himself of both Mortons and precipitating Ellen's madness and her wilderness exile, De Haldimar cuts himself off from potent forces of rejuvenation, love, and creativity. Dedicating himself instead to an aggressively masculine ideal, a sterile abstraction, the law giver and authoritarian parent rejects what Bly calls 'the male mode of feeling' and 'the masculine emotional body' as well as the 'feminine' in himself as in others, banishing emotion, imagination, beauty, and sexuality.[37] The four men he is most adamantly opposed to are strongly associated with these elements. De Haldimar seems incapable of the deep human commitment and intense love manifested in their relationships. It is significant that the Governor – celibate for a decade and a half or so – splits up or blocks these bonds: a jealous, puritanical Shadow King, he separates Clara Beverley and Sir Reginald Morton, Ellen and Frank Halloway, Clara and Everard, haughtily rebuking the latter for his passionate expression of affection for his daughter. In a patriarchal culture where Zeus's negative characteristics are in the ascendant, where human relations are structured according to what Eisler calls the dominator model, women are victimized, but they are not the only victims. As Robert Moore observes, 'Shadow Kings are no more empowering of the males around them than they are the females. Shadow Kings don't want anyone getting stronger and creative around them. Shadow King is always castrating – castrates his sons and castrates his daughters.'[38]

De Haldimar's strained relations with women in particular reflect his contempt for the realm of feeling, intuition, and sensibility with which women are here associated. The numerous American editors of Wacousta appear to share De Haldimar's misogynous leanings. They have been quite thorough in cutting down or totally editing out references to, or scenes involving, women. Besides deleting passages relating to the 'Canadians,' the Ottawas, everyday garrison routine, the landscape, and circle-square imagery, Americanization of the text has also meant diluting anything expressive of that 'vigorous heterosexuality' which John Moss identifies as characteristic of Canadian frontier fiction.[39] American editors, it seems, have attempted to make Richardson palatable to the taste of readers bred on what Leslie Fiedler calls the for-men-only Edens and womanless romances of Cooper and his contemporaries.[40]

De Haldimar's conduct toward Ellen is instructive. Her initial appeal to his sense of mercy and compassion in connection with her accused husband goes unheeded. Irritated by this 'interruption,' he orders that 'the women of the regiment ... be kept out of the way' (I, 70; 40). As a 'Shadow Warrior' (Moore), the Governor may seduce the feminine – as in the case of the naive Clara de Haldimar – but he will not be seduced by it. Women and their values are relegated to the shadows (and the shadow in the male psyche). Before Ellen can be silenced, she wildly contests his authority and denounces his severity. Instead of the *senex* curbing his one-sidedness in the past through a wife he has not had time for and by allying himself to this vibrant young woman (as do Erskine, Blessington, and Charles), the Governor declares war on woman as he does on nature, Wacousta, the French, and the Indians – those marginalized ex-centrics outside the mainstream who surface in such contemporary works as Audrey Thomas's *Intertidal Life* or Leonard Cohen's *Beautiful Losers*. Thus, appropriately, the wild Ellen, befriended by François's earthy daughter Babette (similarly oppressed by De Haldimar and romantically linked with Wacousta) ends her days as an outcast living among the Indians in the wilderness as Wacousta's mate – a listless Persephone abducted and raped by Hades.

In exiling feeling, joy, creativity, and sexuality, and in severing natural bonds, the celibate founder of British North America incorporates the deficiencies of the *senex* and the patriarchy into the social order he establishes. Governor de Haldimar is one of the first of many official social representatives to be a misogynist. Others who swell the ranks include Godfrey's Geoffrey Firebank, MacLennan's Colonel Wain, Callaghan's 'Commander' Groome, Kroetsch's William Dawe, Davies's Dunstan Ramsay, Reaney's Reverend McGillicuddy, O'Hagan's Father Rorty, Atwood's The Commander, and numerous other characters in Atwood, Thomas,

Bersianik, Swan, and Van Herk. Such figures possess negative characteristics of the *senex*. Theirs is often a dislike of intimacy and 'opening up' and a need for body armour to distance themselves from others. At the core of all such figures is fear – fear of their own bodies, fear of not measuring up, fear of letting go, fear of grieving, fear of other men, as well as what Marion Woodman calls 'a patriarchal fear of the feminine.'[41]

No one has to kill a Father Rorty or a 'Commander' Groome, a Dawe, or a De Haldimar: they are already dead inside or dying of wounds of which they remain sadly unconscious. The abstract ideal these wounded king figures enforce is in itself a kind of death force that does violence to men's psyches let alone women's. Each *senex* kills himself in his own way, often through an arrogant act of self-immolation or self-amputation. Psychological dismemberment or what Robertson Davies calls 'psychological suicide' precedes Boy Staunton's actual suicide; as Eisengrim's 'Brazen Head' proclaims, he is killed by himself first of all, his lust for control, power, and respectability having eaten away at his soul. The stone-in-the-snowball which is Boy's trademark is characteristic of most of these shadow kings; the split-off 'brother' with whom they struggle and will not re-member usually proves the keeper of their conscience, whether he be a Dunstan Ramsay, a Chone, a Wacousta, or a David Newman, Darcy's double in Patricia Blondal's *A Candle to Light the Sun*. Certainly not every adult male in a position of power or authority in *Wacousta* or *The Canadian Brothers* abuses it, as the glowing portraits of Blessington and General Brock, to name just two, attest. Nor does Richardson, in contrast to some American novelists counsel, young men to be inordinately suspicious of older males. Yet Governor de Haldimar is not alone in a literature in which we meet more expressions of shadow or wounded-and-wounding kings than sacred ones. The merciless Judge Black in Wiebe's *The Scorched-Wood People* may also be numbered among the wounded and living dead. Riel falls victim to the 'Presbyterian dourness' of this incarnation of 'all-knowing Protestant Ontario.' All Wiebe's authority figures here as in *The Temptations of Big Bear* are as rigid, humourless, and emotionally repressed as Governor de Haldimar. In contrast, the fiery Riel is an animated, articulate orator. Specifically associated at one point with sexuality, the body, and passion, he is an outlaw with a price on his head like Wacousta. Laughing aloud at the words 'Canadian law,' Wiebe's wild man is likewise sustained by a similar vision of 'beauty, love, life.'[42]

Unable to reconnect with the cut-off parts of themselves, many of these shadow kings wither away after their official persona has slipped or been punctured. And all the king's men can't put them together again after this major loss of power and status with which they have identified. The final image of De Haldimar fuses the two strands of imagery connected with him throughout the work which recur with startling frequency in the descriptions of his fellow *senex*-figures. A 'stony coldness' invests the dead man's body as it has his heart, as it will Hagar's, and as a wooden feeling paralyses the Bentleys, and the Commander and his Wife in the nightmarish *The Handmaid's Tale*. 'Bowed down to the dust by the accomplishment of the curse of Ellen Halloway, the inflexibility of Colonel de Haldimar's pride was not proof against the utter annihilation wrought to his hopes as a father by the unrelenting hatred of the enemy his early falsehood and treachery had raised up to him' (III, 367; 541). In keeping with the fixed/fluid patterning in the text, the rigid De Haldimar – the man who would be king and would not be moved – turns to stone while the ever-changing Wacousta-Poseidon descends beneath the border river.

Richardson's gallery of the living dead, of the emotionally and spiritually maimed, is a prophetic one, as the works of other writers, especially those from Southwestern Ontario, testify. His choice of the *senex* has proven a prescient one; that it is particularly apt for this region is the purpose of the rest of this section to show. This survey is of the utmost importance for our understanding of *Wacousta* and especially *The Canadian Brothers* with its emphasis on Gerald Grantham's relationship with his reserved and withdrawn parents. In an editorial in *Alphabet* in 1963, James Reaney makes the brief but suggestive statement that '*Mortvivants* is a good name for what passes as society in our country.'[43] (One is reminded of Toronto *Globe* columnist Richard

Needham's frequent appraisal of Canadians as a people stricken with 'funereal disease.') Richardson's characters to the judges, magistrates, churchmen, and academics in the Donnelly trilogy, *Baldoon*, *The Boy with an R in His Hand*, *Three Desks*, and *The Dismissal* testify to the overwhelming presence of *mort-vivants* in the literature of this region.

Governor de Haldimar, the younger Delme and Murphy, and, to a lesser extent, Judge Grantham in *The Canadian Brothers*, stand squarely at the beginning of a long line of desiccated and pompous establishment representatives in Canadian literature. Scarred by the garrison anxieties of prudery and propriety, they are the progenitors of that fervent upholder of 'the rules of middle-class Canadian respectabilitarianism' whom Scott Symons identifies not as the Wild Man but variously as 'The Blandman,' 'The English Canadian Cube,' the joyless, body-hating, intellect-worshipping 'Civil Serviceable' – in short, 'God's frozen people ... the WASP English Canadian.' For Symons, 'our national smugliness' seems to have reached epidemic proportions in his – and Richardson's – birthplace, 'massive, impenetrable' Southern Ontario.[44] Richardson's imaginative diagnosis of men who shaped this country and his depiction of this region, referred to in *Survival* as 'the heartland of WASP Canada' and personified in *Life before Man*'s 'William WASP, from a good family in London, Ontario,'[45] forecasts Marian Engel's description of Southwestern Ontario as strongly puritanical, moralistic, and judgmental and James Reaney's delineation of 'Southwestern dourness' and of the stony 'Calvinist heart of Souwesto.'[46] De Haldimar's and Grantham's symbolic descendants have certainly spread throughout Souwesto, settling in Munro's Jubilee and Hanratty, Engel's Godwin, Reaney's and Gibson's London-Lucan-Stratford region, Knister's and Elliott's rural townships, and Davies's Deptford. They are also superbly dramatized in the 1990 National Film Board release, *Beautiful Dreamers*, set in nineteenth-century London where they are brought into contact with the Souwesto author of *Cosmic Consciousness*, R.M. Bucke.

Perhaps the most obvious work that bears out the truth of Reaney's observation is Atwood's *Crestwood Heights*-type postmortem on fossilized hearts, *Life before Man*. The rigid, censorious, puritanical Auntie Muriel is the ultimate female version of the *senex*. She is a matriarchal type that Southern-Ontario based Jungian analyst Marion Woodman identifies variously as 'the old petrifying mother' and the Medusa.[47] With 'her eyes, like two pieces of gravel, cold and unreflecting,' she is the very gothic exemplar of all Canadian *mort-vivants*: 'It isn't a living room, because Auntie Muriel cannot be said to live. Auntie Muriel is both the spider and the fly, the sucker-out of life juice and the empty husk ... She should have been sent into the Army. Only in a tank, helmeted, gauntleted, her guns directed at something, anything at all, would she have been happy.'[48]

Hers is an odd double identity, but an appropriate one for this one-woman army of occupation proud of her Southwestern Ontario ancestors. 'Might is right' is a truth as unquestionable for this power-hungry 'wardress' as it is for De Haldimar or Reaney's churchman John McTavish in *Baldoon* or the nature-conquering public officials in Ondaatje's *In the Skin of a Lion*. Malevolent, barricaded inside her own head, fortified by strict ideals of duty, decency, and hard work, dreading her decaying body, she is a death force as malignant and coldly competent as a dozen of Mitchell's Mrs Abercrombies. As much 'a pattern of rigid propriety and decorum of conduct' (III, 141; 417) as Governor de Haldimar, she dresses as self-consciously and immaculately as he or Marshall's Dr Bradley Dunlop. Devoutly materialistic, hers is the accountant mentality – stingy, evasive, egocentric, emotionally constipated – of Richardson's Delme and Murphy, Reaney's McTavish, Davies's Dunstan Ramsay, or of Atwood's own William WASP.

The italicized phrases 'We are the Dead' (from the Canadian war poem *In Flanders Fields* but also found in Orwell's *Nineteen Eighty-Four*) and 'We are the Numb' are the recurrent watchwords for Atwood's *mort-vivants* and *senex* respectively.[49] Auntie Muriel shares De Haldimar's and Mrs Ramsay's granite determination to enforce her own narrow perspective on everything without consulting anyone else. As insolent and insulting as the Governor, she shares Dunstan Ramsay's inability to resist a cruel speech, especially when it entails lecturing on the lapsed morals of her self-indulgent inferiors. Not lacking in De Haldimar's self-righteousness, Auntie Muriel locates herself and the Queen under God on 'the great Chain of Being.' At the very bottom, after 'cockroaches, clothes moths, silverfish and germs,' come 'sexual organs, except those of flowers.' This is the basic operating manual most *senex*-figures come equipped with.[50]

As we move progressively westward into this region towards Richardson's hometown of Amherstburg, such horrendous figures proliferate with alarming frequency. Auntie Muriel's equally invidious counterpart in Munro's Jubilee is 'Our Gothic Mother, with the cold appalling mask of the Shaking Palsy laid across her features ... eyes dead and burning, fixed inward on herself.' This formidable old woman, the twisted, diseased mother of the two contrasting sisters in 'The Peace of Utrecht,' is another dying dinosaur in the land time forgot. She presides magisterially over a 'house of stone' that suffocates life and growth.[51] Emotionally dead, she bleaches all feeling out of her daughters.

Both sisters are intimidated by the complacent, judgmental look on the faces of Jubilee's citizens, 'only one or two whose respectability was ever in question.' 'Certain restrictions of life in Jubilee' – a wickedly ironic name for this town founded by dour Scots Presbyterians – makes it as claustrophobic, herd-minded, and inbred as Richardson's constricted garrisons. Gazing at an old photograph of family members who appear as indestructible as Auntie Muriel does to her descendants, the narrator, the roving sister who has escaped to the west coast, senses that 'They stared back at me with grave accusing Protestant faces, for I had run up against the simple unprepossessing materialism which was the rock of their lives.'[52] While the one sister manages to escape such burial alive, the other, the perversely dutiful, timid, and guilty Maddy, wastes away in a thankless ten-year vigil over their mother.

Trapped in this puritan hurdle-course, she, like Gerald Grantham in *The Canadian Brothers*, is a victim of what Minn in Engel's *The Honeyman Festival* classifies as 'southern Ontario guilt.'[53] She desperately wants to escape like her unconventional sister; but her last words – the last of the short story – convey the increasing paralysis that threatens to turn her into another of these gothic *mort-vivants*: 'Why can't I?'[54] Hers is the same sickening sense of stasis and entrapment which is presented in *The Canadian Brothers* by a series of circular trips which always return the guilty Gerald to the home of his austere, reserved father, in Reaney's seminal poem *The Upper Canadian* through the image of geese who sail round their pond in continual circles, and in Gibson's *Five Legs* by the frenzied circling of Dr Crackell's thoughts in a cerebral labyrinth.

Crackell, that 'veritable pillar of southwestern Ontario's academic community,' could be Governor de Haldimar reincarnated. He is the perfectly domesticated hive personality that De Haldimar's garrison aims to churn out. His cultural conditioning is so complete that it walls out the energies of the body, referred to as 'the unofficial man,' of sexuality (his wife is always 'out of order'), and of the Wacousta figures, 'the wild and thoughtless' Martin Baillie and the impulsive, long-haired Felix, distinguished by his 'instinctive carelessness' and mocking tone.[55] De Haldimar's genes are particularly apparent in Deptford's Ramsays, Scots Presbyterians who consider themselves the guardians of the town's respectability, exemplars of 'common sense, prudence, and right opinions of virtually everything.' Theirs is a 'bred-in-the-bone puritanism' that creates 'a moral monster' in the person of Dunstan Ramsay. Grimly 'serious people,' eminently practical and hard-working, they are moral watch-dogs continually on the lookout for 'very serious breaches of propriety.'[56]

Moving farther west still, into the even more haunted borderlands of Essex County where Richardson grew up and to which he returned from overseas, we encounter the hideously gothic Lethens of Raymond Knister's *White Narcissus* (1929). Though sometimes clumsily written, this short novel is a surprisingly comprehensive medley of all the themes associated with Southwestern Ontario's *senex/mort-vivants* figures. It deserves discussion at some length. In many respects, it bears a striking resemblance to *Wacousta*, suggesting the mysterious and undeniable power of place to which both authors have responded with singular fidelity. As their name and grotesque appearance indicate, Knister's Lethens are denizens of the same stony, cold, and inhuman twilight world as De Haldimar, Auntie Muriel, and 'Our Gothic Mother.' As one of their rural neighbours says of 'the old people,' as they are called, 'they don't seem livin' ... You understand me, they don't seem alive.' Certainly, these 'slowly petrifying people' are 'dead to each other,' literally not having talked to one another in decades.[57] This is De Haldimar's incommunicableness taken to the nth power. They are as self-destructive and inseparable as De Haldimar and Wacousta, Gerald and Matilda.

Mrs Lethen recalls the secretive and withdrawn De Haldimar who is nothing if not calculating. Striving to emulate the impenetrability of his garrison walls, De Haldimar is always on guard and if ever caught out in a moment of surprise, 'instantly resumed his habitual sternness of look and manner' (I, 75; 43). Auntie Muriel also takes a perverse delight in remaining inscrutable. Like these other fortresses unto themselves, closed in and self-absorbed, the sickly white Mrs Lethen is constantly presented bent over her jealously guarded white narcissi. The suffocating, enervating odour of white narcissi lingers throughout the mirror-reflection obsessed literature of this self-enclosed region.

Mr Lethen is seldom referred to by name, known simply as 'the old man' or 'It.'[58] He denies his wife any affection in the same way De Haldimar does his family, the way 'Commander' Groome and Boy Staunton do their wives, the way both Dr Lucan Crackell and Dr Bradley Dunlop think of their spouses as bitches, the way William WASP rapes Lesje, the way Owen's father maintains a constant warfare with his embittered wife in the nearby Perth County of Reaney's Listen to the Wind. Not only alienated from his wife, Lethen plays out a Cain and Abel conflict in rural Ontario terms, haggling over fences and lot sizes with his importunate neighbour. Such territorial disputes and bitter feuds form the backbone of many Southwestern Ontario tales from Wacousta and its sequel and Westbrook, the Outlaw to Baldoon, Listen to the Wind, and the Donnelly trilogy.

Having exiled love, feeling, passion, and pleasure, the Lethens move stiffly about like zombies in the 'oppressive rooms' of a 'decayed house.' As hermetically sealed as Richardson's garrison, as impregnable as Mrs Fullerton's barricaded old gothic house in Munro's *Dance of the Happy Shades*, as constricted as the Donnelly farm or Symons's 'Cube' edifices, as guilt-ridden as Robert Mallon's household in David Helwig's Kingston tetralogy, the Lethen's haunted house has a secretive air and its narrow, dark windows are permanently shut against the outside world. Like De Haldimar and Auntie Muriel, the Lethens see life – or rather existence – as something that can only be maintained inside a heavily armed fortress, at the expense of shutting out nature, sexuality, and their own humanity. Such also seems to be the stance of the inhabitants of the nearby hamlet, aptly named 'Lower Warping,' a cramped place of 'primly closed' gates and 'empty and shrunken streets.' Like the reserved, respectable citizens of Jubilee, they are practical folk; theirs is the 'impervious stolidity' and 'instinctive caution' typical of such a 'circumscribed place' of 'choked vistas.'[59] The Southwestern Ontario of *The White Narcissus* is a breeding ground for the warped, the bent, the crippled.

The protagonist and the woman he loves barely escape this cultural maiming. Richard Milne and Reginald Morton, Ada and Clara, are veritable mirror images of one another. They have, indeed, sprung from the same fertile imaginative soil. Like Morton, Milne is a passionate romantic idealist who finds in the captive Ada Lethen his 'ideal.' She is 'his vision of beatification,' 'the goal which his imagination had held before him in a vision of her.' He, too, is an artist, a writer with a 'bent towards romance in his creative efforts.' As Clara is for Morton, Ada is Milne's muse. Such are 'the twin deities of his life. His urge to expression – and this [woman]. Perhaps she was at the bottom of his urge to write.'[60] Ada is, indeed, the spirit of place – of Can-*ada*. Another goddess-figure in touch with elemental forces, Ada is identified with the landscape of ravines and forests (reminiscent of *Wacousta*) that Milne, a devotee of Pan, delights to explore.

In contrast to the static, immobile characters who surround

him, Milne is a Wacousta figure associated with movement and energy. 'A great rover,' we find him reading *Wilhelm Meister's Wanderjahre*, an important work in the tradition to which *Wacousta* is indebted. A dynamic soul guided by an 'impulsive consciousness,' he, like Wacousta or the wandering Perth County protagonist of Reaney's *Colours in the Dark*, is engaged in a search for beauty and freedom; savouring 'the mystery of the earth and skies' instead of grudgingly wresting a living from the soil, he gives himself up to wonder and awe rather than to the Protestant work ethic. Exuberant, imaginative, and intuitive, he also possesses 'a sense of fatality.' Moreover, Milne has that keen appreciation of paradoxical reversals, of break boundaries, which seems to be particularly pronounced in figures from this region: 'Richard Milne had never ceased to admire the peripety of life.'[61]

Artist, rover, lover, outlaw, he too perceives himself as an outcast enmeshed in an ossified materialistic society. Despite his revulsion to everything the Lethens are and represent, he perceives a very Richardsonian magic complicity between himself and that 'comparative stranger,' Mr Lethen. Facing the other man across a fence, a border that blurs identities, Milne thinks 'It was to him as if the ghost of some lost part of himself were speaking. An angleworm twisted in a shiny clod of freshly turned earth, its two halves separate.'[62]

In a manner recalling the fairy-tale motifs of *Wacousta*, Milne tries through his art and his love to wake Sleeping Beauty from the nightmare of 'Souwesto' guilt, denial, repression, and obsession with duty. The literature of this region abounds in metaphors of bursting out, blossoming forth, or, in the Donnelly trilogy, the whole 'John Barleycorn' gamut of ploughing, first shoots, growth, harvest, threshing, distilling. Seasonal oppositions also crop up in abundance in this rural area: the fiery Milne and the frozen Lethens; Morton and De Haldimar, 'fire and ice' (III, 194; 447), the former burning with desire, associated with a forever springtime Eden with its 'luxuriance of vegetation, that might have put to shame the fertility of the soft breeze-nourished valleys of Italy and France' (III, 212–3; 457), the latter, 'all coldness,' presiding over a garrison in late September that is suffering from unusually chilly weather; Donnelly, 'the hot blooded vital summer,' and Cassleigh, 'the cold frost of sterility ... winter, monstrosity.'[63] For Lethen, De Haldimar, and Cassleigh, as for 'Commander' Groome, that 'gravedigger [whose] got the cold hand,' thawing out entails growing close to the sun again.[64]

The startling fact that the life-destroying forces of this region are rarely verbalized alerts us to what is perhaps most disheartening about Souwesto, as writers from Richardson on have had cause to lament. It is a culture in which no attempt is made at articulation; things go left unsaid. Those who feel the urge to expression doubt themselves, feel guilty, and are either ignored, ridiculed, rebuffed, or punished by the silent majority presided over by a *senex*-figure. It is highly significant, of course, that both Milne and Ada are artists upon whom impinges a terrible, dead silence. Richard Milne and Ada Lethen, however, are not the only maimed artists – fictional or historical – attempting to articulate their community who meet with smug resistance from this silent region. The crippling spirit of Lower Warping also manifests itself in Munro's Jubilee, blocking Del's aspirations as a writer and ostracizing her mother as a reckless, wild woman. Davies's Deptford is another Souwesto town inimical to the wonder and the magic that absorb an Eisengrim, a Reginald Morton, or a Richard Milne. It religiously teaches its citizens lessons in emotional and verbal repression. Souwesto artists like Del, Milne, the three thwarted writers in Gibson's *Five Legs*, and Ada belong to a prominent literary family in English-Canadian fiction whose roots we may trace back to Reginald Morton and Clara Beverley: Morton, the impassioned painter and writer of love letters, an artist exiled from a materialistic garrison society; Clara, a lover of paintings and painters who must conceal this passion from a parent who distrusts and hates art, a withdrawn misanthrope who forbids her to develop her own artistic talents and Lethen-like smothers, but does not extinguish, her natural inclinations.

Wacousta is this group's ancestral voice. Indeed, it is as *voice* that he declares himself throughout the work. For the most part, he is heard and not seen. And it is sound that the visually oriented garrison has no defence against. It is the Mortons who, like the Donnellys, feel compelled to tell their stories. Wacousta's life history takes the form of an intimate and emotional three-and-a-half chapter long flashback. In contrast, in chapter 6, volume 3, detailing De Haldimar's secretive past, there is no direct speech from the Governor whatsoever. Perhaps it is because his inner life is so impoverished and his inarticulateness so crippling that the narrator must reveal the taciturn man who cannot, or will not, reveal himself. Wacousta seems never to tire of speaking – his story ends only because Frederick escapes – and, indeed, he begins telling it over again during his second court martial. This time he is silenced by De Haldimar who threatens at one point to cut out his tongue, then simply to gag him – for it is the trickster or the fool who tells the truth. In this verbal sparring match, De Haldimar's dry legal jargon proves unequal to Wacousta's mordant wit and Hermes-like facility with words. The experienced talker quickly effects an ingenious reversal, turning the Governor into the accused and himself into the prosecutor. The Governor's favourite commands seem to be 'Silence!', 'Hold!', and 'No more questions.' When all values are unquestionable, discussion or debate is superfluous.

When De Haldimar breaks his own silence, it is not usually to initiate conversation – he engages in monologues not dialogues – but to issue orders and prohibitions or deliver insults. He snaps at his inferiors in short staccato outbursts as abrasive as cannon shots; the cannon and the telescope are the Governor's symbols as the thunderbolt and the eagle are those of Zeus. His harsh, solemn tones – the mark of his literary descendants – convey the stern severity, the rigidity of manner, which he seems, on all occasions, to think so indispensable to the maintenance of authority. The Governor is as tight-lipped and secretive as Dunstan Ramsay, the anonymous members of the clandestine Secret Society who swarm across the countryside in the Donnelly trilogy, or the paranoid secret society of Christopher Dewdney's *Fovea Centralis*. De Haldimar keeps all information about himself – and Wacousta – top secret; he has sealed off his past even to his children who thirst for anything pertaining to their parents' lives.

He reserves his greatest censure for those among his soldiers the most articulate, and, therefore, – it is to him a therefore – the most troublesome: Everard, both Mortons, Charles, even François, the talkative *aubergiste*, draw his fire. Erskine, the officer modelled on Richardson's grandfather, has the fool's gift for puns and conundrums which vex that younger version of De Haldimar, the literal-minded Delme.

Anyone casting a comparative glance over this region's literature for the past 150 years since *Wacousta*'s publication might not feel inclined to dispute Northrop Frye's 1958 claim that 'southern Ontario, [is] surely one of the most inarticulate communities in human culture.'[65] It is an observation echoed in Eli Mandel's description of Western Ontario as one of 'those barren places of our imagination'[66] and Marian Engel's comment that 'Western Ontario ... taught us ... to use our imagination because it was such a bleak environment.'[67] In his fascinating interviews with Engel, Godfrey, Munro, and Symons, Graeme Gibson explores many of themes just discussed. They lead him and the aforesaid writers to speculate 'that Southwestern Ontario might become a kind of mythical country, like the American South for example.' He finds that a major concern of most of the writers in his own age group 'has been to come to terms with, in many cases very angrily or in an injured way, with what you [Godfrey] just called the United Church, Puritan or whatever it was, the lack of ability to express, the lack of ability to feel, the imposition of rigidity.'[68] Godfrey responds to such 'Protestant reticence and neuroticism' as 'a chamber of horrors' complicated by the fact that we 'grow up in a society that doesn't ever *think* about itself.'[69] Richardson's comments that he may just as well have published in Kamschatka as in Canada, that 'the non-reading Canadians' could not have cared less whether the author was a Canadian or a Turk, gain in resonance from such later statements.

I have been concerned here at some length with threading out a good part of the tapestry of *senex* and *mort-vivants* which Richardson introduces into our fiction, the better to appreciate his place within, and contribution to, the literary tradition of this region. In this larger context, it becomes clear that *Wacousta* and

The Canadian Brothers plumb deep-seated cultural fears and prolonged national anxieties. With surprising regularity, the same cards arise over and over again no matter who shuffles the deck. Hopefully, such diverse allusions to other novels and plays, especially to those from Souwesto, strengthen our handhold through the labyrinth of Richardson's complex work.

Native Canadian Gothic:
Wacousta as Trickster, 'The Enemy of Boundaries'

More trickster energy seems to be stored in the North American soil than in any continent in the world.

ROBERT BLY, *Iron John*

[Hermes] is the god of the unexpected, of luck, of coincidences, of synchronicty... Whenever things seem fixed, rigid, 'stuck,' Hermes introduces fluidity, motion, new beginnings – and the confusion that almost inevitably preceeds new beginnings.

ARIANNA STASSINOPOULOS, *The Gods of Greece*[70]

Wacousta is an amalgam of border legend and historical personages as well as of gothic and Romantic hero-villains. Wacousta also bears a curious resemblance to the intriguing figure of Trickster in North American Indian mythology. Typical trickster motifs appear throughout the novel. Richardson, we may speculate, was conversant with this body of stories about a shape-shifter in whom opposites merge and who recklessly blurs the boundaries between all manner of things.

This seems possible, given his (alleged) Indian ancestry and his half-Indian relatives; his intimate familiarity with the numerous tribes of the border region attested to in such non-fiction works as 'The North American Indian'; his friendship with John Norton (aka Chief Teyoninhokorawen and the man from 'Wagousta') and with his lifelong hero Tecumseh who took a special interest in this 'product of the mingling of the two races';[71] his knowledge of Indian languages and their circle-square imagery; his contempt for white Christian missionaries who dismiss the Indians as 'pagans'; and his account in an article for *The Literary Garland* of the strong pull to return to the wilderness and live among the Indians. That *Wacousta* may be indebted to local sources of native Canadian gothic should not, then, strike us as inconceivable. As Margaret Atwood states, 'it's not surprising that a large number of Canadian monsters have their origin in native Indian and Eskimo myths.'[72]

The Trickster, with commentaries by Karl Kerényi and C.G. Jung, is Paul Radin's classic study of this ambiguous figure. The anthropologist writes that the most important of the Indian's heroic myth-cycles are connected with Trickster, the Twins, and the Two Boys. The former is a being 'who is always wandering, who is always hungry, who is not guided by normal conceptions of good or evil, who is either playing tricks on people or having them played on him and who is highly sexed.' Opposites meet and merge in him in unpredictable ways. The trickster is above all *'the spirit of disorder, the enemy of boundaries'* (author's italics). No better description of Wacousta could be found. Kerényi's comments serve as a gloss on the confrontation between the orderly European garrison obsessed with fixed borders and rigid demarcations and the gigantic, trickster-like Wacousta who defies borders of all sorts and leaps over walls and abysses with ease:

> ... nothing demonstrates the meaning of the all-controlling social order more impressively than the religious recognition of that which evades this order, in a figure who is the exponent and personification of the body: never wholly subdued, ruled by lust and hunger, for ever running into pain and injury, cunning and stupid in action. Disorder belongs to the totality of life, and the spirit of this disorder is the trickster. His function ... is to add disorder to order and so make a whole, to render possible, within the fixed bounds of what is permitted, an experience of what is not permitted.[73]

Trickster mythology admonishes us, in the interest of wholeness, to let down the walls, to assimilate the dark or night-side of consciousness, however strong the perceived threat of apparent disorder. Such disorder is reflected in the trickster's primary traits, his restless wandering and especially his unbridled sexuality. 'The phallus is Trickster's double and alter ego,' avers Kerényi, linking him as do Bly, Moore, and Bolen with Dionysus and Hermes, both of whom disregard borders and are represented by the phallus; 'Dionysian ecstasy had the same function as the trickster myth: it abolished the boundaries, not least the boundaries of sex.'[74] In *The Shaman's Doorway*, Larsen notes that the deity 'classically associated with orgiastic sexuality, and with the breaking of traditions and boundaries is Dionysus. And it seems to be Dionysus who is stealing the stage from our old aloof *Senex* God-image these days.'[75] Wacousta possesses and is often possessed by a strong sexual force. 'Wacousta has a highly developed sexuality,' writes Margot Northey; 'the sexual atmosphere is startling considering the age and society in which the book was written.'[76] Pronouncing Wacousta 'a sexual prodigy,' L.R. Early finds the lover in the Scottish Garden of Eden 'overwhelmed with sexual adoration.'[77]

Richard De Mille in commenting on Carlos Castaneda's writing declares that 'Trickster is not guided by conventional morality ... Trickster symbolizes rebellion.'[78] He often disrupts protocol. He erases the line between the real and the unreal. Notes Kerényi, Trickster 'operates outside the fixed bounds of custom and law.'[79] One expression of this rebelliousness is his inordinate sexuality; another is the laughter, humour, and irony which permeate everything he does. As George Bowering claims of Sheila Watson's Coyote, Richardson likewise connects his trickster figure 'more with fear than fun.'[80]

Both Coyote and Wacousta arouse terror, mystery, and a brooding sense of nameless menace; they tempt others to despair and seduce them to their deaths. Wacousta's raucous 'Ha! Ha! Ha!' reverberates throughout the romance. It marks those moments when he has confounded the garrison's attempts at order, deflated its pretentious formalities, or ridiculed the onerous obligations of its moribund social order. As we have seen, through his verbal agility during the final court-martial episode, he effects a characteristic reversal, accusing De Haldimar of being the real villain and presenting himself as the unfortunate victim of his rival's machinations.

In 'On the Psychology of the Trickster Figure,' Jung associates Trickster with the doppelgänger, the shadow, and the unconscious. He examines 'experiences of split or double personality' where 'the split-off personality is not just a random one, but stands in a complementary or compensatory relationship to the ego personality. It is a personification of traits of character which are sometimes worse and sometimes better than those the ego personality possesses ... The trickster is a primitive "cosmic" being of *divine-animal* nature, on the one hand superior to man because of his superhuman qualities, and on the other hand inferior to him because of his unreason and unconsciousness.' Those destructive, unheroical traits declare themselves in 'grotesque scurrility' and in 'the unpredictable behaviour of the trickster, of his pointless orgies of destruction' indicative of an 'extremely primitive state of mind.'[81]

Wacousta's excessive treatment of Everard and Clara de Haldimar suggests 'not only the dire extent to which the revenge of Wacousta could be carried, but the actual and gratuitous cruelty of his nature' (III, 187; 442). As De Mille observes, 'Trickster wreaks havoc wherever he goes, destroying lives and making the innocent suffer.'[82] George Bowering, referring to Gary Snyder's account of the passage of the Coyote figure into North American literature, states that 'He is a kind of person, but not one who can be assimilable to the conscious and rational mind.'[83]

This is also Jung's emphasis. For 'unsuspecting modern man,' the trickster motif is manifest whenever 'he feels himself at the mercy of annoying accidents which thwart his will and his actions with apparently malicious intent. He then speaks of "hoodoos" and "ginxes" ... Here the trickster is represented by countertendencies in the unconscious, and in certain cases by a sort of second personality ... I called it the *shadow* ... Radin's trickster cycle preserves the shadow in its pristine mythological form.'[84] As such, Trickster is the perfect shadow for a garrison culture fearful of the present and of the wilderness and clinging to memories of an ideal European order. As Jung notes, 'Anyone who belongs to a sphere of culture that seeks the perfect state somewhere in the past must feel very queerly indeed when confronted by the figure of the trickster.'[85] De Haldimar and the garrison project their shadow onto Wacousta and the Indian. Priding themselves on their reason and restraint, the British soldiers all too frequently lapse into a civilized barbarity indistinguishable from the savagery they decry in their dusky adversaries. Inside them, too, the Shadow Warrior takes aim. When Wacousta is finally captured by the regiment, 'many and various were the opinions expressed as to the manner of death he should be made to suffer ... One was for impaling him alive, and setting him up to rot on the platform above the gate. Another for blowing him from the muzzle of a twenty-four pounder, into the centre of the first band of Indians that approached ... A third was of opinion he ought to be chained to the top of the flag-staff, as a target, to be shot at with arrows only, contriving never to touch a mortal part ... Each devised some new death – proposed some new torture' (III, 306–7; 508).

'The trickster is a collective shadow figure,' explains Jung, touching on concerns such as the tensions between opposites and ironic reversals which preoccupy Richardson. 'Outwardly people are more or less civilized but inwardly they are still primitives ... The conflict between the two dimensions of consciousness is simply an expression of the polaristic structure of the psyche, which like any other energetic system is dependent on the tension of opposites. That is also why there are no general psychological propositions which could not just as well be reversed.' Garrison cultures prove highly susceptible to the appearance of a trickster figure. Though 'so-called civilized man has forgotten the trickster,' his wild energy may be a potent source of renewal and rejuvenation for those leading cramped, conventional lives.[86] Trickster is all impulse, Wacousta 'all enthusiasm, carelessness, impetuosity and independence' (III, 194; 447). 'He wills nothing consciously. At all times he is constrained to behave as he does from impulses over which he has no control. He knows neither good nor evil ...

He possesses no values, moral or social, is at the mercy of his passions and appetites, yet through his actions all values come into being.'[87] Radin's portrait echoes Frye's description of the Byronic hero or the Romantic version of the natural man, one who eludes all moral categories just as nature itself does and who cannot be simply condemned or accepted. Like Davies's wolfish Eisengrim, Wacousta nurses an unappeasable psychic hunger. It is 'revenge, the exclusive passion of the gods' (III, 276; 491) that he hungers for, even as in the Highlands it had been love. The apparently amoral, animal vitality of nature which Trickster embodies is reflected in the fact that he is frequently identified with specific animals, usually the wolf or the coyote, but also the raven, the hare, the fox, and the spider. In *Legends of My People the Great Ojibway*, Norval Morriseau says that the trickster 'Nanabojou called all the wolves his blood brothers.'[88] In *Sacred Legends of the Sandy Lake Cree*, we learn that 'Ma-heegun, the wolf ... is the little brother of Wee-sa-kay-jac, they often travel together in the forest.'[89]

The lycanthropic Wacousta is, of course, associated with wolves. In particular, he is identified with his animal companion, the wolf-dog Onondato. The Indians are described by the Europeans as howling hell-hounds or 'blood-hounds on their scent' (II, 43; 181). 'There is an instinct about me,' says Wacousta, 'enabling me to discover a De Haldimar, as a hound does the deer, by scent' (III, 290; 499). One of the most frequent similes applied to both Wacousta and De Haldimar, Indian and European, is 'cunning, like the fox' (II, 66; 195). In the work's opening pages, Wacousta is mistaken for a wolf. Charles de Haldimar, addressing Everard Valletort, fancies he sees a shadowy blur which may be 'a stray Indian dog devouring the carcass of the wolf you shot yesterday.' 'Be it dog or devil' (I, 49–50; 29), Everard fires and wounds Wacousta. Later, on the fatal bridge, Frederick and Everard see a shapeless object which turns out to be Onondato devouring Halloway's remains. 'The wolf-dog, whose eyes glared like two burning coals through the surrounding gloom' (II, 41; 180), resembles its master who has just been presented as a shadowy creature whose only visible feature is his 'glaring eye' (II, 30; 197).

Wacousta is the leader of a pack of wolf-like figures – many of them doubles and tricksters – prowling the pages of Canadian literature. They overrun Atwood's *oeuvre* and appear in Mitchell's *Who Has Seen the Wind* in the form of wild, wolf-like Young Ben, Brian's double; like Wacousta, Tay John, and Robert Ross, Young Ben is identified with coyotes, Indians, swift movement across open space, and border crossings of various kinds. Like the feral Judith West in Ross's *As For Me and My House* or the great wolf-monster Eisengrim of the Deptford Trilogy, these passionate outcasts are often romantic idealists of deep feeling gifted with powerful imaginations and voices. Interestingly, those works which constitute, in part, an exposition of the puritan conscience, are the ones haunted by wolf-like apparitions nipping at the respectable heels of De Haldimar-like incarnations of authority. This doubling of ostracized wolf-women and wolf-men with establishment manticores and moral monsters is a struggle of 'brothers' first dramatized in *Wacousta*.

'Basically,' notes Radin, despite Trickster's symbolic appearance as wolf or coyote, he 'possesses no well-defined and fixed form ... he is primarily an inchoate being of undetermined proportions, a figure foreshadowing the shape of man.'[90] In *Ojibway Heritage*, Basil Johnston writes that 'Nanabush was essentially an incorporeal being, even when he assumed a physical form.' Endowed with 'the powers of transformation,' 'Nanabush was a paradox.'[91] Jung, too, speaks of Trickster's 'powers as a shape-shifter, his dual nature, half animal, half divine'; he is reminded of certain phenomena in the field of parapsychology, notably the malicious tricks of poltergeists.[92] More often than not, Wacousta is perceived as little more than a shadowy blur, an unreal, malevolent spectre. A fleeting, indistinct shape, he seems to change magically before the strained eyes of the terrorized Europeans. Materializing soundlessly at the side of his enemies at unpredictable moments, Wacousta emerges seemingly from nowhere. This happens to both De Haldimar and his son. When Frederick first encounters the spectral being at the bottom of the border river abyss, he is aware only of a nightmarish hand growing out of the darkness that suddenly grabs him with all the force of an Iron John.

A nexus of transformation and illusion, the ravine resembles 'that world of primordial darkness where everything that is characteristic of the trickster can happen.'[93]

> Clinging to the bushes that lined the face of the precipitous descent, he managed once more to gain the bed of the ravine ... Scarcely conscious of what he did, Captain de Haldimar ... fancied he felt the hot breathing of human life upon his cheek. With a sickly sensation of fear, he turned to satisfy himself whether it was not an illusion of his heated imagination. What, however, was his dismay when he beheld bending over him a dark and heavy form, the outline of which alone was distinguishable in the deep gloom in which the ravine remained enveloped! ... he felt a powerful hand upon his chest; and, with as much facility as if he had been a child, was he raised by that invisible hand to his feet. (II, 189–93; 261–3)

Wacousta's invisibility is often linked to the fact that he runs and leaps with a speed deemed superhuman. Such a flowing ease of movement is characteristic of Trickster, that 'double of the divine trickster of Greek mythology, Hermes.' The patron of athletes, orators, thieves, and wanderers, he is the swift-footed messenger who conducts souls of the dead to Hades – as Wacousta conducts unwilling Europeans to a Canadian underworld. While Wacousta easily grabs others, he no less than Hermes (the Roman Mercury) is as ungraspable as a ball of mercury or quicksilver. Sometimes equated with Satan, 'this Herculean Hermes in his American Indian manifestations' also 'disregards boundaries.'[94] As Robert Lecker has commented, Wacousta defies 'the boundaries between language, race and culture.'[95] Called the God of Significant Passage by Murray Stein, Hermes is for Jean Bolen the god of the threshold, 'the archetype present "betwixt and between" psychological phases ... a liminal god, present in the transitional space.'[96] All the experiences of coincidences, simultaneity, and synchronicity in this story and in *The Monk Knight* may reflect the magical presence of Hermes whom Bolen and Bly explicitly link with such phenomena. Hermes and Trickster are also of key importance in the tale of Iron John, and Robert Moore discusses them in connection with the archetype of the magus or magician. In the terms of my study, Hermes is the border blur and break boundary god par excellence.

Seemingly uncontained by uniform, continuous space, Wacousta appears and disappears with uncanny suddenness, as if by magic. The instantaneous quality of his movements are such that he almost seems to 'teleport,' to borrow a term used to describe the futuristic Hermes figures to be found in science fiction or speculative fiction: 'Wacousta no sooner saw her sink into the arms of her lover, than with that agility for which he was remarkable he was again on his feet, and stood in the next instant at her side' (III, 189; 444); 'The form glided hastily past, brushing the tree with its garments ... and clearing, at a single bound, the belt of underwood that divided the encampment from the tall forest, stood suddenly among the group of anxious and expectant chiefs' (II, 159; 245).

'Trickster is metamorphic, appearing in countless guises,' states Richard De Mille in *Castaneda's Journey*. In his study of what may be the most widely known modern trickster series – the never-ending saga of Don Juan and Carlos Castaneda, another American marriage of males – De Mille sees Trickster symbolically as 'man changing from one character to another with little stability or selfhood.'[97] Castaneda's language is instructive. In these psychic frontier 'tales of power,' Coyote-Trickster, renowned as 'a master of equilibrium,' instructs a rather obtuse, Sancho Panza-like sorcerer's apprentice in 'the balancing arts of the warrior.' Carlos, like everyone, has a 'double' or 'a twin.' He must transcend the limits of reason and give up 'the nagging desire to control everything.' 'Transporting himself over great distances' is accomplished 'by making the self and the world fluid.' Once conscious of the 'notion of his duality' and capable of expanding his identity beyond 'the boundaries in which it is contained,' he will grasp the double-hook nature of existence: 'the art of a warrior is to balance the terror of being a man with the wonder of being a man.'[98] Similar images appear in Richardson's work and other trickster tales from Lynn Andrews to the Greeks.

Morton/Wacousta is nothing if not metamorphic, splintering into myriad fragmented and discontinuous selves since his descent from the mountain-top Eden. In the fluid New World milieu, his identity is so slippery he is described in a variety of conflicting epithets: 'the terrible Warrior of the Fleur de Lis' (II, 80; 203); 'the black warrior' (II, 129; 228); 'the 'white warrior' (II, 74; 199); 'The warrior of the pale face, and the friend of the Ottawa chief' (II, 75; 202); 'a chief of the red skins' and 'a tall spy' (II, 73; 199); 'this terrible and mysterious being' (II, 74; 200); 'monster' (III, 173; 435); etc. There seems to be no end to his names.

As a figure in whom opposites meet and blur, Trickster is the *personification* of ambivalence.' Embodying 'human ambivalence and social ambiguity,' associated with 'reversals and risks of identity,' 'the concrete image of the trickster is ... transformed into the problem of injustice.'[99] In Cree mythology, according to *Indian Legends of Canada*, one of the sayings of Wisakedjak is that 'everything has two names.'[100] Basil Johnston, in *Ojibway Heritage* (Ojibway-speaking people include the tribes featured in *Wacousta*), writes 'that there are two aspects to everything, appearing as opposites ... life and being are paradoxical.'[101] 'As found among the North American Indians,' reports Radin, 'Trickster is at one and the same time creator and destroyer, giver and negator, he who dupes and who is always duped himself.'[102]

Stories about Trickster are often structured around the struggle-of-brothers motif which obsesses Richardson's imagination. Kerényi discusses Hercules and Prometheus, both of whom Richardson associates with Wacousta. Several of the North American tricksters closely resemble Prometheus. 'Prometheus has affinities with the trickster because the cunning he practices on Zeus overreaches itself and turns into stupidity, personified by his own brother ... The profound affinity between these two figures is expressed in the fact that they are brothers. One might almost say that in them a single primitive being, sly and stupid at once, has been split into a duality: Prometheus the Forethinker, Epimetheus the belated Afterthinker.' Such 'a dual being,' he who dupes others and who is duped himself, is found in Wacousta-De

Haldimar.[103] Tricks, disguises, secrets, duplicity, illusion, betrayal, and deception are fundamental to the development of Richardson's story. They are intimately linked to the struggle-of-brothers theme.

Wacousta, likewise, displays his 'Indian ingenuity' (III, 342; 523), his ability to get out of a tight spot – and get others into it –throughout this struggle. The ingenious escape-artist slips into the fort undetected and escapes uncaptured three times. Appropriately, he is caught only when the garrison troops play a trick on him: they hide under the borderland bridge which he is duped into believing unguarded. Wacousta, in turn, cleverly outwits his captors; playing on De Haldimar's anxiety over his reputation, he arranges for his hands to be untied, then turns the flagstaff which is to be his gallows into an escape route. Of course, the famous historical ruse of the Indian lacrosse game, a 'wily stratagem' (II, 175; 253) devised by Ponteac to lull the suspicions of the fort he intends to capture, is itself the central trick around which the story is woven. Wacousta revolves around tricks performed in a hall of mirrors.

The British prove equally adept at playing their parts in this charade. Foiling his enemies with their own weapons of cunning and deceit, matching 'plot' with 'counter-plot' (II, 48; 185), the Governor and his regiment dupe the Ottawas into believing they have been duped in order to deceive the Indians into believing that they, in turn, have been duped previously by the French and Wacousta into the belief that the British are their dire enemies! A tangled web indeed! Its strands extend throughout The Canadian Brothers: the very first incident revolves around another 'stratagem' implemented by Wacousta's cunning descendant, Desborough. That American frontiersman tries to outsmart De Haldimar's great-grandson, Gerald Grantham, the Canadian garrison officer, during the War of 1812 by effecting the safe passage of an American boat down the Detroit River. Gerald, like Frederick, has overheard his adversary's secret plans and likewise pretends to acquiesce in his enemy's suggestions. 'Resolved to appear the dupe they purposed to make me,' his own trickery mirrors 'the rascality of those who, imagining me to be their dupe, were soon to become mine ... a result so opposite to that which they anticipated.'[104]

In another characteristic reversal, Trickster is also 'a forerunner of the saviour' even as 'the individual shadow contains within it the seed of an enantiodromia, of a conversion into its opposite.' Everything flows into its opposite: the apparent threat becomes the means of salvation, breakdown becomes breakthrough. Both Mortons state that they are not what they seem. Paradoxically, as Jung observes, 'the wounded wounder is the agent of healing.'[105] Though striking a satanic pose, Wacousta is, like Lucifer, a light-bearer, spotting gaps in the garrison mentality. He floodlights a vast murky area within the fort itself, exposing its shortcomings and the secrets of its self-appointed bearer of rationality and justice. The Governor's insistence on absolute secrecy in the interests of 'national security' is shown to be only an excuse for a shadow king's own non-accountability and constitutes a personal shielding from the public eye.

Behind an unprepossessing exterior, Trickster hides a valuable treasure. Considering the trickster as a parallel of the individual shadow, the first thing Jung finds standing behind the shadow is the anima. Behind the monstrous Wacousta lies the edenic dream of union with Eve and the land. The recognition of the night-side of consciousness, of the shadow, precedes reintegration; 'the problem constellated by the shadow is answered on the plane of the anima, that is, through relatedness' – what we've seen Bly call 'partnership-thought' and Freeman 'duetting.' Yet a man like De Haldimar, unable to admit his weaknesses to himself or to his family, will also admit of no kinship with Wacousta or the wilderness; the suggestion of any connection to his shadow encounters fierce resistance, as Halloway, Everard, and Charles quickly realize. Balance and wholeness depend upon cultivating the 'feminine' component of the psyche, yet 'it is practically impossible to get a man who is afraid of his own femininity to understand what is meant by the anima.'[106]

Trickster is an ambiguous saviour, embracing loss as well as gain, darkness as well as light, energy as well as order. For Robert Kroetsch, the opposites merge, finally, in the artist-as-

Trickster: the artist 'in the long run, given the choice of being God or Coyote, will, most mornings, choose to be Coyote: he lets in the irrational along with the rational, the pre-moral along with the moral.'[107] Jesus himself makes a similar choice in Rudy Wiebe's *My Lovely Enemy*. We seem to be moving in these later works toward the notion of God given by that sophisticated primitive, C.G. Jung, a few days before his death: 'To this day God is the name by which I designate all things which cross my willful path violently and recklessly, all things which upset my subjective views, plans and intentions and change the course of my life for better or worse.'[108] Or, to quote a lyric from the aptly named *Double Fantasy*, an album by inveterate shape-shifter John Lennon, 'Life is what happens to you / While you're busy / Making other plans.'[109]

More Gothic Outlaws and Border Wolves

[Richardson's] is the fashion in which cultures mythically, rather than historically, handle violence ... I am thinking of the world of Grimm's Fairy Tales, where giants bite off heads while kings chop them off.

DENNIS DUFFY, *Gardens, Covenants, Exiles*[110]

Westbrook, the Outlaw; or, The Avenging Wolf: An American Border Tale (1851), Richardson's last published novel, marks a return to the setting of his birthplace, and features another gothic border monster prowling the wilds of 'Souwesto.' As in other works set in British North America, we are confronted with a grotesque world of shock and terror and shattered hopes, a chamber of horrors reminiscent of the Jacobean tragedians. For Reaney, the story affords 'an archetypal vision of our province's cultural problems.'[111] The tale emerges out of historical incidents such as 'The Battle of the Thames' in the War of 1812 and local legends surrounding the notorious Andrew Westbrook, a farmer who lived near 'the town of Delaware in the London District of Western Canada' and who caught the attention of Richardson's relatives, the Askins.[112] Like Ondaatje, Richardson is again drawn to those historical figures who live on that edge where there is no social fuel and who cast an eerie gothic shadow over the province.

Given Richardson's stressful situation in New York City as – literally – a starving artist during the last years of his life and the serial format in which *Westbrook* first appeared, it is not surprising that it reads more like the hastily sketched blueprint for a much larger and complex work. Like a Wacousta stripped of his romantic sensibility, Westbrook is tall, muscular, uncouth, and robust. There is an expression of mixed cunning and revenge in his eyes. Recalling Desborough, he is 'one of the those wayward and restless spirits – half American, half British – who acknowledged allegiance to neither government, but were too glad, as disappointment, ambition or interest impelled them, to espouse the side of either.' Later, after his atrocities are made public, both sides refuse to acknowledge this border hybrid as a citizen. 'The victim of some of the persons in authority ... he had sworn unmitigated hatred' to the British; he is reported for insubordination to one of Souwesto's father figures, Colonel Talbot.[113] Westbrook feels slighted when the command of the local militia is given to the genteel Captain Stringer (also based on a historical figure) who is the fiancé of his eldest daughter Marian; the grim Westbrook eventually revenges himself by taking their baby and abandoning it in a wolf's den in the dreaded 'forty mile' woods. Pared down to its essentials, *Westbrook* begins to read like a very distressing fairy-tale.

The ogre imprisons the Captain's sister, the beautiful Emily Stringer, in a decaying shanty on the forested banks of the Thames. There he rapes and later murders her. Like Gerald in *The Canadian Brothers*, Captain Stringer, his sister and wife dead, becomes morose and taciturn and hopeless about the future. Detected in his villainy, Westbrook sets out for the American territory across the border. As a spy for the American forces, the outlaw returns to the dark woods, murders Stringer who has just located his lost child, and is himself savagely killed by the enormous she-wolf who has raised 'that inhumanized child.'[114] The wolf has been howling fatefully throughout and has eluded the savage hunter; it has more maternal feelings than Westbrook has paternal ones. But though Romulus and Remus, the twin founders of Rome, were similarly suckled by a she-wolf, this nameless wolf-child of idiotic expression will be the founder of nothing but chaos. Richardson's *Wacousta* tells the story of a gigantic wolf-man; his canon ends with this ominous wolf-child, an apt gothic symbol for the expression of Souwesto angst.

Westbrook's character recalls that of the brutal and monstrous Desborough. Both are border outlaws, traitors, spies, and hunters, openly disdainful of authority and consumed with an inhuman revenge. Like Wacousta, they are associated with the elemental forces of an untamed land. Westbrook shares Desborough's desire for utter seclusion from society. Just as Desborough seeks to tarnish Gerald's reputation, the Iago-like Westbrook, denied promotion in the militia, blackens Stringer's name. Where Desborough murders Major Grantham and Henry, Westbrook brings about the destruction of the respectable Stringer family. Both outlaws are associated with the incest motif; they violate the sanctity of the family so dear to such characters as the Canadian brothers. The atmosphere of *Westbrook* is as sexually charged and violent as that of Davies's nearby Deptford, likewise the locus of incest and rape, or the smouldering family farms in the fiction of Grove and Matt Cohen.

As in *Wacousta* and its sequel, there is a journey out of the civilized world into the nightmare realm of the strange and the terrifying. In the company of Westbrook who has been sent to retrieve her from a convent, Emily Stringer leaves the flower-adorned cottages of Montreal and descends into 'the far west,' 'the wilderness of Upper Canada.' At the heart of this 'semi-barbarous province' is the demonic 'forty mile' woods in which Westbrook's hut is concealed. After crossing the Ottawa river en route to Kingston, 'the comparative wilderness before them announced that they had reached the line which divides Upper from Lower Canada. What a dreary prospect!' The thinly settled wilderness is devoid of all signs of life save where 'some desperately courageous settler was making a herculean attempt to reduce his patch of forest to something like a state of culture.'[115]

In 'a lonely and desolate part of what are called the Highlands, not very far from York, and remarkable for a very steep and dangerous descent into a short valley or ravine,' the licentious Westbrook tries to force himself upon the innocent Emily. She is rescued by the monk Anselmo with whom she has fallen in love in Montreal. Ironically, the Frenchman is disguised as a woodsman; that, and his height and bearing, recall Westbrook with whom he is confused by several characters. A very pale shadow of 'The Monk Knight,' Anselmo has left the church for Emily; he is explicitly connected with Byron's Corsair through the inclusion in the text of the line 'Link'd with one virtue and a thousand crimes.' This is not the only instance of a blurring of identity: Emily whom Westbrook rapes resembles Sophia, his daughter, with whom 'the brutal tyrant' has probably committed incest.[116] Parallels also exist between Anselmo and Minister Winslow who also loves Emily; the relationship of Emily and Anselmo echoes that of Stringer and Marian.

The naive Anselmo, who compares himself and Emily to Abelard and Heloise, expects the Upper Canadian bush to be a romantic forest like that in which the American lovers revel in Richardson's Chicago trilogy (*Hardscrabble, Wau-Nan-Gee,* and its unfinished sequel); the shattering of such expectations becomes a recurring motif throughout Canadian fiction. 'In the forest, we shall be free – no limit shall be there – the grass mantled earth, the womb from which we sprung, shall be our couch,' declares Anselmo in Cooperian accents. The 'forty mile' woods, of course, becomes their common prison and tomb, for Anselmo is also murdered by Westbrook. Like Ellen who alters and degenerates after crossing over the border river with Wacousta, Emily also undergoes a horrific metamorphosis in the bush with Westbrook, her hair turning white overnight. 'This dense and pestiferous wood was as dreary a piece of wood as ever appalled the enterprise, or cursed the vision of the stoutest-hearted explorer ... the forest ... was dense, dark and overrun at the edges with fallen and rotting trees – noxious and creeping vines – and loathsome fungi, from the midst of which the dulled heart of the traveller expected at each moment to see erecting their hideous crests every description of venomous reptile. It was one continuous, low and foetid extent of unwholesome-looking marsh, every mile of which appeared to the unexperienced eye to be tripled, at least.'[117]

'A species of spell, inspired by the lugubrious character of that seemingly interminable swamp' descends upon all who wander through it, Indian and white alike.[118] This recalls the New World wilderness in *Wacousta*. Richardson seems intent on giving the Ontario bush the same resonance as the haunted Black Forest of the German romancers or the dark landscapes of fairy-tales in which evil is as omnipresent as virtue. As Duffy shrewdly observes of Richardson's uses of enchantment, 'His is the fashion in which cultures mythically, rather than historically, handle violence. As in folklore, it does not intrude upon life but remains one of its conditions. I am thinking of the world of Grimm's Fairy Tales, where giants bite off heads while kings chop them off.' Richardson, however, 'so exuberantly breaks every canon of taste' that his blood-curdling tales of horror quite overwhelmed his readers in the 1850s.[119] As Beasley opines, *Westbrook* 'was its own worst enemy owing to its graphic description of a subject which the leaders of American society regarded as morally subversive.'[120]

Interestingly enough, the gothic shadows recede when Richardson leaves the Souwesto setting and depicts the American landscape in *Hardscrabble* and *Wau-Nan-Gee*. These are two of the four major fictional works he published after *The Canadian Brothers* in 1840. (*The Monk Knight* and *Westbrook* are the other two.) I pass over them briefly here since they were consciously designed by a very needy Richardson to cater to an American audience and because they lack the resonance and complexity of his earlier novels. After leaving an indifferent Canada in 1849, Richardson published his two short historical tales in the United States: *Hardscrabble; or, The Fall of Chicago: A Tale of Indian Warfare* (1851) and *Wau-Nan-Gee; or, The Massacre at Chicago* (1852). These were inspired by eyewitness accounts of the attack by native peoples on the American Fort Dearborn at the outset of the Border War of 1812. Richardson is deliberately writing for an American audience; absent are the familiar border dichotomies and the gothic atmosphere of his works set in Upper Canada or British North America. Unprepossessing volumes lacking the sophistication of works like *Wacousta*, they do reveal that sure knowledge of American social mythology which lies behind the creation of the Desboroughs in *The Canadian Brothers*. This is particularly evident in the portraits of several American frontiersmen, including Captain Wells, the impetuous hero Ronayne, and the heroine's father.

The latter is a suspected criminal who lights out for the territory, the 'Far West' of the remote Chicago wilderness, to escape the forces of the law. A restless, resourceful individual pursuing solitude, Heywood is animated by 'his desire of isolation from everything that could be called society.' A hunter, he travels with the Indians in search of game. His daughter, Maria Heywood, abjures the crowded cities for 'the wild but beautiful romantic country.' Unlike the forbidding bush in *Wacousta*, 'the boundless wilderness offered health and freedom.'[121] Obviously, we have entered Cooper territory. There are even Good and Bad Indians, the noble Wau-nan-gee and Pee-to-tum, an inferior version of Magua in *The Last of the Mohicans*.

The hero is the rebellious young Ensign Ronayne, the perfect match for the outlaw's independent daughter. As is not the case in *Wacousta*, the forest solitude nurtures rather than extinguishes their love. A fiery and chivalrous Southerner, Ronayne chafes against military prudence and is respected by the Indians. Unlike Richardson's silently obedient Canadian and British garrison officers, the American soldiers and their officers are openly defiant of the authority of their commanding officer, Captain Headley. They unhesitatingly voice their dissent, repeatedly challenging his command and displaying a contemptuousness not found in their compliant Canadian counterparts. Headley is a strict disciplinarian who recalls De Haldimar; however, he becomes more relaxed and affectionate in the sequel, seeking advice from his stronger and more intelligent wife. Richardson remains unswayed by the American passion for a marriage of males; his imagination still pursues the possibility of a viable heterosexual relationship between the races which received first statement in

Wacousta's Frederick-Oucanasta-Madeline triangle. Wau-nan-gee, 'strange, wildly-loving, fascinating and incomprehensible,' falls in love with Maria.[122]

Not unexpectedly in a Richardson novel, the Indian and the defiant Ronayne mirror one another, although this motif is not rigged out with the usual variations and subtleties. At one point, they are dressed in identical Indian attire and peer at each other through a window. Maria, significantly Richardson's only strictly fictitious character, flees with Wau-nan-gee into the wilderness after the deaths of her husband and parents. The final instalment of this unfinished trilogy was to have been the story of this flight; again, we see Richardson's interest in closing the gulf between an immigrant and an indigenous mentality. Why wasn't it written? David Beasley's conjecture may be correct: '*Hardscrabble* and *Wau-Nan-Gee* created phenomenal interest; it appears, therefore, that the only hindrance to the publication of the third novel was its subject matter.'[123] Perhaps this type of union that did not find expression in North American terms was displaced into the more abstract east-west terms of *The Monk Knight* – only to be greeted with shock and anger.

By this point, the reader will not be surprised to learn that I regard gothic Southwestern Ontario as a kind of mythical country and Richardson as the first writer to give voice to the fascinating world of Souwesto and of the enigmatic Canadian-American border region.

CHAPTER SIX

No End in Sight:
Seeing Double Hooks, Haunted by
No Lack of Ghosts ... and
Making Richardson Safe

I keep coming back to the feeling that there does seem to be such a thing as an imaginative continuum, and that writers are conditioned in their attitudes by their predecessors, or by the cultural climate of their predecessors, whether there is conscious influence or not.

NORTHROP FRYE, 'Conclusion to a *Literary History of Canada*'

The margin or border is the postmodern space *par excellence* ... recent works by Robert Kroetsch, Margaret Atwood, Susan Swan, Rudy Wiebe, Timothy Findley, and, perhaps most obviously, Michael Ondaatje attest to the attraction of boundaries and margins as sites of novelistic investigation.

LINDA HUTCHEON, *The Canadian Postmodern*

To acknowledge the past is not necessarily to be bound by it or to wish to repeat it; it is to recognize the continuing shaping of the set of tendencies which supplies a context for composition in the present... In this sense traditions also exist only in retrospect; they are the mind's acknowledgment of connection and continuity all the while the pen is spelling out disparities and differences in the present and celebrating the possibility of literary distinction.

Continuity/discontinuity: connection/fragmentation.

W.H. NEW, *Dreams of Speech and Violence* [1]

'Fifty years ago,' observes Margaret Atwood in her 1977 essay 'Canadian Monsters: Some Aspects of the Supernatural in Canadian Fiction,' 'this was Canada, or rather this was the image of it which everyone seemed to believe in: a dull place, devoid of romantic interest and rhetorical excesses, with not enough blood spilled on the soil to make it fertile, and above all, ghostless.'[2] For our first professional native-born poet-novelist, however, Canada was haunted by no lack of ghosts. Richardson anticipates Atwood's notion that important images and archetypes in Canadian literature as well as deep-seated cultural fears are tied to the concepts of doubles, monsters, and ghosts, gothic creatures who roam the blurred borders of nightmare. Over a mercurial twenty-nine year writing career, Richardson experimented with the romance form, especially the descent narrative, and created a strange and marvellous cast of characters and settings: giants, witches, vampires, spectres, cannibals, demon-lovers, shadow kings, *mort-vivants*, tricksters, wolf-men and snake-women, babies raised by wolves, titanic figures who celebrate dionysian sexual energy and merge ecstatically into one another, spiral paths leading up to mountain-top Edens, a pet deer named 'Fidelity,' mazes, bottomless abysses haunted by grieving wild men with wolf-dogs, prosaic factually-detailed garrisons lost in fantastic space, bloody battles between cultures, fateful coincidences, carnivalesque inversions and contradictions, bizarre metamorphoses, halls of mirrors, stories-within-stories, doppelgängers ...

As our first national prose epic composed of *Wacousta* and *The Canadian Brothers* testifies, our story, riddled with uncertainties and anxieties, ambiguities and duplicities, is far from unexciting. For Richardson, this was both a country with and without a mythology. He set out both to map and imaginatively to construct myths of origins and beginnings, possible identities, and hidden cultural selves for a people who have been careless with or inattentive to their own cultural tradition. Berating Ontario for being indifferent enough 'to let Richardson starve to death, an exile in New York,' James Reaney, who imaginatively adapted Richardson's epic to the stage, shares Atwood's view that as a culture we are not as flat and lacking in resonance as we were once led to believe. Richardson, he notes, 'always had far more American readers than Canadian ones; yet, you know, he didn't want that. He wished for a "National Canadian Literature" – his phrase, and he also tried to get his history of the 1812 War used as a school text in preference to the "American trash" the teachers were using. No, Ontario's story is not dull. It will, certainly, after these nightmares have been put on the boards, not be a duller place to live in either.'[3]

Since Richardson wrote *Wacousta* over one hundred and fifty years ago in unnamed country amid a bookless people, the tradition he sought to initiate has become a great deal clearer. The stories he tells, charged with menace and mystery and the concrete particularities of place, dramatize conflicts, double hooks, paradoxes, and preoccupations that most of the people of his age saw rather abstractly, if at all, but to which he gave human and imaginative dimensions – thus making visible an 'invisible' people. The stories he does *not* tell are not told because he successfully fulfilled his first task: 'uninventing' the world according to the American Cooper and the British Scott, that he might see and give authentic utterance to a new land, to a different, local place, to *here*. As opposed to their more ordered and optimistic national visions, his result in different narrative structures which simultaneously brandish and frustrate epic expectations as well as celebrate and question myths of nation-building. This generates unsettling border tales of trickery and betrayal that emphasize the unreliable and unstable, the fragmentary and incomplete. Nor are images of a fractured country perpetually in a state of emergency and bordering on dissolution out of place in today's political climate.

As a witness to and constructor of characteristic patterns of expression and sets of tendencies, of the discontinuities and contradictions of our regional and national existence, in his best work Richardson has opened up this place for literary purposes, shown us multiple images of ourselves, perhaps even spoken the myths that might bind us collectively. A journey through the Richardson canon brings back no final answer – but some interesting and perplexing questions. In addition to 'How do you write in a new country?'[4] I've suggested that the most significant and troubling of these have to do with the ironic tensions and paradoxes generated by borders, tensions which are an expression of a fundamental dualism in Canadian art and society. The multiple borderlines in Richardson's major works signal psychological as well as topographical dichotomies and double binds; such a strategy of cultural dialectic and interplay – and the refusal of any easy resolution of contraries or any final, single, definitive inscription of nationality or selfhood – is of central importance to our fictional and national heritage.

As Richardson tells it, the myth of the border is the coincidence of opposites. Canada the borderline case fascinates him, with its problems of identity which seem to be problems of equilibrium. In Richardson's phantasmagorical border region, worlds collide as well as coincide and conflate, complementing and running into one another; such carnivalesque 'double crossing' provides the touchstone for his epic's thematic, imagistic, archetypal, and structural patterns. Doubles, twins, or doppelgänger figures of descent imagery are generated by this border-blur and break-boundary process. Richardson's predilection for such slippery, contradictory figures, as I have noted more than once, seems to issue from a psyche obsessed with balancing or undoing/unfixing one element or force with another. Whether in the twin configurations of group or cultural identity, or in his repertoire of doubles and complementary personalities, Richardson envisions two equal and opposite forces balancing at a common point along an uncertain and wavering borderline. Casting De Haldimar and Wacousta as the two poles of the Canadian psyche of the time, Grantham and Desborough as representative Canadian and American, the Monk Knight and the Baron as Apollonian and Dionysian figures, he is unable to see them except as equally matched opposites in mutual dependency, woven together in a very tightly interconnected universe. 'Dull, simple, amazing and unfathomable'[5] – such is the disconcerting, inexplicable doubleness of Richardson's contradictory border-blur world no less than of Munro's paradoxical and frequently grotesque one, or that of other writers from this distinct region. This issues in an ironic double or 'blurred' vision and voice and an abiding sense of interrelationship and interdependence that highlights and challenges boundaries of all kinds; it is an imaginative legacy that modern – and especially postmodern – writers and critics have lately come to appreciate. 'Perhaps,' as Robert Kroetsch notes in *The Lovely Treachery of Words* (1989), 'we tell a blurred story because the story is blurred.' [6]

One of my concerns has been to examine Richardson's claim – paradoxically, an ex-centric's claim – to the title of 'The Father of Canadian Literature.' Paternity suits are often long and drawn-out affairs, and this is no exception. It has thus been necessary in this study to range freely throughout Canadian, American, and British literature, that we might better realize that our interest in this seminal writer belongs in this larger context. Having cast my net widely, I have sought to substantiate a statement made in the Introduction to the effect that in the work of our first poet-novelist are adumbrated imaginative patterns which illuminate the work of Richardson's successors in the canon of English-Canadian fiction. Such an allusive approach to an author who works through association and spiralling repetition, though dictated by the nature of this study's objectives, may also be as much cultural as personal in origin. As Atwood notes of this 'love for synthesis,'

> The Canadian habit of mind, for whatever reason ... is synthetic. 'Taste' and 'technique' are both of less concern to it than is the ever-failing but ever-renewed attempt to pull all the pieces together, to discover the whole of which one can only trust one is a part. The most central Canadian literary products, then, tend to be large-scope works ... Give the same poem to a model American, a model English and a model Canadian critic: the American will say 'This is how it works'; the Englishman 'How good, how true to Life' ... the Canadian will say 'This is where it fits into the entire universe.'[7]

W.R. Riddell's 1923 statement that later poets and novelists would return to Richardson's material and weave out of it fresh stories seems more and more prophetic from the perspective of today. I have already commented on the adaptation of Richardson's fiction and non-fiction by Don Gutteridge and James Reaney; Frank Davey's long poem about North American myths, *The Louis Riel Organ and Piano Company* (1985), begins with a section entitled 'Wacouster,' a satirical revision of the De Haldimar-Wacousta relationship. Richardson is increasingly coming to be seen as an ancestral voice of the Canadian imagination, a poet-novelist with a good sense of the conventions of romance and tragedy who turns these forms to his country's own emerging cultural needs, and as a map-maker identifying the habits, attitudes, and deep concerns of the country that gave him birth.

This new perspective on 'The Father of Canadian Literature' is dramatized most tellingly, perhaps, in the figure of Lou, the historian-heroine of *Bear* by Souwesto writer Marian Engel. After reclaiming her body, feelings, and sexuality from the cold storage of a patriarchal and puritanical past in Southwestern Ontario, Lou sets out from her wilderness island carrying only two prize possessions: Bewick's *Natural History* and 'the first edition of *Wacousta*.' Returning afresh to society, 'she would make these two books safe.' Lou finds the autographed *Wacousta* beside Trelawny's remembrances of Byron and Shelley in the library of Colonel Cary, a nineteenth-century eccentric romantic. At home in the wilderness, with a bear for a companion, Colonel Cary has met Richardson who – in the best Emily Carr fashion – kept a pet deer, ponies, and dogs. Against regulations, Lou decides to take the original *Wacousta*: 'There were other valuable books ... but nothing, so far, to equal *Wacousta*. Strange I have never read it, she thought, but I won't read this copy. Get myself a reading copy from Toronto and compare the texts. Well, Cary, you were somebody after all if you knew Richardson.'[8]

Notes

1 Introduction

1 James Reaney, 'An ABC to Ontario Literature and Culture,' *Black Moss: Halloween 3*, 2:3 (Spring 1977) 3. In his 'A Letter from James Reaney,' in *Black Moss: Halloween 1*, 2:1 (Spring 1976) 8, Reaney refers to *Wacousta* as 'our first prose romance and obsessed with our great national problem of borders.' The three quotations preceding the first chapter are from the following sources: James Reaney, Letter, *Globe and Mail* Nov. 4 1977; Robert Kroetsch, *The Lovely Treachery of Words: Essays Selected and New* (Toronto: Oxford University Press 1989) 109; Leslie Monkman, 'Canadian Historical Fiction' in *Queen's Quarterly* 94:3 (Autumn 1987) 637.

2 Dennis Duffy, *Gardens, Covenants, Exiles: Loyalism in the Literature of Upper Canada/Ontario* (Toronto: University of Toronto Press 1982) 45

3 Kroetsch, *Treachery* 154

4 Linda Hutcheon, *The Canadian Postmodern: A Study of Contemporary English-Canadian Fiction* (Toronto: Oxford University Press 1988) 174

5 David Beasley, *The Canadian Don Quixote: The Life and Works of Major John Richardson, Canada's First Novelist* (Erin: The Porcupine's Quill 1977) 17. See also my chapter-length biography of Richardson in 'The Borders of Nightmare: A Study of the Fiction of John Richardson,' PH D dissertation (Queen's University 1984).

6 George Woodcock, review of *The Canadian Don Quixote*, *Globe and Mail* 29 Oct. 1977, 39

7 Beasley, in *The Canadian Don Quixote* (197), ends his study with this excerpt from Richardson's obituary in *Pick's*: 'The Major was a queer fish in some respects, and a very eccentric Christian.'

8 Judge W.R. Riddell's description as quoted by James T. Tallman, introduction, *The Journal of Major John Norton*, by Major John Norton, ed. Carl F. Klinck and James T. Tallman (Toronto: The Champlain Society 1970) cxiii. Brant names the white Norton 'Chief Teyoninhokorawen.' ('Teh' means 'Two' or 'Dual Nature,' a suitable name for Norton and Morton/ Wacousta.)

9 Major John Richardson, *The Guards in Canada; or, The Point of Honour* (Montreal: H.H. Cunningham 1848) 26. See also 41–43, 4, 13, 23.

10 Woodcock, review of *The Canadian Don Quixote* 39

11 *Tecumseh; or, The Warrior of the West: A Poem, in Four Cantos, with Notes by John Richardson*, introduction W.F.E. Morley (1828; rpt Ottawa: The Golden Dog Press 1978) canto 4:38, 68

12 Major John Richardson, 'A Trip to Walpole Island and Port Sarnia's in *Tecumseh and Richardson: The Story of a Trip to Walpole Island and Port Sarnia*, ed. A.H.U. Colquhoun (Toronto: Ontario Book Co 1924) 64, 68. See also 57, 51, 70–71.

13 Major John Richardson, 'A Canadian Campaign, by a British Officer,' in *The New Monthly Magazine and Literary Journal* 19:1 (1827) 162

14 Terry Goldie, *Fear and Temptation: The Image of the Indigene in Canadian, Australian, and New Zealand Literatures* (Kingston: McGill-Queen's University Press 1989) 13. With the exception of certain comments in my introduction and in the section on Wacousta as Trickster, my interest, like Goldie's, is in the image of the indigenes, a white image, thus the use of the term 'Indian.' To quote Goldie again, 'Because this study is about the image rather than the people the image claims to represent, I use that synchronic designation of conquest, "Indian," throughout in reference to Canadian native peoples' (6).

15 Michel Foucault, 'Truth and Power,' *Power/Knowledge: Selected Interviews and Other Writings 1972–1977*, trans. Colin Gordon et al, ed. Colin Gordon (New York: Pantheon Books 1980) 133; Joseph Campbell, *The Hero with a Thousand Faces* (1949; rpt New York: Princeton/Bollingen 1973) 337

16 Michel Foucault, *The Archaeology of Knowledge*, trans. Sheridan Smith (New York: Harper and Row 1976) 23. See also Hutcheon's chapter 'The Postmodern Challenge to Boundaries' in *The Canadian Postmodern* 78–106.

17 Michael Ondaatje, *Coming through Slaughter* (Toronto: Anansi 1976) 96. See also Ann Wilson, 'Coming through Slaughter: Storyville Twice Told,' in *Descant* 42, 14:4 (Fall 1983). For a discussion of equally matched opposites in mutual dependency in Robert Kroetsch's work, see Rosemary Sullivan's 'Summing Up,' in *Crossing Frontiers: Papers in American and Canadian West-*

ern Literature, ed. Dick Harrison (Edmonton: University of Alberta Press 1979) 154.

18 Robertson Davies, Fifth Business (Toronto: Macmillan 1970) 7. See chapter 5 n14 re my ensuing comment on the gothic and its sister genres.

19 Alice Munro, Lives of Girls and Women (1971; rpt New York: Signet 1974) 210

20 Leslie Fiedler, 'Canada and the Invention of the Western,' in Crossing Frontiers 96

21 Major John Richardson, Eight Years in Canada ... (Montreal: H.H. Cunningham 1847) 92

22 In 'An Immigrant's Song,' by Urjo Kareda, Saturday Night 92:12 (December 1983) 48

23 Woodcock, review of The Canadian Don Quixote 39

24 Monkman, 'Canadian Historical Fiction,' in Queen's Quarterly 637–8. This is an excellent article on the subject.

25 Such phrases appear throughout Richardson's autobiographical writing. See 'A Trip to Walpole Island and Port Sarnia,' ed. Colquhoun, 67; Eight Years 11, 107, 93, 106; 'Preface,' Wacousta, rev. ed. (New York: Dewitt and Davenport 1851) vi; The Guards 43

26 Major John Richardson, The Monk Knight of St. John: A Tale of the Crusades (New York: Dewitt and Davenport 1850) 79, 121. For a fuller discussion of this work see my article 'Double Entendre: Rebel Angels and Beautiful Losers in John Richardson's The Monk Knight of St. John' in Canadian Literature 128 (Spring 1991).

27 Richardson, Eight Years 141, 144

28 In Personal Fictions: Stories by Munro, Wiebe, Thomas, & Blaise, ed. Michael Ondaatje (Toronto: Oxford University Press 1977) 227

2 Wacousta

1 James Reaney, Colours in the Dark (Vancouver: Talon Books 1971) 5; in 'Scott Symons,' Eleven Canadian Novelists, interviewer Graeme Gibson (Toronto: Anansi 1973) 311; Dennis Lee, Savage Fields: An Essay in Literature and Cosmology (Toronto: Anansi 1977) 42, 56; Audrey Thomas, Blown Figures (Vancouver: Talon Books 1974) 388

2 Marshall McLuhan, 'Canada: The Borderline Case,' in David Staines, ed., The Canadian Imagination: Dimensions of a Literary Culture (Cambridge, MA: Harvard University Press 1977) 232–47. Interestingly, Hutcheon in The Canadian Postmodern (52) argues that 'contemporary Canadian novelists ... despite themselves, I suspect – are McLuhan's true spiritual heirs.'

3 The 1967 NCL edition of *Wacousta* is, as Douglas Cronk attests, 'the worst edition of *Wacousta* yet produced'; every aspect of the romance has been affected by the omission of 40,000 words. See Douglas Cronk, 'The Editorial Destruction of Canadian Literature: A Textual Study of Major John Richardson's *Wacousta; Or, The Prophecy*' MA dissertation (Simon Fraser University 1977) 29.

4 Richard Chase, *The American Novel and Its Tradition* (London: G. Bell and Sons 1957) 54

5 Carl F. Klinck, introduction, *Wacousta; or, The Prophecy* (Toronto: McClelland and Stewart 1967) xii

6 John Moss, *Patterns of Isolation in English Canadian Fiction* (Toronto: McClelland and Stewart 1974) 50

7 Northrop Frye, *Divisions on a Ground: Essays on Canadian Culture*, ed. James Polk (Toronto: Anansi 1983) 49, 54

8 Eli Mandel, *Another Time* (Erin, Ont.: Press Porcépic 1977) 68

9 Eli Mandel, 'The Border League,' in *Crossing Frontiers* 105

10 Dick Harrison, introduction, *Crossing Frontiers* 7

11 Mandel, 'Border League,' in *Crossing Frontiers* 118

12 Carl Ballstadt, *Major John Richardson: A Selection of Reviews and Criticism* (Montreal: Lande Foundation 1972) 26

13 Mandel, *Another Time* 85

14 Richardson, 'Introductory,' *Wacousta; or, The Prophecy* 2

15 Sir Walter Scott, introduction, *Rob Roy*, Waverley Novels II (Edinburgh: Robert Cadell 1831) viii

16 Frye, *Divisions* 20

17 Robert Lecker, 'Patterns of Deception in *Wacousta*,' in *The Canadian Novel: Beginnings* II, ed. John Moss (Toronto: NC Press 1980) 48. In the same volume, consult my article '*Wacousta*: The Borders of Nightmare.'

18 Northrop Frye, *Bush Garden: Essays on the Canadian Imagination* (Toronto: Anansi 1971) 183

19 Northrop Frye, 'Haunted by No Lack of Ghosts,' in *The Canadian Imagination* 27

20 Major John Richardson, *The Canadian Brothers; or, The Prophecy Fulfilled: A Tale of the Late American War*, 2 vols. (Montreal: A.H. Armour and H. Ramsay 1840) I, 190. The pagination is the same in the 1976 University of Toronto reprint, introduced by Carl F. Klinck.

21 Margaret Atwood, *The Journals of Susanna Moodie* (Toronto: Oxford University Press 1970) 62–63. In *Survival: A Thematic Guide to Canadian Literature* (Toronto: Anansi 1972), Atwood speaks of civilization's constructs as square and nature's forms as circular.

22 Margaret Avison, 'Intra-Political,' in *Poetry of Mid-Century 1940–1960*, ed.

Milton Wilson (Toronto: McClelland and Stewart 1964) 106

23 Frye, *Divisions* 168

24 Lee, *Savage Fields* 20, 27. Lecker also sees such symmetry reflecting the need to control.

25 Frye, *Divisions* 170

26 Ibid. 58

27 Atwood, *Survival* 120

28 John G. Neihardt, *Black Elk Speaks* (New York: Pocket Books 1972) 164–65. See also *The Hero's Journey: The World of Joseph Campbell*, ed. Phil Cousineau (New York: Harper & Row 1990) 8, 10, 208–9, and Joseph Campbell and Bill Moyers, *The Power of Myth* (New York: Doubleday 1988) 88–9, 100, and *Hero* 41–2.

29 John Fire/Lame Deer and Richard Erdoes, *Lame Deer: Seeker of Visions* (New York: Pocket Books 1972) 100–02

30 Frye, *Bush Garden* 226

31 Lee, *Savage Fields* 21

32 These quotations, previously identified, are essential for an understanding of Richardson's myth of the borderline as the coincidence of opposites. The first paragraph of Janette Turner Hospital's novel *Borderline* (Toronto: Seal 1987) is apposite here as well: 'At borders, as at death and in dreams, no amount of prior planning will necessarily avail. The law of boundaries applies. In the nature of things, control is not in the hands of the traveller ... But at borders there is never an ordinary course of events.'

33 Robert Kroetsch, *Treachery* 15

34 Frye, *Bush Garden* 199–201

35 See also Atwood's *The Edible Woman*, Ross's *As For Me and My House*, Connor's *The Sky Pilot*, Knister's *White Narcissus*, O'Hagan's *Tay John*, Laurence's *The Stone Angel*, and Richardson's *The Canadian Brothers*. I use the 'border' river in its symbolic sense as does Richardson; I am not referring to the Detroit River which is the historical border river only in *The Canadian Brothers*.

36 Mandel, 'Border League,' in *Crossing Frontiers* 115

37 In C.G. Jung and M-L. von Franz, eds., *Man and His Symbols* (London: Aldus Books 1964) 38; Campbell, *Hero* 58. See also *Hero* 97, 30, 36–37, 245–6, 79, 51, 90.

38 Frye, *Bush Garden* 200–01

39 Al Purdy, *Purdy Selected* (Toronto: McClelland and Stewart 1972) 21–22

40 Atwood, *Journals* 39

41 Joseph Conrad, 'Heart of Darkness,' in *Three Short Novels*, introduction, Edward Weeks (1899; rpt New York: Bantam 1960) 62–63, 47

42 Frye, *Bush Garden* 141, 199

43 Ibid. 200

44 Atwood, *Journals* 13

45 Quoted in Dick Harrison, introduction, *Crossing Frontiers* 8

46 Margaret Atwood, 'Progressive Insanities of a Pioneer,' in *15 Canadian Poets*, ed. Gary Geddes and Phyllis Bruce (Toronto: Oxford University Press 1970) 170

47 Frye, *Bush Garden* 226

48 Frye, *Divisions* 55. See also D.G. Jones, *Butterfly on Rock: A Study of Themes and Images in Canadian Literature* (1970; rpt Toronto: University of Toronto Press 1970).

49 Robertson Davies, 'Gleams and Glooms,' in *One Half of Robertson Davies* (New York: Penguin 1978) 239–40

50 This subtitle is borrowed from Marshall McLuhan's *Understanding Media: The Extensions of Man* (New York: Signet 1964), a key document in the argument of this and following chapters.

51 Sinclair Ross, *As For Me And My House*, introduction, Roy Daniells (1941; rpt Toronto: McClelland and Stewart 1957) 38

52 Conrad, *Heart of Darkness* 79, 59, 56, 72, 58

53 In 'Scott Symons,' in *Eleven Canadian Novelists* 311–15; Scott Symons, *Combat Journal for Place D'Armes* (Toronto: McClelland and Stewart 1976) 60–5, *passim*; 'Scott Symons' 312

54 Frye, *Bush Garden* 225

55 Quoted by Eli Mandel, 'Ecological Heroes and Visionary Politics,' in *Another Time* 107

56 Compare Richardson's use of the telescope to Ondaatje's and Atwood's use of the camera.

57 McLuhan, *Understanding Media* 88

58 Frye, *Bush Garden* 250

59 Lecker, 'Patterns of Deception in *Wacousta*,' in *The Canadian Novel: Beginnings* 53

60 Atwood, *Survival* 122

61 Lee, *Savage Fields* 16–18, 21

62 Margaret Atwood, *Surfacing* (Toronto: PaperJacks 1972) 57

63 Atwood, *Journals* 12; Margot Northey, *The Haunted Wilderness: The Gothic and Grotesque in Canadian Fiction* (Toronto: University of Toronto Press 1976) 23–24

64 Ibid. 19

65 Margaret Atwood, *The Circle Game* (Toronto: Anansi 1966) 75

66 McLuhan, *Understanding Media* 49

67 Frye, *Divisions* 144
68 Northrop Frye, *The Secular Scripture: A Study of the Structure of Romance* (Cambridge, MA: Harvard University Press 1976) 103
69 Davies, 'Gleams and Glooms,' in *One Half* 240
70 In 'Robertson Davies: The Bizarre and Passionate Life of the Canadian People,' in Donald Cameron, *Conversations with Canadian Novelists: Part One* (Toronto: Macmillan 1973) 38
71 In 'Robert Kroetsch: The American Experience and the Canadian Voice,' in *Conversations* 85. John Moss compares *Wacousta* to Kroetsch's *But We Are Exiles* in his *Patterns of Isolation* 39–42.
72 In 'Robert Kroetsch,' in *Conversations* 93
73 In 'Rudy Wiebe: The Moving Stream is Perfectly at Rest,' in *Conversations* 151
74 Lee, *Savage Fields* 21
75 Mandell, *Another Time* 93

3 Border Doubles

1 Frye, *Divisions* 49, 55; Michael Ondaatje, *In the Skin of a Lion* (Toronto: Penguin 1988) 134
2 See Masao Miyoshi, *The Divided Self* (New York: New York University Press 1969); Ralph Tymms, *Doubles in Literary Psychology* (Cambridge: Bowes and Bowes 1949).
3 See Margaret Atwood, 'Superwoman Drawn and Quartered: The Early Forms of *She*,' in *Second Words: Selected Critical Prose* (Toronto: Anansi 1982).
4 Edward F. Edinger, *Ego and Archetype: Individuation and the Religious Function of the Psyche* (Baltimore: Penguin 1972) 100
5 McLuhan, 'Borderline,' in *Canadian Imagination* 247
6 For instance, see Hutcheon's *The Canadian Postmodern*.
7 Matt Cohen, *The Sweet Second Summer of Kitty Malone* (Toronto: McClelland and Stewart 1979) 176; Tom Marshall, *Rosemary Goal* (Toronto: Oberon 1978) 99, 117
8 Hugh MacLennan, *The Watch That Ends the Night* (1958; rpt New York: Signet 1959) 341, 343
9 Quoted by Peter Thomas, 'Priapus in the Danse Macabre: The Novels of Robert Kroetsch,' in *The Canadian Novel in the Twentieth Century*, ed. George Woodcock (Toronto: McClelland and Stewart 1975) 286
10 Robert Kroetsch, *The Studhorse Man* (New York: Pocket Books 1971) 119

11 Northrop Frye, *A Study of English Romanticism* (New York: Random House 1968) 30–31
12 Frye, *Secular Scripture* 141
13 Frye, *English Romanticism* 31
14 Tymms, *Doubles* 30
15 William Blake, 'The Marriage of Heaven and Hell,' in *Blake: Complete Works*, ed. Geoffrey Keynes (London: Oxford University Press 1966) 157
16 Quoted by Robertson Davies in 'The Canada of Myth and Reality,' in *One Half* 286
17 Robertson Davies, *The Manticore* (New York: Curtis Books 1972) 115
18 Jones, *Butterfly* 81
19 See J. Stewart Reaney's description of the Donnellys in *James Reaney*, Profiles in Canadian Drama Series (Toronto: Gage Educational Publishing 1977) 66–67.
20 Arianna Stassinopoulos, *The Gods of Greece*, quoted by Jean Shinoda Bolen, *Gods in Everyman: A New Psychology of Men's Lives and Loves* (1989; rpt New York: Harper & Row 1990) 72; Bolen, *Gods* 78–79
21 Bolen, *Gods* 78, 72–97
22 Ibid. 91, 74, 78
23 Robert Bly, *Iron John: A Book about Men* (New York: Addison-Wesley 1990) 5
24 Richardson, *Guards* 42, 12
25 Bly, *Iron John* 47
26 Ibid. 43, 6
27 Ibid. 14, 8, 47
28 Ibid. 26
29 In 'Death is a Happy Ending: A Dialogue in Thirteen Parts' (with Diane Bessai), in *Figures in a Ground: Canadian Essays on Modern Literature Collected in Honour of Sheila Watson*, ed. Diane Bessai and David Jackel (Saskatoon: Western Producer Prairie Books 1978) 208–9
30 Robin Mathews, *Canadian Literature: Surrender or Revolution*, ed. Gail Dexter (Toronto: Steel Rail 1978) 14
31 Robert Kroetsch, *The Studhorse Man* (New York: Pocket Books 1971) 55
32 Jones, *Butterfly* 72–3. My following comments on Grove echo Jones. See Marion Woodman's *Addiction to Perfection: The Still Unravished Bride* (Toronto: Inner City 1982).
33 Warren Tallman, 'Wolf in the Snow,' in *Contexts of Canadian Criticism* 236; Michael Ondaatje, *The Collected Works of Billy the Kid* (Toronto: Anansi 1970) 28–9; Frederick Philip Grove, *The Master of the Mill*, introduction R.E. Watters (1944: rpt Toronto: McClelland and Stewart 1969) 264, 287–8, 229, 227

34 Perry Nodelman, 'The Collected Photographs of Billy the Kid,' in *Canadian Literature* 87 (Winter 1980) 68
35 Bly, *Iron John* 33
36 L.R. Early, 'Myth and Prejudice in Kirby, Richardson, and Parker,' in *Canadian Literature* 81 (Summer 1979) 30
37 Bly, *Iron John* 85
38 Bolen, *Gods* 54–69
39 Bly, *Iron John* 98–99
40 Ibid. 33
41 Riane Eisler, *The Chalice and the Blade: Our History, Our Future* (New York: Harper & Row 1987) xvii–xxiii, 146–7, 170. Mac Freeman's fascinating concept of 'duetting' and of 'duocentric' rather than egocentric orientation is more complex than I can suggest here. See 'Is Infant Learning Egocentric or Duocentric? Was Piaget Wrong?' in *Pre-and-Peri-Natal Psychology Journal* 2:1 (Fall 1987) 25–42 and his newsletter *Wellspring* with its emphasis on 'Human Partnering.' For more information on goddess cultures see publications by the authors I've listed, and Barbara Walker's *The Woman's Encyclopedia of Myths and Secrets* (San Francisco: Harper & Row 1983), Adele Getty's *Goddess: Mother of Living Nature* (London: Thames and Hudson 1990), Judith Duerk's *Circle of Stones: Woman's Journey to Herself* (San Diego: Lura Media 1990), and the NFB films *Goddess Remembered* and *The Burning Times.*
42 Frederick Philip Grove, *Fruits of the Earth*, introduction, M.G. Parks (1933; rpt Toronto: McClelland and Stewart 1965) 22, 36; Grove, *Our Daily Bread*, introduction, D.O. Spettigue (1928; rpt Toronto: McClelland and Stewart 1975) 5, 11; Grove, *Fruits* 40; Grove, *Bread* 11
43 Robert Moore, *Rediscovering Masculine Potentials* (Wilmette, IL: Chiron 1988, 4 casette tapes; tape 1:'The King'). See also Robert Moore and Douglas Gilette, *King, Warrior, Magician, Lover: Rediscovering the Archetypes of the Mature Masculine* (San Francisco: Harper San Francisco 1990) 49–73.
44 Quoted by Bolen, *Gods* 45
45 Bolen, *Gods* 45–52
46 Ibid. 53–55

4 The Canadian Brothers

1 James Reaney, 'Topless Nightmares, Being a Dialogue with Himself by James Reaney,' in *Halloween 2: Topless Nightmares* (Fall 1976) 4; W.H. New, *Articulating West: Essays on Purpose and Form in Modern Canadian Literature* (Toronto: New Press 1972) xvi; Susan Swan, *The Biggest Modern Woman of the World* (Toronto: Lester & Orpen Dennys 1983) 273–4

2 Frye, *Secular Scripture* 53. Interestingly, in writing the postmodernist *What the Crow Said*, Kroetsch was 'directly influenced by Frye's *The Secular Scripture*. It had become a kind of bible to me' (*Lovely Treachery* 160). See also Campbell's *Hero* 36-7, 77-89, 245-6 for patterns about the stages in the heroic journey.

3 Richardson, *Wacousta; or, The Prophecy* np

4 J.E. Cirlot, *A Dictionary of Symbols* (New York: Routledge and Kegan Paul 1962) 115

5 Quoted by Jones, *Butterfly* 42. See Campbell's *Hero* 109-26.

6 Frye, *Secular Scripture* 104-5

7 Frye, *English Romanticism* 53

8 Ibid. 141. See also Jean Bolen's discussion of Medea in *Goddesses in Every Woman: A New Psychology of Women* (San Francisco: Harper & Row 1984) 61-2 and the reference to Medea in Barbara G. Walker's *The Woman's Encyclopedia of Myths and Secrets* 628.

9 John Keats, *Lamia* and *Endymion*, in *John Keats: Selected Poetry and Letters*, ed. R.H. Fogle (New York: Holt, Rinehart and Winston 1968) 254, 271, 109, 106, 84, 107, 106, 42

10 Miyoshi, *Divided Self* 79

11 Samuel Taylor Coleridge, *The Rime of the Ancient Mariner*, in *Coleridge: Poetical Works*, ed. Ernest H. Coleridge (London: Oxford University Press 1969) III, 11. 192-4, 194

12 Frye, *Secular Scripture* 102-3, 113

13 Ibid. 104, 108

14 Ibid. 140

15 Edinger, *Archetype* 161

16 Jay Macpherson, 'Narcissus: Some Uncertain Reflections,' in *Alphabet: A Semiannual Devoted to the Iconography of the Imagination* 1 (1960) 56

17 Frye, *Secular Scripture* 42-3

18 Macpherson, 'Narcissus,' in *Alphabet* 1 (1960) 50; Jones, *Butterfly* 85

19 Macpherson, 'Narcissus,' in *Alphabet* 2 (1961) 70

20 Ibid.

21 Lee, *Savage Fields* 21, 56, 88

22 Frye, *Secular Scripture* 156, 108

23 McLuhan, 'Borderline,' in *Canadian Imagination* 247

24 Frye, *Secular Scripture* 115

25 Ibid. 113

26 Frye, *English Romanticism* 61

27 Frye, *Secular Scripture* 118

28 James Reaney, letter, *Globe and Mail* 4 Nov. 1977

29 Mario Praz, *The Romantic Agony*, trans. Angus Davidson (London: Oxford University Press 1951) 205–6
30 Frye, *Secular Scripture* 114, 123, 129
31 Ibid. 108
32 Cirlot, *Dictionary* 150–1
33 Jones, *Butterfly* 88
34 Frye, *Secular Scripture* 140
35 Ibid. 145, 58, 145, 122
36 Ina Ferris, 'Morley Callaghan and the Exultant Self,' in *Journal of Canadian Studies* 15 1 (1980) 15
37 Jay Macpherson, 'The Death of Animals,' unpublished essay
38 Frye, *Secular Scripture* 114
39 Ibid. 114
40 John Moss, *A Reader's Guide to the Canadian Novel* (Toronto: McClelland and Stewart 1981) 232; George Bowering, *A Short Sad Book* (Vancouver: Talonbooks 1977) 111
41 Lawrence, *Studies* 1

5 The Shadow Cast by Southern Ontario Gothic

1 In 'Alice Munro,' in *Eleven Canadian Novelists* 248; in 'Timothy Findley,' in *Eleven Canadian Novelists* 138; Robertson Davies, *High Spirits* (London: Penguin 1982) 2. See Alice Munro, *Who Do You Think You Are?* (Toronto: Macmillan 1978) 16 for the phrase 'the other side of dailiness.'
2 Margaret Avison, *History of Ontario* (Toronto: W.J. Gage & Co 1951) 42
3 Frye, *Bush Garden* 140–1, 225
4 D.H. Lawrence, *Studies in Classic American Literature* (1923; rpt New York: The Viking Press 1961) 47, 51
5 Frye, *Bush Garden* 191
6 Carl F. Klinck, 'Literary Activity in the Canadas: 1812–1841,' in *Literary History of Canada: Canadian Literature in English*, ed. Carl F. Klinck et al (Toronto: University of Toronto Press 1965) 137–38
7 Klinck, Introduction, *Wacousta* ix
8 Hutcheon, *Canadian Postmodern* 61–77
9 Germaine Warkentin, 'Exploration Literature in English,' in *The Oxford Companion to Canadian Literature*, ed. William Toye (Toronto: Oxford University Press 1983) 246
10 Frye, *Bush Garden* 199
11 Leslie Fiedler, *Freaks: Myths and Images of the Secret Self* (New York: Simon and Schuster 1978) 93

12 Frye, *Bush Garden* 174
13 Leslie Fiedler, *Love and Death in the American Novel*, rev. ed. (New York: Stein and Day 1966) 140
14 Donna Bennett, 'Criticism in English,' in *The Oxford Companion to Canadian Literature* 161
15 Mandel, *Another Time* 139
16 W.F. Axton, Introduction, *Melmoth the Wanderer* (1820; rpt Lincoln: University of Nebraska Press 1967) vii
17 Ibid. xi
18 D.P. Varma, introduction, *The Romance of the Forest*, foreword by Frederick Garber (1797; rpt New York: Arno Press 1974) xiv–xxvii
19 Both Scott and Cooper are not responsive to the *meaning* of the Gothic, although each on occasion adopts its trappings.
20 Fiedler, *Love and Death* 135
21 Mary Shelley, *Frankenstein, or The Modern Prometheus* (1817; rpt New York: Collier Books 1961) 65
22 Shelley, *Frankenstein* 173, 83–4, 115, 172
23 Harold Bloom, *Ringers in the Tower: Studies in Romantic Tradition* (Chicago: University of Chicago Press 1971) 126
24 Lord Byron, *The Giaour*, in *Byron: Poetical Works*, ed. Frederick Page (London: Oxford University Press 1969) 11. 943–5, 260
25 Bloom, *Ringers* 126
26 Byron, *Lara*, in *Byron*, 1:17, lines 289–94, 307
27 John Milton, *Paradise Lost*, in *John Milton: Complete Poems and Major Prose*, ed. Merritt Y. Hughes (New York: Odyssey Press 1957) 1:584–604, 226–7
28 For an in-depth discussion of the gothic and Richardson, see chapter 8, 'Literary Influences: Gothic and Romantic Literature,' in my thesis, 'The Borders of Nightmare: A Study of the Fiction of John Richardson,' PH D dissertation (Queen's University 1984). See also I.S. MacLaren's article in *Recovering Canada's First Novelist: Proceedings of the John Richardson Conference*, ed. Catherine Ross (Erin: Porcupine's Quill 1984) 49–62.
29 Bly, *Iron John* 226; New, *Articulating West* xxiv
30 Axton, *Melmoth* x
31 Stephen Larsen, *The Shaman's Doorway: Opening the Mythic Imagination to Contemporary Consciousness* (New York: Harper Colophon Books 1976) 208. See also Marion Woodman's *The Ravaged Bridegroom: Masculinity in Women* (Toronto: Inner City Books 1990) for a ground-breaking exploration of the psychological impact of patriarchy and a re-evaluation of the feminine principle.
32 Campbell, *Hero* 337

33 Larsen, *Shaman's Doorway* 213
34 Quoted by Larsen, *Shaman's Doorway* 208
35 Hugh MacLennan, *Barometer Rising* (1941; rpt Toronto: McClelland and Stewart 1960) 217, 208, 217, 134–5
36 Larsen, *Shaman's Doorway* 215
37 Bly, *Iron John* 98, 85
38 Moore, *Rediscovering Masculine Potentials*, cassette 1
39 Moss, *Isolation* 37
40 See Cronk's thesis on the 'editorial destruction' of Richardson.
41 Woodman, *Ravaged Bridegroom* 16
42 Rudy Wiebe, *The Scorched-Wood People* (Toronto: McClelland and Stewart 1977) 26, 84, 51, 181
43 James Reaney, editorial, *Alphabet* (1963)
44 In 'Scott Symons,' in *Eleven Canadian Novelists* 311–15; Scott Symons, *Combat Journal for Place D'Armes* (Toronto: McClelland and Stewart 1976) 60–5, passim
45 Atwood, *Survival* 189; Margaret Atwood, *Life before Man* (Toronto: McClelland and Stewart 1979) 186
46 See 'Marian Engel,' in *Eleven Canadian Novelists* 107–8; James Reaney, *14 Barrels from Sea to Sea* (Erin, Ont.: Press Porcépic 1977) 140, 17
47 Woodman, *Ravaged Bridegroom* 17
48 Atwood, *Life before Man* 119–20
49 Ibid. 137
50 Ibid. 279
51 Alice Munro, 'Our Gothic Mother' and 'The Peace of Utrecht,' in *Dance of the Happy Shades* (Toronto: McClelland and Stewart 1968) 199–201
52 Munro, 'The Peace of Utrecht,' in *Dance* 191, 194, 206
53 Marian Engel, *The Honeyman Festival* (Toronto: Anansi 1970) 14
54 Munro, 'The Peace of Utrecht,' in *Dance* 210
55 Graeme Gibson, *Five Legs/Communion*, introduction, Leon Edel (1969; 1971; rpt Toronto: Anansi 1979) 49, 43, 79
56 Davies, *Fifth Business* 12; Robertson Davies, *World of Wonders* (1975; rpt New York: Penguin 1977) 38; Davies, *Fifth Business* 255, 13, 4
57 Raymond Knister, *White Narcissus*, introduction, Philip Child (1929; rpt Toronto: McClelland and Stewart 1962) 81, 57, 43, 36
58 Ibid. 83
59 Ibid. 118, 39, 19, 53–4
60 Ibid. 110, 45, 63, 105, 110
61 Ibid. 55, 20, 39, 95, 50
62 Ibid. 89, 87

63 J. Stewart Reaney, *James Reaney* 63, 69
64 Morley Callaghan, *Close to the Sun Again* (Toronto: Macmillan 1977) 126
65 Frye, *Bush Garden* 91
66 Mandel, *Another Time* 130
67 In 'Marian Engel,' in *Eleven Canadian Novelists* 108
68 In 'Dave Godfrey,' in *Eleven Canadian Novelists* 248
69 Ibid. 171
70 Bly, *Iron John* 228; quoted by Bolen, *Gods* 162
71 Beasley, *Canadian Don Quixote* 17
72 Margaret Atwood, 'Canadian Monsters: Some Aspects of the Supernatural in Canadian Fiction,' in *Canadian Imagination* 101
73 Paul Radin, *The Trickster: A Study in American Indian Mythology*, introduction, Stanley Diamond (1956; rpt New York: Schocken Books 1972) 155; Karl Kerényi, 'Trickster in Relation to Greek Mythology,' in *Trickster* 185. As readers of Radin's work, Terry Goldie's *Fear and Temptation*, and Gaile McGregor's *The Noble Savage in the New World Garden* are no doubt aware, the use of trickster is inevitably a 'white' appropriation and rendering of 'native' content, however sympathetic to native perspectives. Radin's study, in particular, offers a Euro/ethnocentric definition and usage of the trickster motif. Robert Bly's casette *The Naive Male* (Ally Press, St Paul MN 1988) offers a North American perspective on trickster, connecting the male god of trickery to betrayal and naiveté, qualities evident in the young De Haldimar and Morton respectively.
74 Kerényi, 'Trickster in Relation to Greek Mythology,' in *Trickster* 182, 188
75 Larsen, *Shaman's Doorway* 217
76 Margot Northey, *The Haunted Wilderness: The Gothic and Grotesque in Canadian Fiction* (Toronto: University of Toronto Press 1976) 21
77 Early, 'Myth and Prejudice,' in *Canadian Literature* 30
78 Richard De Mille, *Castaneda's Journey* (Santa Barbara: Capra Press 1976) 110
79 Kerényi, 'Trickster in Relation to Greek Mythology,' in *Trickster* 185
80 George Bowering, 'Sheila Watson, Trickster,' in *Modern Times: A Critical Anthology*, The Canadian Novel III, ed. John Moss (Toronto: NC Press 1982) 214
81 Carl Jung, 'On the Psychology of the Trickster Figure,' in *Trickster* 201, 203–4. See also Marie-Louise von Franz's *Patterns of Creativity Mirrored in Creation Myths* (Dallas: Spring Publications 1986) 63–4, 186.
82 De Mille, *Castaneda's Journey* 110
83 Bowering, ' Sheila Watson, Trickster,' in *Modern Times* 215
84 Jung, 'On the Psychology of the Trickster Figure,' in *Trickster* 202

85 Ibid. 203
86 Ibid. 208–9
87 Radin, *Trickster* xxiii. See Frye, *English Romanticism* 31.
88 Norval Morriseau, *Legends of My People, The Great Ojibway*, ed. Selwyn Dewdney (Toronto: McGraw-Hill 1965) 20
89 James R. Stevens, *Sacred Legends of the Sandy Lake Cree* (Toronto: McClelland and Stewart 1971) 20
90 Radin, *Trickster* xxiv
91 Basil Johnston, *Ojibway Heritage* (Toronto: McClelland and Stewart 1976) 159–60
92 Jung, 'On the Psychology of the Trickster Figure,' in *Trickster* 195
93 Ibid. 206
94 Kerényi, 'Trickster in Relation to Greek Mythology,' in *Trickster* 188, 182, 186, 189
95 Lecker, 'Patterns of Deception in *Wacousta*,' in *The Canadian Novel: Beginnings* 58
96 Bolen, *Gods* 169
97 De Mille, *Castaneda's Journey* 108
98 Carlos Castaneda, *A Separate Reality: Further Conversations with Don Juan* (New York: Simon and Schuster 1971) 130; *Tales of Power* (New York: Simon and Schuster 1974) 161, 48, 252, 48, 53, 17; *Journey to Ixtlan: The Lessons of Don Juan* (New York: Simon and Schuster 1972) 315
99 Stanley Diamond, introduction, *Trickster* xiii
100 Ella E. Clark, *Indian Legends of Canada* (Toronto: McClelland and Stewart 1960) 10
101 Johnston, *Ojibway Heritage* 58
102 Radin, *Trickster* xxiii
103 Kerényi, 'Trickster in Relation to Greek Mythology,' in *Trickster* 180–1
104 Richardson, *Canadian Brothers* I, 128–32
105 Jung, 'On the Psychology of the Trickster Figure,' in *Trickster* 211
106 Ibid. 211
107 In 'Death is a Happy Ending,' in *Figures* 209
108 Quoted in Edinger, *Ego and Archetype* 101
109 John Lennon and Yoko Ono, *Double Fantasy*, Geffen Records, XGHS 2001, 1980. See also Robert Bly, *The Naive Male*.
110 Duffy, *Gardens* 52–4
111 Reaney, 'An ABC to Ontario Literature and Culture,' in *Halloween* 3 3
112 Major John Richardson, *Westbrook, the Outlaw; or, The Avenging Wolf: An American Border Tale* (1851; rpt Montreal: Grant Woolmer Books 1973) 1
113 Richardson, *Westbrook* 1, 7, 57

114 Ibid. 73
115 Ibid. 29, 42, 8, 45
116 Ibid. 51, 40, 4
117 Ibid. 42, 9–10
118 Ibid. 10
119 Duffy, *Gardens* 52–4
120 Beasley, *Canadian Don Quixote* 189
121 Major John Richardson, *Hardscrabble; or, The Fall of Chicago: A Tale of Indian Warfare* (New York: Robert M. Dewitt 1855) 69; Major John Richardson, *Wau-Nan-Gee; or, The Massacre at Chicago: A Romance of the American Revolution* (New York: H. Long and Brother 1852) 94, 41
122 Richardson, *Wau-Nan-Gee* 16
123 Beasley, *Canadian Don Quixote* 176

6 No End in Sight

1 Frye, *Bush Garden* 250; Hutcheon, *Canadian Postmodern* 4, 81; W.H. New, *Dreams of Speech and Violence: The Art of the Short Story in Canada and New Zealand* (Toronto: University of Toronto Press 1987) 99
2 Atwood, 'Monsters' in *Canadian Imagination* 99
3 Reaney, 'Topless Nightmares,' in *Halloween* 2 9
4 See Kroetsch's comment in *Lovely Treachery* (147) that 'it is the first task of the Canadian writer to uninvent the world.' My use of the words 'bookless' and 'visible/invisible' echoes passages from the first essay in Kroetsch's collection (9, 6). See also Kroetsch's notes on 'pattern of contraries' such as 'record and invent' in 'On Being an Alberta Writer,' in *Open Letter* 5:4 (Spring 1983) 76, Hutcheon's reflections on this in *Canadian Postmodern* 19, and the title of her conclusion.
5 Alice Munro, *Lives of Girls and Women* (1971; rpt New York: Signet 1974) 210
6 Kroetsch, *Lovely Treachery* 129
7 Atwood, 'Eleven Years of *Alphabet*,' in *Second Words* 94
8 Marian Engel, *Bear* (Toronto: Seal Books 1976) 102

Index

Alphabet, 128, 172

American cultural/literary motifs, 142, 148, 153, 157–8, 199, 201, 206; American Adam, 22, 164; and Canada, 110; editorial practices, 96; and history-writing, 21; independent loners, 70, 81; individualism, 17; marriage of males, 84, 199; outlaws, 20, 24, 106, 115, 145–6; sharp boundaries, 23

American South, 19–20, 150, 182

Andrews, Lynn, 191

Atwood, Margaret, 22, 133, 214n.56; and Canadian tradition, 4, 202–3; and doubleness, 6, 19, 34, 68, 189; and establishment representatives, 13, 104–5, 170, 173; and gothic, 17, 78, 160; and Indian mythology, 184; and straight line/curve motif, 59–60; and synthesis, 206. Works: 'Canadian Monsters: Some Aspects of the Supernatural in Canadian Fiction,' 202; *The Circle Game*, 65; *The Edible Woman*, 213n.35; *The Handmaid's Tale*, 108, 161, 170, 172;

The Journals of Susanna Moodie, 48, 50, 63–5; *Progressive Insanities of a Pioneer*, 52; 'Superwoman Drawn and Quartered: The Early Forms of *She*,' 76, 215n.3; *Survival*, 39, 173, 212n.21; *Surfacing*, 63, 65, 146

Audubon, John James, 8

Avison, Margaret, 34; *History of Ontario*, 157

Axton, W.F., 161–2, 166

balance; balancing, 15–16, 28, 50, 108, 130–1; in *The Canadian Brothers*, 148; of De Haldimar and Wacousta, 73, 85, 127, 194; of equal opposite forces, 12, 14, 31–4; of European culture and wilderness, 10–11, 62, 154; of order and disorder figures, 15, 96–7; Richardson's fascination with, 5, 70, 205; and Trickster, 191

Ballstadt, Carl, 30

Beasley, David, x, 10, 199, 201, 209n.7; *The Canadian Don Quixote: The Life and Works of Major John*

Richardson, Canada's First Novelist, 7

Beautiful Dreamers, 173

Beckwith-Hart, Julia Catherine, 9

Beddoes, Thomas Lovell, 142–4; *The Bride's Tragedy*, 121; *Death's Jest Book*, 121, 162; *The Second Brother*, 162

Bersianik, Louky, 171

Big Bear, 11

Black Elk/Hehaka Sapa, 39–40

Blake, William, 86, 129, 140

Blondal, Patricia: *A Candle to Light the Sun*, 171

Bloom, Harold, 164

Bly, Robert: and Davies, 104; and descent, 141; and father-son bond, 106; and Hermes, 190; and mythopoetic men's movement, ix, 14, 99; and patriarchy, 18; and *senex*, 167–9; and Trickster, 19, 185, 194; and wounds, 101; and Zeus, 108, 147. Works: *Iron John: A Book about Men*, 14, 92–5, 104, 106–7, 166, 183, 189, 191; *The Naive Male* (cassette), 222n.73, 223n.109

Bolen, Jean Shinoda, 15, 18–19, 99, 144, 167; and goddess cultures, 107; and Hermes, 190; and Trickster, 185; and Zeus, 105, 108–9. Works: *Goddesses in Everywoman: A New Psychology of Women*, 218n.8; *Gods in Everyman: A New Psychology of Men*, 14, 92, 105

border blur, 6, 15–17, 23, 56, 66, 203, 205; and Atwood, 65; between autobiographical and fictive, 20, 158; and *The Canadian Brothers*, 150; and descent narratives, 116; between European and Indian, 78;

and gothic, 32, 157; and identity, 61, 72–3, 76, 179, 188–9, 205; and national epics, 153; and origin of term, 5; and Poseidon, 93; and postmodernism, 206; and Trickster, 183, 191–2; in *Wacousta*, 43–54; in *Wuthering Heights*, 25

borders, key statements on: and border legend, 19; and the border river, 15–16, 67; Canadian border *vs* American frontier, 12, 81; by Chase, 29; and doubles, 16, 18, 29, 31, 82, 111, 131, 161, 205; by Frye, 29; and identity, 13, 56, 66–7, 79, 147; by McLuhan, 27, 29, 58, 81; by Mandel, 29–30; by Morton, 29; by Moss, 29; as *the* postmodern space, 202; as Richardson's focus, 4–5, 10, 209n.1, 213n.35

Bosch, Hieronymous, 136

Boulding, Kenneth, 67

Bowering, George, 13, 15, 20, 22, 30, 185–6; *Burning Water*, 82; *A Short Sad Book*, 152

Brant, Chief Joseph, 10

break boundaries, 12, 16, 28, 157; in *The Canadian Brothers*, 111, 115, 125–6; and doubles, 205; and origin of term, 5–6; and romance, 126; and Trickster, 184, 191; in *Wacousta*, 58–69; and *White Narcissus*, 179; and Woodman, 25

Brock, General Isaac, 8, 21, 24, 146, 149

Brontë, Emily, 21, 25; *Wuthering Heights*, 12, 25, 32, 83–4, 143, 164

Bucke, R.M.: *Cosmic Consciousness*, 173

Buckler, Ernest: *The Mountain and the Valley*, 73, 91

Burning Times, The, 217n.41. *See also* feminist perspectives

Byron, Lord George Gordon, 21, 84, 122, 136, 188, 207; as strong influence on Richardson, 158. Works: *The Giaour,* 164; *Lara,* 165; *Manfred,* 124

Cain and Abel, 74, 101, 140–1, 149–50, 177; Canadian Cain *vs* American Adam, 22, 84; in Frye, 12

Callaghan, Morley, 97, 104. Works: *Close to the Sun Again,* 105, 122, 170–1, 177, 180; *It's Never Over,* 147; *The Loved and the Lost,* 13, 89–90; *More Joy in Heaven,* 146; *A Passion in Rome,* 147

Campbell, Joseph, 13, 15, 33, 47, 167; and ascent narratives, 144, 148; and descent narratives, 22, 116–8, 133; and monsters, 159; and romance, 126. Works: *The Hero's Journey: The World of Joseph Campbell,* 213n.28; *The Hero with a 1000 Faces,* 213n.28, 218nn.2,5; *The Power of Myth,* 213nn.28, 37

Canadian Brothers, The. See Richardson, John: *The Canadian Brothers; or, The Prophecy Fulfilled*

carnivalesque, x, 91, 131, 203, 205

Carpenter, Edmund: *The Eskimo and his Art,* 57

Carr, Emily, 207

Castaneda, Carlos, 185, 191

Chase, Richard, 28–9, 43, 68, 83, 131

Children of Peace, 23. *See also* Willson, David

Christ, Carol, 99

circles and squares, 12, 28, 93, 151,

169, 184; as Atwood's terms, 212n.21; in *The Canadian Brothers,* 137–44; in *Wacousta,* 34–43

Cirlot, J.E., 140; *A Dictionary of Symbols,* 118

Clark, Ella E.: *Indian Legends of Canada,* 192

Cohen, Leonard: *Beautiful Losers,* 13, 43, 55, 60, 82, 87, 89–90, 146, 170, 211n.26

Cohen, Matt, 30; Salem novels, 82, 197

Cohen, Nathan, 156

Coleridge, S.T.: *Christabel,* 121; *Remorse,* 163; *The Rime of the Ancient Mariner,* 123; *Zapolya,* 163

Connor, Ralph: *The Sky Pilot,* 213n.35

Conrad, Joseph, 81; *Heart of Darkness,* 49, 55–6, 136, 148

Cooper, James Fenimore, 7, 12, 51, 220n.19; and American myth, 24–5; and denial of gothic, 157–8; and his frontier *vs* Richardson's border, 12, 31–2, 163–4, 198, 200, 204; and national epics, 150, 152–5; and Richardson and Scott, 21–2; and view of history, 149; and womanless romances, 170. Works: *The Last of the Mohicans,* 7, 154–5, 200; Leatherstocking Tales, 31, 44, 63–4

Crawford, Isabel Valancy, 90

Crestwood Heights, 173

Cronk, Douglas: MA thesis, 6, 212n.3, 221n.40

Curnoe, Greg, 18

Dacre, Charlotte: *Zofloya, the Moor,* 162

Daly, Mary, 107
Davey, Frank: *The Louis Riel Organ and Piano Company*, 207
Davies, Robertson: and Bly, 104; and documentary detail, 44; and *enantiodromia*, 54, 67–8; and equally matched opposites, 5, 16, 83–97; and gothic, 6, 17, 22, 78, 156; and Kroetsch, 16, 99; and *senex*, 13, 18; and wolf-double, 19. Works: 'The Canada of Myth and Reality,' 86; Deptford trilogy, 101, 173–4, 176–7, 180–1, 189, 197; *Fifth Business*, 16, 170–1; *The Manticore*, 86, 104–5; *The Rebel Angels*, 162, 211n.26; *World of Wonders*, 55, 121, 162, 188
De Haldimar-like establishment representatives in Canadian literature, 13, 22, 33, 100, 105, 171, 173
De Mille, Richard: *Castaneda's Journey*, 185–6, 191
descent narrative, 4, 29, 203, 205; and Bowering, 15; and Campbell, 15, 22; in *The Canadian Brothers*, 110–55; characteristics of, 33; and Frye, 15–16
Dewdney, Christopher, 18, 44; *Fovea Centralis*, 181
documentary realism and mythic patterning, blurring of, 122, 149, 153–4; in contemporary writers, 30; and Hutcheon, 111, 158–9; and Southern Ontario writing, 16, 20–1, 44–5, 195–6
doubles; doppelgängers; doubleness: and Atwood, 17; and Blondal, 171; border phenomena of, 5–6, 23, 33, 40–2, 205–6; and Canadian psyche, 9, 11, 18; in *The Canadian*

Brothers, 33–4, 129, 141, 147; and contemporary writers, 5, 82; and Cooper and Scott, 22, 31; and descent narratives, 15–16, 33, 67, 127; and Frye, 29, 67, 126; and Hawthorne, 28; and Jung, 186; and Keats, 123; and postmodernism, 5, 22; Richardson's fascination with, 5–6, 9–10, 15, 21, 35, 204; and struggle-of-brothers theme, 12, 16, 111, 127, 163; and Trickster, 186, 191; in *Wacousta*, 36, 46, 53, 62, 66, 69–109; and wolf-like figures, 19, 189
Drew, Wayland, 157
Duerk, Judith: *Circle of Stones: Woman's Journey to Herself*, 217n.41
Duffy, Dennis, 18, 41; *Gardens, Covenants, Exiles: Loyalism in the Literature of Upper Canada/Ontario*, 195, 199
Durham, Lord, 8

Early, L.R., 102, 185
Edinger, Edward F., 127; *Ego and Archetype: Individuation and the Religious Function of the Psyche*, 78
Eisler, Riane, ix, 99, 167, 169; *The Chalice and the Blade: Our History, Our Future*, 14, 107; *The Partnership Way*, 14, 107
Elliott, George, 173
enantiodromia, 25, 54, 67, 194
Engel, Marian, 13, 25–6, 156, 173, 182, 221n.46; *Bear*, 207; *The Glassy Sea*, 82; *The Honeyman Festival*, 175

fairy tales, 93, 169, 179, 196, 199. See also *Grimm's Fairy Tales*
father-son relationship, 105–9, 112

feminist perspectives, ix, 14, 92, 99, 101, 107. *See also* Bolen, Jean Shinoda; Christ, Carol; Daly, Mary; Eisler, Riane; Gilligan, Carol; Spretnak, Charlene; Starhawk; Stone, Merlin; Teish, Luisah; Woodman, Marion

Ferris, Ina, 147

Fiedler, Leslie, 20, 160, 170; *Freaks: Myths and Images of the Secret Self*, 159

Findley, Timothy, 20–2, 30, 44, 97, 111, 202; on gothic Southern Ontario, 17, 156; *The Wars*, 151, 189

Foucault, Michel, 13, 103

Franz, Marie-Louise von, 168; *Patterns of Creativity Mirrored in Creation Myths*, 222n.81

Frazer, Sir James G.: *The Golden Bough*, 128

Freeman, Mac, x, 107, 194, 217n.41

Frye, Northrop, 4, 13, 53, 147–8, 160; and Beddoes, 121; and Byronic heroes, 188; and descent narratives, 15, 33, 116, 119, 136, 139, 145; and doppelgängers, 29, 43; and gothic, 49, 67, 159–60; and immigrant and indigenous mentalities, 11, 34–5; and the land, 46–7, 56, 58; and Southern Ontario, 182; and struggle-of-brothers theme, 12, 143–4. Works: 'Conclusion to a *Literary History of Canada*,' 202; *Divisions on a Ground: Essays on Canadian Culture*, 36, 67, 69; *The Secular Scripture: A Study of the Structure of Romance*, 15, 67, 126, 152; *A Study of English Romanticism*, 83, 223n.87

Getty, Adele: *Goddess: Mother of Living Nature*, 217n.41

Gibson, Graeme, 17–18, 157, 173, 176, 182; *Five Legs*, 102, 177, 180; *Perpetual Motion*, 89, 105

Gillette, Douglas, 108. *See also* Moore, Robert

Gilligan, Carol, 107

goddess cultures, 107, 217n.41. *See also* feminist perspectives

Goddess Remembered, 217n.41

Godfrey, Dave, 182; *The New Ancestors*, 170

Godwin, William, 18; *Caleb Williams*, 163

Goethe, Johann Wolfgang von, 120, 163

Goldie, Terry: *Fear and Temptation: The Image of the Indigene in Canadian, Australian, and New Zealand Literatures*, 11, 210n.14, 222n.73

gothic: and Atwood, 17, 48, 203, 211n.18; in *The Canadian Brothers*, 153, 156–201; in Canadian literature, 17, 25, 156–201; and Coleridge, 121, 123; and Cooper and Scott, 22, 32, 220n.19; and Frye, 49, 67, 159–60; and *Hardscrabble*, 20, 198–9; and Hawthorne, 28; and identity, 47, 74; and Keats, 123; and nineteenth-century writers, 18; and author's PHD thesis, 220n.28; and Purdy, 48; and Southern Ontario, 17, 19, 82, 156–201; and Symons, 56; and *Wacousta*, 156–201; and *Wau-Nan-Gee*, 20, 198–9; and *Westbrook*, 20, 153, 195–201; and *Wuthering Heights*, 25

Graves, Robert, 139

Grimm's Fairy Tales, 93, 195
Grove, F.P., 13, 100, 104–5, 108, 197, 216n.32; *Fruits of the Earth*, 107; *The Master of the Mill*, 82, 100–1; *Our Daily Bread*, 108; *Over Prairie Trails*, 91
Gutteridge, Don: *Tecumseh*, 39, 207

Haggard, Rider, 76; *She*, 139
Harrison, Dick, 30
Hawthorne, Nathaniel, 28, 48, 164
Heavysege, Charles: *The Advocate*, 101
Helwig, David: the Kingston tetralogy, 178
Henry, Alexander the Elder, 20; *Travels and Adventures in Canada and the Indian Territories*, 159
Hillman, James, x, 99
Hoffmann, E.T.A., 163
Hogg, James, 18; *The Confessions of a Justified Sinner*, 163–4
Homer: *The Odyssey*, 125
Hospital, Janette Turner: *Borderline*, 213n.32
Hutcheon, Linda, 5, 26, 28, 111, 159; *The Canadian Postmodern: A Study of Contemporary English-Canadian Fiction*, 4, 202, 210n.16, 211n.2, 215n.6, 224n.4

Indians/Native peoples 3, 8–9, 11, 19, 24, 33, 39, 170; and use of term 'Indian,' 210n.14; and Trickster, 183–95
In Flanders Fields, 174

Johnston, Basil: *Ojibway Heritage*, 189, 192
Jones, D.C., 4, 89, 100, 128, 143,

216n.32; *Butterfly on Rock: A Study of Themes and Images in Canadian Literature*, 99, 214n.48
Jones, Ray, x, 99
Jung, C.G. and Jungian references, 14, 25, 78, 92, 127, 167–8, 174; and border blur, 47; and *enantiodromia*, 194; on God, 195; and opposites coinciding, 16, 68, 76, 95; and Trickster, 19, 184; 'On The Psychology of the Trickster Figure,' 186–7, 189

Kaufman, Michael, x, 99
Keats, John, 144; *La Belle Dame Sans Merci*, 123; *Lamia*, 123
Kerenyi, Karl, 19, 184–5, 192
King, Mackenzie, 67, 86
Klinck, Carl, 29
Knister, Raymond, 18, 156, 173; *White Narcissus*, 176–80, 213n.35
Kroetsch, Robert, 1, 13, 26, 43, 97, 99, 104, 133; and borders and gaps, 4–5; and Canadian literature, 22, 96, 145; and Frye, 15, 224n.4; and opposites in balance, 14, 16, 68, 74, 96, 194, 210n.17; and postmodernism, 78, 202, 204n.4; and regional myth, 30; and Trickster, 194–5. Works: *Alibi*, 82; *Badlands*, 82, 105, 170–1; *But We Are Exiles*, 55, 68, 89, 215n.71; *The Lovely Treachery of Words*, 206, 218n.2, 224n.4; 'On Being an Alberta Writer,' 224n.4; *The Studhorse Man*, 82, 99; *What the Crow Said*, 218n.2

Lame Deer/John Fire, 40
Lampman, Archibald, 89

Larsen, Stephen, 168; *The Shaman's Doorway: Opening the Mythic Imagination to Contemporary Consciousness*, 18, 167, 185

Laurence, Margaret, 82, 104; *The Stone Angel*, 105, 172, 213n.35

Lawrence, D.H., 160; *The Spirit of Place*, 155; *Studies in Classic American Literature*, 157

Lecker, Robert, 32, 59, 190, 213n.24

Lee, Dennis, 4, 37, 83; and opposites coinciding, 43, 130–1; *Savage Fields: An Essay in Literature and Cosmology*, 27, 60–1, 68

Lee, John, x

Lennon, John: *Double Fantasy*, 195

Le Pan, Douglas: *Coureurs de bois*, 86; *The Deserter*, 12, 87, 90, 145–6

Lewis, Monk, 18; *Alonso the Brave*, 162; *The Castle Spectre*, 162

Literary Garland, 11, 184

love triangles, 6, 12, 41, 70, 77, 80–1, 86, 201; list of, in *Wacousta*, 76

McGregor, Gaile: *The Noble Savage in the New World Garden*, 222n.73; *The Wacousta Syndrome: Explorations in the Canadian Langscape*, 6–7

MacLaren, I.S., 220n.28

MacLennan, Hugh: *Barometer Rising*, 168; *The Watch that Ends the Night*, 13, 55, 82, 90, 170

McLuhan, Marshall, 43, 57, 83, 116, 131, 211n.2; 'Canada: The Borderline Case,' 5, 27–9, 68, 77, 81; *Understanding Media: The Extensions of Man*, 67, 214n.50

Macpherson, Jay, 63, 118, 127–8, 147, 160

Mandel, Eli, 47, 57, 68, 182; *Another Time*, 29–30; 'Atwood Gothic,' 160; 'The Border League: American "West" and Canadian "Region,"' 30

Marshall, Tom: *Rosemary Goal*, 82, 174, 177; *Voices on the Brink: A Border Tale*, 11

Mathews, Robin, 97

Maturin, Charles Robert, 18, 161; *The Fatal Revenge*, 162; *Melmoth the Wanderer*, 162

Meade, Michael, x, 14–15

Melville, Herman, 45, 164

men's movement, ix, 14, 99, 101; and the De Haldimar-Wacousta relationship, 92–5; and Zeus and the patriarchy, 105–9. *See also* Bly, Robert; Gillette, Douglas; Hillman, James; Jones, Ray; Kaufman, Michael; Lee, John; Meade, Michael; Moore, Robert; Stein, Murray; Wilson, Tim

Milton, John: *Paradise Lost*, 162, 165

Mitchell, W.O.: *Who Has Seen The Wind*, 13, 19, 55, 90–1, 100, 174, 189

Miyoshi, Masao, 70–1, 123

Moers, Ellen: *Literary Women*, 160

Monk Knight, The. See Richardson, John: *The Monk Knight of St. John*

Monkman, Leslie, ix, 1, 22; 'Canadian Historical Fiction,' 211n.24

Moore, Brian: *I Am Mary Dunne*, 82

Moore, Robert, x, 14, 18, 99, 107, 168, 170, 191; and shadow kings, definition of, 108, 169; and Trickster, 185. Works: *King, Warrior, Magician, Lover: Rediscovering the Archetypes of the Mature Masculine*, 14, 108, 217n.43; *Rediscovering*

Masculine Potentials (cassette), 217n.43

Morley, William F.E., x

Morriseau, Norval: *Legends of My People the Great Ojibway*, 188

Morton, W.L., 29

mort-vivants, 18, 120–1, 166–83, 203

Moss, John, 4, 18, 29, 41, 63, 68, 170; *A Reader's Guide to the Canadian Novel*, 152; *Patterns of Isolation in English-Canadian Fiction*, 215n.71

Munro, Alice, 6, 182; and American South, 20; and documentary realism, 44; and gothic, 17, 78, 156, 178, 205; and Jubilee, 173, 175, 180. Works: *Dance of the Happy Shades*, 175, 177–8; *Who Do You Think You Are?*, 219n.1

mythological figures and patterns: Apollo and Dionysus, 76, 205; and Bly, 108, 190; and Bolen, 92, 105, 108–9, 185, 190; and Campbell, 15, 116–7, 133; and Canada, 11, 49, 111, 154, 203; Circe, 15, 136, 139; and Cirlot, 118, 140; crippled tyrant, 167–9; and Frye, 116, 159; and Hades, 120–1, 170; Hermes, 14, 19, 190; and Meade, 14–15; Medea, 218n.8; Medusa, 174; Narcissus, 16, 33, 87, 110, 126–9, 147; Pan, 178; Persephone, 170; Polyphemus, 133–7; Poseidon, 14, 112–4, 122, 139, 172; and Southern Ontario, 19, 201; Trickster, 183–95; Venus, 64, 75, 77, 142; The Wild Man, 91–5; and Woodman, 174; Zeus, 14, 99, 105–9. *See also* Trickster

National Film Board, 173, 217n.41

Needham, Richard, 172–3

New, W.H.: *Articulating West: Essays on Purpose and Form in Modern Canadian Literature*, 110, 166; *Dreams of Speech and Violence: The Art of the Short Story in Canada and New Zealand*, 202

Nichol, b.p., 5, 47

Nodelman, Perry, 100

Northey, Margot, 18, 41, 63, 160, 185

Norton, John, 10, 183, 210n.8

Nowlan, Alden: *Various Persons Named Kevin O'Brien*, 82

O'Hagan, Howard, 19; *Tay John*, 13, 55, 63, 90, 170–1, 189, 213n.35

Olson, Charles: *Call Me Ishmael*, 51–2

Ondaatje, Michael, 5–6, 16, 22, 160, 202, 214n.56; and border blur, 47; and documentary realism, 111; and equally matched opposites, 14; and historical subjects, 20, 195. Works: *The Collected Works of Billy the Kid*, 37, 43, 60–1, 90, 100; *In the Skin of a Lion*, 69, 174

Ontario. *See* Southern Ontario/ Southwestern Ontario ('Souwesto')

opposites, equally matched in balance: and the border, 11–12, 15–17, 28, 32, 34, 58, 62–3, 81, 116, 130–1, 205; and Brontë, 25; in *The Canadian Brothers*, 74, 118, 140, 145, 151; and Canadian psyche, 86, 96; and Cooper and Scott, 31; and Davies, 5, 67–8, 86; and doubles, 85, 163; and von Franz, 168; and Frye, 43, 53; and Hospital, 213n.32; and Kroetsch, 5, 68, 210n.17, 224n.4; and Lee, Dennis,

43; and love triangles, 76; and McLuhan, 5; and Ondaatje, 14; and Shelley, Mary, 25; and Trickster, 183–4, 187, 192

Orwell, George: *Nineteen Eighty-Four*, 174

Ostenso, Martha: *Wild Geese*, 105

Oxford Companion to Canadian Literature, The, 159–60

Pacey, Desmond, 10

Page, P.K.: *The Sun and the Moon*, 63

paradoxes; paradoxical inversions. *See* border blur; break boundaries

parallels; correspondences. *See* spiralling repetition and replay; parallels; interconnections

patriarchy, 105–7, 169; and Bolen, 93; and Bly, 106–7; and De Haldimar, 18, 97, 100, 107–9, 169; and Eisler, 107, 169; and Engel, 207; and feminist writers, 107, 220n.31; and goddess cultures, 107; and modern Canadian literature, 169–71; and Moore, Robert, 169; and war on women, 23; and Woodman, 171, 220n.31. *See also* Bolen, Jean Shinoda; Bly, Robert; Eisler, Riane; Moore, Robert; Woodman, Marion

Pick's, 9

Ponteac (historical figure), 9, 24, 30, 158

postmodernism, xi, 89, 210n.16, 211n.2; and the border, 202; and Frye and Kroetsch, 218n.2; and gothic, 161; and Richardson, 1, 3, 21–2, 78, 82, 159, 161, 206. *See also* Hutcheon, Linda

Pratt, E.J., 37, 56, 157

Praz, Mario: *The Romantic Agony*, 139

Purdy, Al: *The Runners*, 48

Radcliffe, Ann, 9, 19, 161; *The Italian*, 162; *The Romance of the Forest*, 162

Radin, Paul: *The Trickster: A Study in American Indian Mythology*, 19, 184, 186, 188–9, 192, 222n.73

Reaney, James, ix, 10, 13–15, 97, 127, 133, 209n.1; and adaptation of Richardson's work, 207; and documentary and myth, 44, 111; and gothic, 17, 156–7, 160; and Ontario, 3, 203; and Richardson's ancestry, 3; and Richardson as 'Father of Canadian Literature,' 1, 3, 26, 138–9; and 'Souwesto,' 18–22, 78, 173; and *Westbrook*, 195. Works: *Alphabet*, 128, 172; *Baldoon*, 157, 170, 173–4, 177; *The Boy with an R in his Hand*, 173; *Colours in the Dark*, 27, 179; *The Dismissal*, 173; *The Donnelleys: A Trilogy*, 13, 55, 63, 89–90, 146, 173, 177–81; *14 Barrels from Sea to Sea*, 221n.46; *Halloween*, 110; *Listen to the Wind*, 177; *The St. Nicholas Hotel*, 105; *Three Desks*, 173; *The Upper Canadian*, 176; *Wacousta!*, 30, 34, 39

Reaney, J. Stewart: *James Reaney*, 216n.19

Richardson, Major John: ancestry of, 3, 8–11, 20, 80, 176, 195; as borderline case, 10; as critic of 'progress' and garrison mentality, 23, 94, 211n.25; as eccentric as Emily Carr, 207; as 'ex-centric' writer, 4–5, 7, 24, 203; as 'Father of Canadian Literature,' 1, 3, 9, 26,

206–7; and (alleged) Indian ancestry and familiarity with native peoples, 3, 10–11, 182–3; later years of, 196; personae of, 8–9; as soldier and POW, 8, 158. Works: *The Canadian Brothers; or, The Prophecy Fulfilled: A Tale of the Late American War*, 110–55; and the border, 28, 213n.35; and border blur, 47; and doubles, 129–30; and establishment representatives, 13, 173; and father-son bond, 106, 172; and gothic, 166; and history, 21, 35; and Munro, 175–6; as national epic, 4, 24, 20, 183, 203; and outcasts, 55, 63; and Poseidon, 92; and spiralling repetition and replay, 130–1, 134–8, 149; and *Wacousta*, 1, 15, 17, 34, 65, 70, 72, 74, 89, 109, 111–2, 116–9, 151–2, 158, 177, 193; and *War of 1812*, 21, 39, 159; and *Westbrook*, 196–7; and Woodcock, 21; 'A Canadian Campaign, by a British Officer,' 11; *Ecarté; or, The Salons of Paris*, 30, 153; *Eight Years in Canada ...*, 20; *Frascati's; or, Scenes in Paris*, 73, 84, 153; *The Guards in Canada; or, The Point of Honour*, 94; *Hardscrabble; or, The Fall of Chicago: A Tale of Indian Warfare*, 20, 198–201; *The Monk Knight of St. John: A Tale of the Crusades*: author's article on, 211n.26; and doubles and triangles, 5, 73, 76, 83; and feminist perspectives, 14; and romantic macabre, 121; and sexual theme, 9, 95, 201; and spiralling repetition and replay, 138, 190; and vampire motif, 120; and Wacousta-like outcasts, 55, 146–7; and war on women, 23; and *Westbrook*, 198–9; *Tecumseh; or, The Warrior of the West: A Poem, in Four Cantos, with Notes by John Richardson*, 11, 30, 39; 'A Trip to Walpole Island and Port Sarnia,' 11; *Wacousta; or, The Prophecy: A Tale of the Canadas*: and break boundaries, 27–58; and connections to *The Canadian Brothers*, 1, 15, 17, 34, 65, 70, 72, 74, 89, 109, 111–2, 116–9, 151–2, 158, 177, 193; and doubles, 69–105; 'Eden' flashback in, 31, 86–91, 97, 127, 141, 164, 181, 185; and gothic, 156–95; as national epic, 4–6, 20, 22, 24–5, 30–2, 152–5, 203; textual history of, 6–7, 96, 169–70; *Wau-Nan-Gee; or, The Massacre at Chicago: A Romance of the American Revolution*, 20, 198–201; *Westbrook, The Outlaw; or, The Avenging Wolf: An American Border Tale*, 20, 30, 55, 153, 176, 195–9

Richler, Mordecai, 13, 68; *The Apprenticeship of Duddy Kravitz*, 101
Richter, Jean Paul, 85, 163
Riddell, W.R., 206
Riel, Louis, 10–11, 13, 171–2
romance, key statements on: and borders, 5–6, 116, 125; and Brontë, 21; by Campbell, 33, 116, 126; by Chase, 28–9; by Frye, 12, 33, 67, 116, 126; and Mary Shelley, 21
Ross, Catherine: *Recovering Canada's First Novelist: Proceedings of the John Richardson Conference*, 220n.28
Ross, Sinclair, 13, 19; *As For Me And My House*, 54–5, 90, 172, 189, 213n.35

Sartre, Jean-Paul, 68

Schlegel, Friedrich, 85

Scott, Chris, 111; *Antichthon*, 13, 82, 96, 161

Scott, D.C., 89; *At Gull Lake: August 1810*, 75

Scott, Sir Walter: and Cooper and Richardson, 21–5, 152–5, 204; and doubles, 163; and dual worlds, 32; and gothic, 158, 220n.19; and historical view, 149; and national epics, 150, 152–5. Works: *Guy Mannering*, 126; *Rob Roy*, 31, 126; Waverley Novels, 31–2, 66

senex, 18, 114, 166–83

Shakespeare, William, 32; *Hamlet*, 52; *Othello*, 142, 197

Shelley, Mary, 21, 25; *Frankenstein; or, The Modern Prometheus*, 162–5

Shelley, Percy Bysshe, 18, 165, 207; *Alastor*, 124–5; *St. Irvyne; or, The Rosicrucian*, 162–3; *Zastrozzi; A Romance*, 162

Snyder, Gary, 186

Southern Ontario/Southwestern Ontario ('Souwesto'), x, 3, 10–11, 32, 156–201, 203, 207; as gothic region, 19–20, 49, 65, 110, 156–201; and Grove, 107; and Kroetsch, 89; and origin of term 'Souwesto,' 18; and writers from, 16–20, 25, 30, 82, 86

Spettigue, Douglas, x

spiralling repetition and replay; parallels; interconnections: and border, 5, 12, 31, 41, 107; in *The Canadian Brothers*, 130–1, 134–8, 149; definition of, 27–8; and doubles, 22; and feminist perspectives, 14, 107; and McLuhan, 27–8; in *The Monk Knight*, 138; in *Wacousta*, 42, 60, 72, 75, 78–83

Spretnak, Charlene, 99, 107

Starhawk, 107

Stassinopoulos, Arianna, 108; *The Gods of Greece*, 92, 183

Stein, Murray, 190

Sterne, Laurence, 9

Stevens, James R: *Legends of the Sandy Lake Cree*, 188

Stevenson, Robert Louis: *Dr. Jekyll and Mr. Hyde*, 164

Stoker, Bram: *Dracula*, 120

Stone, Merlin, 107

struggle-of-brothers theme: and Brontë, 25; in *The Canadian Brothers*, 111–2, 121–2, 143; and doubles, 16; and Frye, 12; and gothic, 166; and Narcissus, 127; and other nineteenth-century works, 162–3; and Mary Shelley, 25; and Trickster, 192–3; and twentieth-century Canadian works, 171, 189; in *Wacousta*, 83–91; and women, 22

Sullivan, Rosemary: 'Summing Up,' in *Crossing Frontiers: Papers in American and Canadian Western Literature*, 210n.17

Swan, Susan, 171, 202; *The Biggest Modern Woman of the World*, 110

Symons, Scott, 13, 27, 55–6, 173, 178, 182; *Combat Journal for Place D'Armes*, 87

synchronicity, 9, 130, 147, 183, 190. *See also* Spiralling repetition and replay; parallels; interconnections

Tecumseh (historical figure), 8, 11,

21, 110; as Richardson's lifelong hero, 183

Teish, Luisah, 107

Thomas, Audrey, 25, 27, 170; *Intertidal Life*, 170

Thompson, Tom, 47

Thoreau, Henry David, 20

Tolkien, J.R.R.: *The Hobbit or There and Back Again*, 125

Toronto *Globe and Mail*, 172

Trickster, 19, 39, 52–3, 181, 203, 210n.14, 222n.81; as paired with *senex*, 167; in *Wacousta*, 183–95; as 'white' appropriation, 222n.73. *See also* Radin, Paul: *The Trickster*

Tymns, Ralph, 70–1

vampires; demon-lovers; gorgons; wendigos, 66, 140, 144, 157, 164, 203; in *The Canadian Brothers*, 117–23

Van Herk, Aritha, 171; *No Fixed Address: An Amorous Journey*, 13, 89

Varma, D.P., 162

von Franz, Marie-Louise. *See* Franz, Marie-Louise von

Wacousta. *See* Richardson, John: *Wacousta; or, The Prophecy: A Tale of the Canadas*

Wacousta-like outcasts from established Canadian culture, 12–13, 19, 22, 55, 89, 146, 171, 179

Walker, Barbara: *The Woman's Encyclopedia of Myths and Secrets*, 217n.41, 218n.8

Walpole, Horace: *The Castle of Otranto*, 161–2

War of 1812: in *The Canadian Brothers*, 15, 17, 111, 149, 193; and gothic, 158; and *Hardscrabble*, 199; and national identity, 8, 30, 154, 204; and Richardson's experiences, 20; and *Wau-Nan-Gee*, 199; and *Westbrook*, 195. *See also* Richardson, John: *War of 1812*

Warkentin, Germaine: 'Exploration Literature,' 159

Watson, Sheila, 5; *The Double Hook*, 55, 62, 128, 146, 185

Wiebe, Rudy, 20–1, 30, 68, 111, 202; *My Lovely Enemy*, 195; *The Scorched-Wood People*, 13, 90, 162, 171; *The Temptations of Big Bear*, 96, 171–2

Willson, David, 23

Wilson, Tim, x

wolf-like figures, 19, 203; in later works, 195–201; paired with establishment manticores, 188–9

women, war against: by establishment representatives, 13, 169–71; made slaves of men, 23, 110, 220n.31

Woodcock, George, 9–10, 21

Woodman, Marion, ix, 25, 167, 171, 174; *Addiction to Perfection: The Still Unravished Bride*, 25, 98–99, 216n.32; *The Pregnant Virgin: A Process of Psychological Transformation*, 25; *The Ravaged Bridegroom: Masculinity in Women*, 220n.31

Wordsworth, William: *The Borderers*, 163; *The Brothers*, 163

Young, Edward, 18; *The Revenge*, 117